Raising Voices

Raising Voices

Creating Youth Storytelling Groups and Troupes

Judy Sima
Kevin Cordi

2003
Libraries Unlimited
Teacher Ideas Press
A Member of Greenwood Publishing Group, Inc.
Westport, Connecticut • London

Library of Congress Cataloging-in-Publication Data

Sima, Judy
    Raising voices : creating youth storytelling groups and troupes / Judy Sima, Kevin
Cordi.
      p. cm.
    Includes bibliographical references and index.
    ISBN 1-56308-919-X
    1. Storytelling. 2. Children's stories. I. Cordi, Kevin.
    GR72.3.S55   2003
    808.5'43—dc21   2003047631

British Library Cataloguing in Publication Data is available.

Library of Congress Catalog Card Number: 2003047631
ISBN: 1-56308-919-X

First published in 2003

Libraries Unlimited, 88 Post Road West, Westport, CT 06881
A Member of the Greenwood Publishing Group, Inc.
www.lu.com

Printed in the United States of America

The paper used in this book complies with the
Permanent Paper Standards issued by the National
Information Standards Organization (Z39.48-1984).

P

In order to keep this title in print and available to the academic community, this edition
was produced using digital reprint technology in a relatively short print run. This would
not have been attainable using traditional methods. Although the cover has been changed
from its original appearance, the text remains the same and all materials and methods
used still conform to the highest book-making standards.

Contents

Section I: Getting Started

Section II: Growing Your Storytelling Group

Section III: Performing and Beyond

Section IV: Storytelling Resources

List of Reproducibles

Acknowledgments

I first thank my coauthor and storytelling colleague Kevin Cordi, who asked me to coauthor the book I had always dreamed of writing but never took the first step toward making it a reality. I am indebted to my friend Dr. Karen White, who read every word of this book many times over and whose assistance, friendship, suggestions, and encouragement were invaluable.

My thanks, too, to the many Talespinners and their families who have shared their stories and ideas with me over the years. From them I have gained patience, vision, and the experience contained in this book. I would like to express a special thanks to the graduated Talespinners who responded to my requests for their feedback (Heidi Bennett, Lori Stone, Theresa Johnson, Jon Napper, Lauren Sroka, Jennifer D'Uva, Brandon Yuker, Jamie Favreau, and Mary Loomis Muzzarelli), and to Brittany Finch, who allowed us to include her story. As a teacher, my main motivation is to make a difference in the lives of my students. Their enthusiastic and honest responses helped me realize the importance of my work. A most grateful thank you to Marilyn Flam, my volunteer storytelling coach, whose unfailing dedication nurtured Talespinners over the years and who finds these kids as delightful, amazing, and interesting as I do.

I am grateful for the storytellers and friends who have given their time and ideas to help make this book possible, especially Gwen Calvetti, who read our early efforts and gave valuable suggestions. Thank you, too, to my friends and fellow storytellers in the Parent-Tellers, Detroit Story League, Northlands Storytelling Network, and the National Storytelling Network who taught, guided, networked, accepted, encouraged, listened, and nurtured me along my journey.

Thank you to all of my colleagues at Chatterton Middle School who tolerated the interruption of their classes and schedules; to the administrators of the Fitzgerald Public Schools who gave me time, space, and resources; and especially my former principal, Joy Holman, who recognized the creativity in me.

I would like to dedicate this book to my husband, Jerry Sima, who wouldn't let me quit; to my children, Jennifer and Joey, who loved me anyway; and to the Fitzgerald Family who made it all possible.

—Judy Sima

A book of this kind does not create itself; it takes a great amount of time, thought, and work. I am fortunate that each chapter of my life has in some way become a chapter for this book. From the hundreds, even thousands, of students, who have shared their stories and ideas with me, I have gained experience and insight. I have learned from my family, both my personal and storytelling families. Most of what I have learned has come from listening to others. Without their voices, my voice would not be heard.

First of all, I would like to thank my friend, professional storyteller, and fellow storytelling coach Judy Sima, whose craft in language and experience has helped this book become a complete resource. Next, I would like to thank my in-house editor Michael Smorowski whose ideas kept me on track, and Barbara Ittner of Libraries Unlimited, who helped this book from process to product. Thank you for all your valuable work. My thanks, too, to my mother and father, Mr. and Mrs. Lyle

G. Cordi, who told me my first stories; Hanford High School principal Leslie Stephens, assistant superintendent Dr. James Spence; The National Storytelling Network; Doug Williams, Jennifer Wooley and Jose Gonzales for helping to create Voices of Illusion; my students, teachers, and colleagues; and most of all everyone who listens to stories. Our children and their stories are our legacy. Let us help them find their voice. "We do make a difference by the stories we tell."

—Kevin Cordi

A Note to the Reader

Folktales and stories have a way of taking on a life of their own. They travel from person to person and place to place. Many times their origins have been lost, and they take on the flavor of their new surroundings. So it is with lessons, games, and activities. They are shared and passed along by dedicated teachers, librarians, and storytellers. Many of the activities we have included came from workshops we have attended over the years and adapted for our own use and situation. Some are original and our own creation. Wherever possible, we have given credit to the individuals who first introduced us to the game or activity. We would especially like to thank the storytellers who have allowed us to use and adapt some of the activities included in Chapters 3 and 4: Donna Boudreau, Mary Hamilton, Cynthia Changaris, Tom McCabe, Jean-Andrew Dickmann, and Finley Stewart.

Judy Sima and members of the Chatterton Talespinners

Kevin Cordi and members of the Voices of Illusion

Storyteller's Pledge

As a Storyteller and Story Listener
I give myself permission
To Have Fun
To Laugh
To Take Risks
To Make Mistakes
To Tell Stories
I Know
Stories
Connect
Us
And
I
Am
Connected
To Story.
Let the Stories Begin.
Let the Stories Begin!
Let the Stories Begin!!!
—Written by Kevin Cordi

Establish a tradition with your youthful storytellers by beginning each meeting with a ritual. Create a mood and atmosphere that makes storytelling inviting and special. Dim the lights, light a candle, move to a special place, ring a bell, or simply begin with the Storyteller's Pledge.

Introduction

The Value of Youth Storytelling

From Our Experience: *"Storytelling has inspired me to become more confident and learn to rely on myself as a person. When you first find a story you learn it by yourself. Then you present it to friends and your coach. You don't stress as much as when you are on stage for a public performance. Storytelling has made me blossom. I am not as shy as I used to be, and I have tons of people skills. I know what to say and when to say it."*
—Dawn Escobar, senior, Hanford High School

"Telling stories helped me become a better writer. By learning the stories (and having to improvise whenever I forgot a piece) I learned a lot about how stories are formed and effective techniques for narrating. I also learn several different versions of the same fairy tales, which showed me that there is no one right way to do something. We also did stuff that was good for the community. It is an important lesson to learn; if you have a gift, it's more fun to share it with others than to just amuse yourself."
—Theresa Johnson, Talespinners graduate, 1992

Imagine sitting in a carpet-filled room listening to a fifth-grade boy retelling an Old Jack tale or a young teenager's personal story relating how she feels about her brother moving to Hawaii. Picture a high school student recounting the classic misadventures of Peter Pan or a twelve-year-old retelling her own version of "The Little Red Hen" to a group of kindergartners. Envision a camping trip on which a Boy or Girl Scout shares a story about a gift that could be held in his or her hand. Marvel, as we have, at the students who speak of their grandmother's smile, their mother's heart, or their friend's kind words. Imagine an older sister and younger brother telling a tale of sibling rivalry in tandem or a petite nine-year-old telling the classic story of "Little Red Riding Hood" in Arabic. Imagine kids sharing their ideas, building stories, and coming together to enjoy time laughing, crying, wondering, and appreciating one another.

Now you can do more than imagine. Focusing on the primary adage "everyone has a story to tell," we have answered the call to create a handbook that explains the "nuts and bolts" of designing and building a club in which stories are appreciated, learned, and told. Young people are searching for ways to be heard. They have stories to tell. Most often their stories are compressed into talks over the phone, or time between classes; worse yet, sometimes their stories are never told. By forming storytelling groups and troupes, we believe we have found an innovative, proven way to help youngsters recover lost time and raise their voices in story.

We created this book for anyone who is involved with youth and who enjoys working with young people. It is written for anyone who loves a good story and knows the power that comes from listening to our youth. Most of us can remember that quiet student who sat in the back of the classroom, the child who was too shy to check out a book, the gawky teenager who stammered when trying to express himself, and the kid who stayed home because she doesn't think she has any friends. We can also relate to the class clown, the overachiever, the daydreamer, and the child with an overactive imagination or a burst of creativity who desperately needs to express it. Using storytelling to reach all children, shy or outgoing, bright or educationally challenged, our book is meant to be an effective guide for helping youngsters find their voices and empower their creativity.

In traveling throughout the country to schools, libraries, group centers, and community halls, we have been asked, "How do you teach children and teenagers to tell stories? How do you build a youth storytelling group?" For many years, we have been answering these questions in workshops and articles written for educational journals. Now we have compiled all the information, advice, examples, and suggestions into one complete volume. Within the pages of this book, we have detailed the process of building a youth storytelling group, from setting goals and getting organized, to activities and exercises for learning and improving storytelling skills. We also provide advanced strategies to ensure the longevity of your group or troupe. It is geared toward librarians who want to help children and young adults connect to books, educators who are looking for a program to build literacy skills, parent organizers who are seeking a safe learning environment for their children, and community leaders who want to build successful programs that help children and young adults reach out to find the stories in their town. Regardless of your goals, we know this book will empower you to connect more with young people.

Focusing on children or young adults in grades four through twelve, this book provides

- Specific suggestions for getting started, from determining your goals to recruiting students, establishing rules, and structuring the meetings

- Step-by-step activities and games to teach and strengthen the story-learning process

- Ideas and guidelines for sharing and performing students' stories

- Advanced techniques for coaching youth storytellers, raising funds to support the group, and ideas for creating a traveling troupe of tellers

- A comprehensive annotated list of books, tapes, props, and Web sites for student and adult leader use

- Testimonials, suggestions, and stories from students for whom storytelling has made a difference

And so much more.

Youth and the Storytelling Renaissance

Over the past thirty years, there has been a resurgence in storytelling and the oral tradition. People all over the United States have rediscovered the joy of sharing stories. Those who want to be storytellers have formed guilds, leagues, clubs, and groups with the sole purpose of telling and listening to stories. Nearly every weekend and on many evenings during the year, you can find large and small storytelling events, festivals, or conferences being held somewhere in the United States. Workshops, seminars, and college courses that teach the art of storytelling are becoming more and more prevalent, and there is a plethora of storytellers who are willing to share what they know with others. Storytellers have been taking their passion and craft into schools, libraries, and other centers where youngsters can be found. Young people of all ages have begun to learn and retell stories they have read in books or heard from teachers, librarians, parents and grandparents, Boy and Girl Scout leaders, church leaders, and storytellers. Many youth storytellers have been meeting on a weekly, monthly, and sometimes daily basis to listen and tell stories to one another and audiences beyond their school or youth groups.

Our youth love stories. They relish an old familiar folktale told in a new way. They ask to hear the story about the day that they were born or what their town was like years ago. Myths and legends amaze them. Ghost stories spark interest and raise delightful goose bumps. They always want to know, "Is that true? Did that really happen?" Not only do children crave and hunger to hear stories, they also wish to tell their own stories. They want to tell about their day at school, the antics of their pets, their secret wishes, or their favorite book or movie.

Children's voices are invaluable. With our overloaded curriculums, we often rush to complete a lesson only to race through another or arrange a new activity, when taking time to listen to our students would be more beneficial. How often do we provide places where children are allowed to "raise their voices" so they will understand how important they truly are in their communities and schools? By forming a storytelling group or troupe, we raise not only voices, but also students who believe in the power of their own words and actions.

When young people tell stories in a youth storytelling group, they are building a legacy. Just as no one knows where a droplet of water runs, no one knows where the wellspring of youth tellers now forming across the country will end. It begins with an adult who has good intentions and inspires others to tell stories on a regular basis. Students now carry their stories across the country as they travel from one place to another.

Special Note: *As you embark on this most wonderful journey, consider taking part in the Voices Across America Youth Storytelling Project, which Kevin founded in 1997. In the first year of its existence, more than sixty storytelling clubs registered with the program—from Lake Charles, Louisiana, to Albuquerque, New Mexico. Interest in the program is growing daily, with requests coming from nearly every state and from Canada and Australia as well. You, too, can join this fast-growing movement and the future of storytelling. To register your group, e-mail Kevin D. Cordi, "Voices Across America" Coordinator: KCtells@youthstorytelling.com. You can also register online at www.youthstorytelling.com.*

Benefits of Storytelling for Young People

Storytelling is the ultimate teaching tool. Unlike television, in which learning is passive, with storytelling young people actively participate in learning, constantly interpreting images created in their minds through a story's words. By retelling a story they have heard or read, they transfer those images into their own words. Unlike computer learning, storytelling encourages face-to-face interaction. The storyteller needs the listener's reaction to know if the story has left its mark. With these skills acting in concert, a true educational environment is formed. Without someone to hear the story, there is no storytelling.

The following are just some of the areas in which building a youth storytelling group or troupe can make a difference.

Storytelling Increases Literacy

Teachers often have trouble motivating students to read. Although many students simply do not want to pick up a book, they do respond to storytelling. Rafe Martin, children's author and storyteller, once said, "Stories are trapped in books, it is the storyteller who sets them free." Often students need an invitation to discover good books. What better way to unlock the pages than to tell a book's story to a nonreader?

Youth storytelling groups and troupes are places where kids discuss their favorite books, examine folktales, create their own tales, and work together to create a special storytelling community. Watch the folklore collection at your media center (398.2) disappear off of the shelves as a group of students prepares a high-energy performance based on well-known fairy tales. By having student storytellers tell stories on topics such as immigration, endangered species, Latin America, or the American Civil War, you'll find they are willing to read and research before and after the project.

Leading English and reading teachers agree that storytelling is a highly effective tool for teaching both reading and writing. The National Council of Teachers of English Committee on Storytelling has adopted a Storytelling Statement:

> Students who search their memories for details about an event as they are telling it orally will later find those details easier to capture in writing. Writing theorists value the rehearsal, or prewriting, stage of composing. Sitting in a circle and swapping personal or fictional tales is one of the best ways to help writers rehearse.
>
> Listeners encounter both familiar and new language patterns through story. They learn new words or new contexts for already familiar words. Those who regularly hear stories subconsciously acquire familiarity with narrative patterns and begin to predict upcoming events. Both beginning and experienced readers call on their understanding of patterns as they tackle unfamiliar texts. Then they re-create those patterns in both oral and written compositions. Learners who regularly tell stories become aware of how an audience affects a telling, and they carry that awareness into their writing.
>
> Both tellers and listeners find a reflection of themselves in stories. Through the language of symbol, children and adults can act out through a story the fears and understandings not so easily expressed in everyday talk. Story characters represent the best and worst in humans. By exploring story territory orally, we explore ourselves—whether it is through ancient myths and folktales, literary short stories, modern picture books, or poems. Teachers who value a personal understanding of their stories can learn much by noting what story a child chooses to tell and how that story is uniquely composed in the telling. Through this same process, teachers can learn a great deal about themselves.
>
> Story is the best vehicle for passing on factual information. Historical figures and events linger in children's minds when communicated by way of a narrative. The ways of other cultures, both ancient and living, acquire honor in story. The facts about how plants and animals can develop, how numbers work, or how government policy influences history—any topic, for that matter—can be incorporated into story form and made more memorable if the listener takes the story to heart. (National Council of Teachers of English Committee on Storytelling, 1996)

Once they have learned to tell their stories, consider sending your youth storytellers to lower-grade classrooms during inclement weather or during programs such as "March Is Reading Month." This will strengthen the younger children's listening skills and encourage them to read. As your students become known as "The Storytellers," you will watch them develop confidence, poise and effective speaking skills while their self-esteem rises to new heights.

Storytelling Serves as an Effective Conflict Resolution Model

Group counseling and peer mediation counselors use stories to help students connect with one another. Professional storyteller Dan Keding often relates an old Croatian saying that he learned from his grandmother: "You can never hurt a man once you know his story." It is usually what is not said that builds anxiety and conflict. As young people tell their stories and listen to each other, they learn to be flexible and understand one another.

Students often carry a hidden fear that others won't like them or that they will be embarrassed by their actions. We all know of troubled youths who refuse to discuss their problems with adults or other students. Storytelling can help group counselors or nurses with the healing process. Often youngsters bottle their anxiety until it can only be released through anger. By talking about these fears in the form of story, students can understand that they are not alone with their fears. Real listening and real talking—the type that is encouraged by a youth storytelling group or troupe—can build real understanding. By truly listening to our students, we can help alleviate tension, which will cause them to be more conscious of each other's needs.

Storytelling Develops a Sense of Collaboration

A local town council or Rotary group might wish to preserve the history of its community. Members may be concerned that few people, especially the young, will ever learn it. A youth storytelling group can help a town make connections to its past by exploring the stories of places in their hometown, as well as the lives and contributions of the people who built it. Your club can visit a senior center or nursing home in your community and listen to the stories of the elders, then retell those tales for an evening of family stories. The young tellers can celebrate the high and low points of the community by telling the history of the town. Working collaboratively with adult civic and historical groups can help not only the students, but the entire town as well.

From Our Experience: *Voices of Illusion, my storytelling group, discovered from researching our town's history that, during World War II, an airplane carrying mail from the soldiers crashed. One man took it upon himself to deliver all the mail to the soldiers' families. My students shared this information with a local English teacher. When she heard their story, she replied that it was her grandfather. Imagine the questions that ensued. The students also discovered that in the small town of Hanford, population 41,000, Amelia Earhart often flew to the local "big band" dances at the civic center to meet another pilot, Mary Packwood, a Hanford resident. We also recently learned of a local man who worked with Neil Armstrong before Armstrong went to work for NASA. And we are still investigating the old school that was torn down, hoping to find out if there might just be a few ghost stories hanging around there. An amazing learning experience occurs when kids take an interest in telling the stories of their community. —Kevin*

Storytelling Is a Cooperative Art

Unlike football and basketball tryouts or auditions for the school play, there are no tryouts or auditions in a storytelling group. The only prerequisite is a commitment to learning how to tell and listen to stories.

Often students come to the group feeling that they have to outdo each other. Once the meeting begins, however, they realize that they don't have to compete with anyone; they simply tell their story in a way they think will work. When youngsters hear real praise and positive comments the first time they begin to realize that others are truly listening to them, they always express how wonderful it is. We have seen so many young people return meeting after meeting because they know it is a warm, friendly place where they can take risks and tell a story without any fear of hurtful criticism or pain.

In her book *Storyteller, Storyteacher*, Marni Gillard reminds us of the importance of telling in an environment of cooperation rather than competition. She suggests that a noncompetitive atmosphere will enable all students, not only the select few who want or think they need competition, to learn:

> My goal is to teach children—and colleagues—how to support each other's individual quests and common goals. I no longer want to encourage the kind of striving that perpetuates loneliness or the hurt and embarrassment of losing, in school or out. I couldn't get competition off the playground or out of the magazine drives or other teacher's classrooms when I worked at a particular school, but I gently weeded it out of my own room every time it sprang up. The kids who missed it were the one ones who always managed to win, the ones addicted to winning. Once freed from the burden of constantly competing, those children eventually relaxed and let their learning stretch in new directions. They became less afraid to take risks and to be not so great at something. Their learning took off. The struggle to stay on top takes time and energy away from learning. Exploration of the unknown is too scary to attempt if you have to be right all the time. (Giallard, 1996, pp. 182–83)

Storytelling Builds Imagination Skills

Albert Einstein said, "Imagination is more important than knowledge, for while knowledge points to all there is, imagination points to all there will be." Storytelling arouses curiosity and an interest to find answers. By exploring imaginary worlds in stories, young people can create places that they wish they could see in real life, or they may simply use stories to escape the feeling of boredom with their lives.

Youth storytellers use their imaginations continuously as they relate their stories. Storytelling is a comfortable base to build skills that allow youngsters to question and explore their curiosities. Because telling stories works from the storyteller's language base and the reaction of the audience, the experience is alive. Students use their imagination to place themselves in the story and can feel free to become giants, warriors, princesses, or villains. As one youth teller stated, "Every story you tell has a little bit of you in it."

In the book *Sit Tight and I Will Swing You a Tale*, author Greg Denman reminds us of how listening to stories can help children learn and build their imagination:

> My research and experience bear witness to the fact that from the earliest years, children listen and listen intently. During the preschool and primary school years, children's imaginations and their ability to visualize are unhampered by a rigid sense of reality. They are free to delight in the mere sound of words and the way sounds blend together as they roll off the storyteller's or reader's tongue. They are also free to surrender themselves to the rhythm of a poem or tune or a story helps children focus their thoughts, which theorists maintain is the foundation for a well-developed imaginative and intellectual life in adulthood. (Denman, 1991)

Storytelling Fosters Cultural Understanding

Storytelling helps keep culture alive. As Anishinabek storyteller Gilbert Oskahoose once related to storyteller Dan Yashinsky, "When legends are lost, the people die." Young people who tell stories begin to understand not only other cultures, but their own heritage as well. We have found that many students develop a renewed interest in their Cherokee, Philippine, Hispanic, or Irish heritage because they heard a story about their culture. They have literally said, "I'm Russian, do you know any more Russian tales?" Students begin to identity and relate to their own cultural background once they understand the stories from that culture.

Storytelling Is a Personal Experience

Storytelling allows us to relate to each other as people and to share feelings with one another. Students often see storytelling time as a means to express a real feeling, such as how it feels to lose a loved one, how it feels to be scared, how going to Grandpa's makes them happy, or the feeling of other personal moments. These "living language experiences" engender community with other tellers, an invaluable experience.

> Language is the most powerful, most readily available tool we have for representing the world to ourselves and ourselves to the world. Language is not only a means of communication, it is a primary mark of personal identity. (NCTE, 1996, language standard, p. 12)

Storytelling Can Teach Spiritual Lessons

A Sunday school instructor may want to teach the story of Daniel in the Lion's Den but have trouble starting. When he or she asks the youth group for help, they can begin to study not only this tale but many others as well. They will have a great time discussing just how to portray the lion and what type of man Daniel was and studying the Bible to make sure their depictions are accurate. Soon this storytelling group may become a regular feature at the Sunday evening service.

Who Should Join a Storytelling Group or Troupe

Belonging to a youth storytelling group is a valuable experience for any young person. There are many youngsters that find storytelling groups especially enriching and beneficial. A youth storytelling group is a company of three or more youths who gather to tell stories. Although they may travel occasionally to tell others their stories, they are primarily concerned with sharing stories with each other. A storytelling troupe is a company of three or more storytellers who travel as storytelling performers. They seek out new venues to tell stories and study all the intricacies involved in the art of storytelling, including styles of telling, performance management, the storytelling code of ethics, and much more.

Students with Special Needs

We have had many students that other teachers said should not take part in storytelling because of their disabilities or special needs: "They would never be able to learn the material." Often these children are overlooked when it comes to the more competitive arenas of sports, student government, theater, chorus and band, newspaper, yearbook, and other student clubs and organizations. A storytelling club provides a safe haven where young people of all talents and abilities experience success—a place where kids are appreciated, accepted, and encouraged to do their best without fear of ridicule or failure.

From Our Experience: *I remember the day I questioned the adage, "Everyone can tell a story." The special education teacher brought three severely handicapped students to my storytelling class: Lupe was nonverbal and had cerebral palsy, Chris was a blind student who had memory retention problems, and Jeff had a disease that confined him to a wheelchair with straps. He, too, was nonverbal and often confrontational.*

I had said that everyone could tell a story, and here was my test. At first, I asked myself, "What am I going to do?" After my initial misgivings, however, I began to focus on these students' strengths rather than their weaknesses. The results were amazing to me, but just the natural path for them.

Lupe was a gifted artist. Sometimes with her group or by herself she would paint a story with big pieces of butcher paper and attach them to her wheelchair. As she wheeled in a circle, her story would unfold as a living painting like a flipbook or comic book. Chris became so comfortable with the class that he was honest about his blindness and shared a story called "Blind Date" in which he revealed that he had never gone on a date, let alone a blind date. A week later he had the courage to go on his first date. Jeff, although nonverbal, became the lion, and with his tremendous roar, performed in "The Lion and the Ashiko Drum" by Jamal Koram dressed in full regalia to an audience of 350. His mother later shared with me that outside of meeting the world wrestler Hulk Hogan, she believes this was the highlight of his life. —Kevin

English Language Learners (ELL)

Youngsters whose primary language is not English often have difficulty in school. Because storytelling as a form of learning is found in all cultures, ELL students respond to stories as a way of learning the language. Students can also "see" the stories from the way the teller shares the tale, and this helps students connect meaning to the words. It also allows students to use their own language base to build a story. We have worked with a vast number of second-language learners, and when they are in a nonthreatening environment, not only does their storytelling ability increase, but the awkwardness they feel because of the language barrier diminishes and they form lasting friendships.

Teenagers

Youth librarians are always looking for ways to involve more kids. Despite efforts at arranging tours, canvassing the schools, giving book talks, and providing vivid displays, teens may not see the library as a gathering place. By forming a storytelling group the library can become the place where teens and preteens invest their time and creative energy. They will see the public library as a place where they can find more rich stories to read and tell, offsetting the misconception of the library as a place to visit infrequently or only if they need to do that once-a-year term paper.

Young people can meet monthly to share tales based on selected themes, or they can present storytelling programs for preschoolers and younger elementary students at the library. The demand will soon rise for books on folktales, fairy tales, biographies, and so much more. Having a storytelling group or troupe will definitely boost circulation.

Boy Scouts and Girl Scouts

A Scout leader can use a storytelling group to entertain the troop with Native American legends or ghost stories at an evening campfire or to teach serious lessons on fire safety or the importance of group cohesion. Youth storytellers can assist in teaching merit badges, moral and ethical choices, and the negative affects of name-calling, or "How Not to Get Lost in the Woods." Scouting was built on making wise choices in all kinds of situations. Why not choose storytelling to help Scouts learn about making good decisions?

Student Writers

Many of our students have found their story by writing it out. Students have gone on to publish their work. Because storytelling is the unofficial cousin of writing, one should embrace the other. Students need to tell their stories before they discover the writer within. When they discover their storytelling voice, their writing voice will often follow.

The Storytelling Report Card: Six Principles Of Youth Storytelling

Storytelling gives children and young adults a voice. We have coached countless numbers of young people who were classified as "nonreaders," "lazy," "troublemakers," or "disadvantaged," "as well as "gifted." As they became involved in telling stories, we watched these labels disappear. Over time they discovered that other students as well as adults enjoyed listening to them; they realized that their voices were invaluable.

Case in Point: *When Lacy Chaffin, a sophomore at Hanford High School, returned from presenting at the National Storytelling Conference in Kansas City, she confided, "Mr. Cordi, I was so scared to be there. I knew everyone there would be a professional storyteller, and what did I have to tell him or her? However, shortly after I arrived, I realized that I had much to share, and when well-known storytellers thanked me for my work with my storytelling troupe, it was then that I knew I had a voice. I think this is the first time someone ever really listened to what I, a teenager, was saying."* —Kevin

---

Students may ask, "What will I get out of being in a storytelling group? Why should I join a storytelling group? To illustrate the benefits students receive when joining a youth storytelling group or troupe, we have developed a "Storytelling Report Card." Share it with your students. Use it as a starting point to discuss the advantages of joining, and in no time your students will be telling other potential members.

A: Youth Storytelling Instills APPRECIATION

The first goal of youth storytelling is to teach appreciation of the efforts of everyone involved with the group. Every student feels valued because everyone listens to his or her story. Every student is also appreciated for listening to stories told by others.

When this appreciative atmosphere is established, worthwhile learning occurs because of the praise in the room. The more students are personally involved, the more they are able to see the potential within themselves. Not only will they be less reluctant to tell a story, they also are able to transfer that skill to performing on stage, delivering a speech, or singing in the church choir.

From Our Experience: *It took hours of coaxing to bring Shannon to our storytelling meeting and when she arrived, she tried to hide in a corner like she did in the classroom. Upon entering the room, however, my group of storytellers came over, shook her hand, and told her how wonderful it was to have her at the meeting. During the course of the meeting, each storytelling student officer took a personal interest in making Shannon feel comfortable. Then she was encouraged to tell a story. Her brief sentences were honestly praised by many of the student tellers. It took a while, but soon she was telling more and more stories. Later she became a troupe member. From the beginning of the meeting, my students honestly appreciated her role as teller and listener.* —Kevin

Young storytellers not only learn to appreciate each other, they also learn to appreciate storytelling as an art. Unlike television and cinema, storytelling is a living art form. It depends on reactions from live audiences. Many students learn audience skills at sporting events and rock concerts where there is little connection between what is happening on stage and what is going on in the audience. Storytelling develops a very real appreciation for a live performer who creates a direct connection with every single person in the audience.

Case in Point: *A shy seven-year-old girl once approached me after telling stories and said, "I never knew stories could be this real." She had read a book with a similar story, but after hearing it told aloud, she said, "I can see it now." For her it became a living, tangible experience, one I am sure she will never forget. She was also a valuable connection to my story. When I tell stories, I always remember this event and see the little girl's face.* —Kevin

B: Youth Storytelling Creates a Sense of BELONGING

Children of all ages have a need to "belong." This accounts for students forming their own peer groups and even cliques in school. In a youth storytelling troupe or group, all students are connected because they share the desire to tell stories. From the athletic to the "gifted," each student has a story to tell. In a storytelling troupe or group, no student is neglected, because regardless of ability, age, or level, every child loves to tell and listen to stories. Each weekly or monthly meeting the student can share his or her new story or simply listen to the stories of others.

When the elements of competition are eliminated, there is no pressure to "out do" one another; instead the environment becomes one that welcomes everyone involved. The goal of self-improvement is stressed rather than competition. As young people experience their own uniqueness in an atmosphere of sharing, belonging becomes second nature. Purchasing group T-shirts, hats, buttons or vests, as well as providing storytelling performances, planning parties, and taking non-storytelling trips also creates pride in the group. This type of collaborative work in turn creates a real desire to participate in all club activities.

From Our Experience: *At first Michelle, a freshman, said she would come to the storytelling meeting but would only write stories. She came to meeting after meeting and listened to each story and teller being praised. She heard more and more tellers sharing their work. Instead of ridicule or public embarrassment, Michelle witnessed a warm sense of belonging. Soon she was not only telling stories but also expressing a sincere interest in helping everyone in the group. She became co-chair of our storytelling group and even told at the National Youth Storytelling Olympics in Tennessee. I firmly believe that, like most children, if Michelle hadn't had a warm environment, she would have never gone beyond her writing stories phase, but because of her peers, she is now a published writer, teller, storytelling activist, and role model. —Kevin*

C: Youth Storytelling Builds CONFIDENCE

We tell youngsters we are proud of them when they give a public speech or perform because, as adults, we feel a great deal of anxiety when asked to speak in front of a group of people. Performing is something their parents or teacher fear and that, for some reason, they should fear it as well. Unfortunately, our society encourages children to fear something that should be viewed as worthwhile and inviting rather than difficult. Unlike public speaking or even performing on stage in a formal setting, storytelling groups soon learn that there is "fun" instead of fear when telling a story (and giving a speech). Children and teens can tell stories sitting on the floor, standing up, with another person or even as an ensemble of thirty people. Storytelling can take place in a kindergarten classroom, a community center, a library, or even at home. Students see storytelling not as a scary obligation, but more like a gift exchange. When children share their lives, imaginations, and favorite stories with others, they are giving a gift. As Cheyenne storyteller and writer Lance Hansen once said to me, "Stories are gifts. It is up to us to take them and receive them." Fear is replaced by confidence because the environment and the attitude are one of comfort, not pain.

From Our Experience: *Young Chris came to the storytelling meeting knowing he did not do well in school and that his personal behavior was unruly, but I had talked him into coming. He reluctantly showed up and listened to the stories. I noticed other students who knew his reputation were staying away from him. Yet when he told the story "When Did Polar Bears Learn to Dance," the response was enthusiastic. After hearing the students' energetic comments and experiencing the supportive atmosphere, he began to tell more and more. His teachers told me later that they noticed his personal and social behavior had also changed in class. Chris had the confidence to share his gift for telling stories, which transferred to better learning in the classroom. He overcame his initial fear of meeting people by telling his stories. At one point, no one expected him to finish school. Recently he informed me of his scholarship to Chico State and his plans to study overseas in Holland.* —Kevin

D: Youth Storytelling Provides DIRECTION

In a storytelling group, members know why they are learning stories. There is usually a performance goal in mind. Smaller steps lead to larger goals, from telling a story to a partner, to telling in front of the group, to performing for an audience of preschoolers or senior citizens, and even producing a troupe compact disc. Unlike some clubs that only last a season, a storytelling group can go on indefinitely, as more and more calls pour in requesting tellers for shows.

As young people perform for Rotary clubs, libraries, board meetings, elderly homes, and child-care centers, they realize the joys and satisfaction of sharing their talents and abilities with others. Soon, students become involved with helping others, and from this altruism a real sense of community and place develops. Storytelling also provides direction for life. The skills and self-confidence learned in storytelling serves them well as they continue their education, seek jobs, and become contributing members of society.

From Our Experience: *When I started my first Talespinner group in 1987 my goal was to have the kids perform at the nursing home where my mother was living. It turned out to be an enriching experience for both the Talespinners and the residents. They also performed at the elementary school. The next year, we were invited to tell our stories at the regional school librarians' meeting. As the years went on, one of our first outings for the season was always to the early childhood center where wide-eyed, adoring preschoolers gave new Talespinners the confidence to tell their stories.* —Judy

> **From Our Experience:** *In 2000, my students heard about the National Storytelling Conference and were given an invitation to showcase their work. Even though the cost was more than $11,000, they worked extra hard by performing more shows, enlisting donations from the community, and even creating an audiotape on nonviolence and storytelling to fund the efforts. It was the students' commitment to excel that provided the direction, and because of this ownership in their storytelling troupe and group, they achieved their goals. —Kevin*

E: Youth Storytelling Fosters EXCELLENCE

In a storytelling group, the group encourages and supports individual improvement and group excellence rather than seeking to be the best as determined through competition between members. True excellence begins to build when the coach realizes that "the teller is more important than the story." For some students, this is the first time they have spoken in front of others. Initially they may feel they're on shaky ground. Yet after watching other members of the group succeed, youth tellers develop their own skills and set goals to improve in their storytelling. In an atmosphere of praise, students will meet more goals than not. Excellence becomes not only the goal of the group, but the individual teller.

> **Case in Point:** *Young Garrett always told long complicated stories and at one time even became arrogant about his telling. Initially he felt he was a better storyteller than anyone else, and he was not afraid to voice this opinion. Even though this caused a few raised eyebrows, the students continued to praise his efforts. Over time Garrett began to accept feedback. He eventually began to let down his need to "be the best." Instead, he listened and over time became a valuable member of our storytelling club. He slowly realized that this is not a place to brag but a place to share. Garrett became vocal in giving as well as receiving honest praise. —Kevin*

F: Youth Storytelling Is FUN

The last goal, but definitely one of the most important, is that storytelling is fun! If it "ain't fun, it ain't anything." The first item on the agenda should be, "How can we make this the most enjoyable educational experience that it can be?" Activities are selected and designed to make learning and strengthening skills exciting as well as useful. When learning is fun, kids keep coming back. As adult leaders see their young charges have a good time while growing and maturing into competent storytellers they, too, find fun and fulfillment. Often, leaders find themselves grinning from ear to ear during performances or when a teller masters a particularly challenging story.

A vibrant storytelling club will also do more than storytelling; they have pizza parties, storytelling and theater games, joke fests, or simply share their days. Sometimes the group takes a "Storytelling Break" to go to a festival and hear other storytellers or takes a non-storytelling outing to the movies, a bowling alley, or some other event unrelated to story. This lets kids know it is okay not to have a story prepared each week, that simply taking the time to talk is highly useful. The subject of the conversation often makes it to the next meeting and helps give the group a distinct personality.

Basically, we never forget to have fun! When a storytelling club becomes too much like a business, then students stop coming to the meetings. At all times, even the times when you are preparing for certain shows, students should feel free to laugh and have time to share ideas, make jokes, and tell other stories. After all, having fun is a quintessential ingredient to the storytelling experience. A good coach never forgets that!

Case in Point: *Kids of all ages love music as well as telling stories. When we noticed a decrease in enrollment at our club, we went out and purchased a karaoke machine and had a "Krazy Karoake Night." This was a night when we could laugh at our efforts to sing rock and roll and even rap. Some of the storytellers showed us yet another talent in their singing ability. Sure enough, by the next meeting our attendance had grown. We had forgotten what fun it was just to sing a song.* —Kevin

---

By joining a storytelling troupe or group, each child is given a voice—a voice that can tell stories. Children will once again relish in the classic tales such as *Winnie the Pooh* and *Alice in Wonderland,* and they will marvel at new tales told by wonderful children's authors such as Frank Asche, Mem Fox, or Jane Yolen. Children and teenagers will delight in creating their own stories, whether it is a personal tale of that wonderful aunt who lived near the haunted forest or an original tale about a boy's wish to find the girl of his dreams. Regardless of the tale, young people will see the profound joy in listening to each other's stories. With the help of a good story coach, our children will be ready to join in the modern storytelling revival and may even show adults a few twists and turns on the wonderful road to sharing stories.

References

Denman, Gregory. *Sit Tight, and I'll Swing You a Tale: Using and Writing Stories with Young People.* Westport, Conn.: Heinemann, 1991.

Gillard, Marni. *Storyteller, Storyteacher: Discovering the Power of Storytelling and Teaching.* New York: Stenhouse, 1996.

National Council of Teachers of English and the International Reading Association. *Standards of English Language Arts.* Urbana, Ill.: NCTE, 1996.

The National Council of Teachers of English Committee on Storytelling. *Position Statement on Storytelling.* Urbana, Ill.: Author. Statement may be found on the organization's Web site (www.ncte.org/positions/teaching_storytelling.shtml).

Section I

Getting Started

You don't need to be an accomplished storyteller to successfully coach a youth storytelling group or troupe. Enthusiasm and a love of young people and stories are the most important requirements. Chapter 1 helps you determine your goals and objectives and gives pointers for recruiting students, finding a place to meet, organizing your meeting space, and gathering supplies. Once the initial preparations have been completed, Chapter 2 helps you to set up a structure for your meetings, establish rules, choose a name for your group, and determine a meeting plan or agenda. Some of you will want your members to hone their storytelling skills quickly so they can begin performing for outside groups such as nursing homes and preschools. For others, simply improving reading and communications skills may be the primary goal, and you will want to keep storytelling within the confines of your own classroom or library. Still others may wish to use storytelling as an entertaining yet educational way to engage young people. In an effort to meet the needs of most adult leaders, we have included two suggested step-by-step outlines for a six- or a ten-week storytelling course. Although the goals may differ, the basic organizational structure is the same. With thoughtful planning, you'll get off to a good start and keep the excitement growing.

Chapter

Initial Preparations

Defining Your Goals and Objectives

How exactly do you organize a youth storytelling group? The best way to start is to determine your own goals and objectives. Why do you want to start a group, and what do you want the young people in your group to do? What do you hope your students will gain from the experience? Who else will your efforts affect? And don't forget to ask, "What's in it for me?" If you are not getting something out of it, you'll soon find yourself feeling stressed out and resentful. It is important for you, as the adult leader, to have a clear idea of what you want to accomplish. Then, once the group has been formed, you can let the students define their goals and together you can decide how best to accomplish these goals.

What you see as the purpose of your group is the overall guiding vision that determines your goals. How you set out to meet those goals will help formulate your objectives. Your goals and objectives will guide the way you organize and run your meetings. If one of your primary goals is to encourage students to read and appreciate folk literature, your objective will be to spend more time reading and listening to stories. If your desire is to teach young people how to communicate and have them perform for other groups in the school or community, your objective will be to spend a greater amount of time practicing and perfecting speaking and listening skills. If your goal is to give students many opportunities to tell stories but not to have them perform for outside audiences, your objective will be to have them learn stories on their own and come to meetings prepared to tell them, presenting outside the group only once in a while.

> **Case in Point:** *When I created the Talespinners back in 1987, I wanted my middle school students to feel the same excitement and sense of accomplishment that I felt when telling stories to an appreciative audience. My first goal was to increase my students' self-confidence and self-esteem, but I also had two other goals in mind. First, I wanted to use storytelling as a vehicle for community service. Next, I wanted to use storytelling to teach lessons of tolerance and acceptance by bringing my storytellers in contact with people different from themselves.* —Judy

Once you have a clear picture of your own goals, then you can set objectives of what you want your students to accomplish to attain those goals. Much like the upward steps on a staircase, the objectives will move your young people toward success. You may decide to let the students determine the group's objectives and structure of the meetings, particularly if one of your goals is to have a student-run organization. This works especially well with high school students. If you allow students to determine some or all of the goals for the group, you must be willing to give up at least partial control. With younger students, it is better to determine the goals and objectives yourself and, after stating them, allow input from participants.

Explain your feelings about storytelling and why you have formed a storytelling group at the first meeting with your high school students. Allow students to express the reasons they came to the meeting and what they would like to gain through involvement in a storytelling club. List their goals and yours on the chalkboard or a flip chart. Discuss the goals, combining or expanding so that everyone feels that they have been heard. Next, brainstorm and list possible ways of meeting these goals, then vote and prioritize the list. Everyone should agree, but make sure you retain veto power if any of their suggestions violate school policy or your own comfort level.

Sample Goals and Objectives

- *Goal:* To improve students' communication skills (i.e., reading, writing, listening, speaking).

  Objectives:
    - Students will be able to summarize and retell, in their own words, the folktales they have read.
    - Students will be able to summarize and retell stories that they have written based on personal experience.
    - Students will be able to perform a story they have learned to younger children in the elementary school.

- *Goal:* To improve students' self-esteem, poise, and self-confidence.

  Objectives:
    - Students will be able to tell stories in front of their peers.
    - Students will be able to tell a story they have learned to a variety of audiences.
    - Students will be able to create a tellable story from a personal experience.

- *Goal:* To use storytelling as a vehicle for community service.

  Objectives:
    - Students will be able to tell confidently at least one story in front of an audience.

– Students will be able to choose stories to tell for a variety of audiences and situations (e.g., nursing homes, homeless shelters, preschools, children's hospitals).

– Students will be able to conduct a storytelling festival to raise funds for charity.

- *Goal:* To give students a place to swap stories.

Objectives:

– Students will be able to locate books and stories on a variety of cultures and subjects (e.g., Native American tales, tall tales, Greek myths, historical stories, Irish fairy tales).

– Students will be able to select, learn, and practice stories to tell outside of meetings.

– Students will be able to tell stories in front of their peers with confidence.

– Students will be able to give feedback to help others improve their storytelling.

Things to Consider When Setting Your Goals

- With what age group do you want to work?

- Who do you need to contact to get started?

- How much time are you willing to devote to running a storytelling group?

- Do you want your storytelling club to perform for outside groups?

- What skills do you want your students to learn?

- What can be done to build poise, confidence, and group support?

- How can you help students take ownership of the group?

- Who will tell stories and how often?

- Who will coach the students and how will they coach each other?

- Do you want the students to run the meetings?

- How much input do you want from students in determining the group's goals and objectives?

- Will you use adult volunteers?

Case in Point: *When I started Voices of Illusion, I simply wanted to have a place to tell stories with my students. I didn't know that they would empower themselves to build upon my goal and become a pioneering storytelling youth group for others to follow. Every year in Voices of Illusion, we examine previous objectives and determine new ones. We try to concentrate on one to three objectives that we want to accomplish during the school year. This helps instill a sense of pride when the objectives are completed and motivation to accomplish still more the following year.*
—Kevin

Keeping your goals in mind as you become organized and reviewing them periodically will help to keep you focused and moving along the path you have set for yourself and your students. As your goals become clarified, you may find new objectives along the way. If you are intrigued by storytelling but don't have a clear vision in mind, use some guideposts listed in the "Storytelling Report Card" and other "Whys" of storytelling described in the Introduction to help set your goals.

Finding a Time and Place to Meet

Where and when your storytelling group meets will depend on the particular circumstances and the background of your students. Schools have a ready-made clientele from which to draw. Churches, public libraries, scouting troops, and Boys and Girls Clubs have their own particular set of students, although recruiting them may take more effort. If you are a freelance storyteller or volunteer, the first step is to find an organization willing to sponsor a storytelling club. You may find the best way to begin is to engage the support of a single teacher or the school's media specialist who can identify a group of specially selected students or a single classroom. As a volunteer, ask if meetings can be held during the school day, during enrichment or activity periods.

After-school meetings once or twice a week for an hour or two work well in middle and high schools where there are other ongoing after-school activities. Meeting once or twice a week during lunch works well in elementary schools where students are bused home immediately after school. In a public library, church, or recreation center, meeting once a month may be the only option, but you can still meet your goals. In such situations, schedule your meetings for time periods of an hour and a half or two hours so that you can accomplish as much as possible. Inform your young people that they will be expected to do much of the work of learning and practicing stories outside of meetings.

Keep the meeting day and time consistent. When scheduling your meeting time, consider other extracurricular activities that may conflict, such as sporting events, band practice, and other clubs. If you are unable to avoid a scheduling conflict, try to make arrangements with the other coaches or club sponsors so that students will not have to choose between one activity and the other. Many activities such as sports have a limited season. Perhaps your members can attend storytelling meetings once a week and then be permitted to skip on the day of a sports meet or game. If the coach will not allow your students to miss practice, then let them work on stories at home and join the meetings when the sports season is over.

If you are working with elementary and middle school students, you will want to make most of the decisions regarding time and place. With high school students, allow them to help make some of the decisions. Because you may be competing with sports, jobs, and other school activities, the success of your group will depend on how much time students are willing and able to commit.

The best space to meet is one where furniture can be moved easily to accommodate a variety of activities. In a school, the media center or a classroom works well. You want the space to be comfortable and large enough for the students to spread out for partner and small group activities, but not too large that you have difficulty having them come back together when you call them. Other places to consider include meeting rooms or classrooms at the public library or a church or synagogue, Boys and Girls Clubs, an apartment or condominium clubhouse, or even in a private home if the group is small enough. Access to a copy machine is also helpful.

Make sure that the room can be reserved for the use of your storytelling group on a regular basis and ask if there is a closet where you can store books and supplies. If your club is meeting in a classroom or space that is not your own, be sure to remind your students to respect the property of others and not to touch anything that does not belong to them. Be sure to put everything back the way you found it before you leave.

Tip for the Adult Leader: *I've moved meetings around to accommodate other school activities and provided kids with a calendar to keep track, but it became too confusing and difficult to remember, so now we're back to Wednesdays after school from 3:00 to 4:00 P.M. Talespinners compete with student council, sports, and other activities. I work with other club sponsors and coaches to allow my students to attend storytelling practices once in a while, and I excuse tellers when they have to prepare for a game or special event. —Judy*

Things to Consider in Setting Up Your Meetings

- Who will sponsor the group (e.g., school, public library, church, youth center)?
- How often will you meet?
- How long will the meetings last?
- Are the meetings in a convenient location?
- Does the meeting day and time conflict with other events or organizations?
- What arrangements can you make for students who wish to participate in other after-school activities?
- Have you confirmed the meeting dates and place with the building principal or other person in charge?

Recruiting Students

How you find participants will depend largely on your role in the school or community and from where you plan to recruit your prospective members. Teachers and media specialists usually have a captive audience from which to draw. In this capacity, it may be a matter of limiting participants rather than trying to entice students to join. Finding a place and time might be the biggest obstacle.

You will need to consider the best way to get the word out about your new club. If you're a teacher or school librarian, talk about it to your students one-on-one, or make an announcement to the class. Advertise your first meeting by displaying colorful posters and signs in school hallways, the media center, the cafeteria, and in areas where students congregate. Have announcements made over the school's public address system or closed-circuit televisions. Consider running a short ad over the local cable TV channel. In public libraries, churches, parks and recreation centers, or other youth centers, it is helpful to advertise in newsletters, put up posters, and simply encourage "regulars" to try storytelling. Talk with other club sponsors or youth group directors in your organization to discover what method works best for them.

Perhaps some students have heard you tell stories and want to learn to tell stories themselves. There may be a group of students who have been to a storytelling event and have asked you to help them organize a storytelling club. You have a ready-made set of allies and supporters with which to begin. You will still need to sit down with them to determine your goals and objectives and find a place and time to meet, but they are probably eager to help and have many ideas.

Word of mouth is always the best advertisement, so put them to work recruiting friends and classmates.

> **From Our Experience:** *A young high school student had approached me about forming a storytelling club after school. We started by having four students tell ghost stories in the basement of the school. The first story time lasted for more than four hours, and we began to plan our next meeting together. Soon the students were actively recruiting new members. We quickly grew to sixteen members, and today we are a storytelling troupe that performs from forty to seventy shows a year. We have even helped to create troupes at a nearby middle school and at a different high school in the same county. We have gone on to record five cassette tapes, one video, and two compact disks. We started very small and from this small group, we grew. Based on the ideas of the founding student members, we continue to flourish today. —Kevin*

Starting small and growing is the best plan of action. Although your enthusiasm and zeal may make you want to involve every young person, a small group allows you to become familiar with your own strengths and limitations as well as those of your students. When the group is too large, it is easy to rush through the learning process instead of taking the time to nurture and savor each stage of growth.

Don't be concerned if it seems you are not immediately attracting the number of students you wanted. Word of mouth is always the best advertisement. As members talk about their experiences, others will want to join in the fun. Part of the joy of working with youth is watching the group blossom over the days and months. Time builds a successful storytelling group, and by taking one small step at a time, the group will flourish. Soon you will likely have the opposite problem—"How do I find someone to help me with all these kids?"

> **From Our Experience:** *My first group of Talespinners back in 1987 consisted of nine girls and one boy. Having recently discovered the joys of storytelling myself, I wanted to share the excitement with my students. At first I was disappointed that my invitation to join the storytelling club had not attracted more students, but this group of ten was bright, energetic, and enthusiastic. Together we explored the story learning and practicing process and a variety of games that kept the meetings fun. Much of what I currently do with my students is based on the experiences with this first group. We visited an elementary school in the district and told stories to the younger students. We even took a school bus to the nursing home where my mother was living. The students learned what it is like to perform in less than optimal conditions. Over the next two years other students, some younger and still others who were friends or siblings of the original ten, joined the group. Talespinners quickly grew in popularity, and now we average around twenty-five storytellers each year. —Judy*

One of the best ways to drum up enthusiasm and attract potential youth storytellers is to have them see and hear stories told. Invite yourself into classrooms and tell a story or two. Teachers usually enjoy the break and may be willing to talk up the club after you leave.

If you are just learning to tell stories yourself, invite or hire a freelance storyteller to perform. Professional storytellers can be found in the National Storytelling Network's Directory of Storytellers (www.storynet.org) or try online searches for storytelling organizations in your state. Find out if your state has an arts and humanities council that includes storytellers in their listing or directory. Check the council's Web site or request a brochure or catalog. In many states, these directories list only performing artists who have been approved after having submitted an application and tape. Arts and humanities councils often provide small grants or some funding for programs featuring one of their performers. Ask your local public librarian, school media specialist, or storytelling league or guild, or call the chamber of commerce for the names of storytellers they might recommend.

You may want to plan a storytelling event in the media center, public library, church, or recreation center as a kickoff to initiate your group and attract members. Invite or train a few students ahead of time to tell a story and make them the featured tellers of the event. Allow time after the performance for a storytelling game or activity such as "Partner Storytelling," described in Chapter 3. In this game, the students retell the story they have just heard to a partner and take the story home to tell someone else.

If the group turns out to be smaller than you had hoped, offer an incentive such as a bookmark or a treat to any student who comes to the first meeting with a friend. Serve refreshments after the program. This will keep potential members from rushing off when the storytelling is over. Pizza is an inexpensive hit with kids, and serving snacks allows participants to socialize and ask questions on an informal basis.

Have permission slips or application forms available (see Figure 1.1). Be sure to let participants know the date, time, and place of the first meeting and whom to call if they have further questions. The application form should include your goals for the group or what you hope to accomplish. Clearly state the place, date, and time of the first meeting. Leave a place for the parent or guardian's signature as well as their home and work phone numbers.

If you are planning to take your group on a number of field trips or performances outside the building, consider asking for permission for all outside performances on your application form. Let parents know that you will be sending home reminders before each outing. A presigned agreement can save many headaches on the day of the field trip when some of your tellers undoubtedly will have forgotten their permission slips. When sending reminders, include any special directions, such as bringing a bag lunch or what is considered appropriate clothing, and state whether parents are invited to join the excursion. It is also advisable to give parents an estimate of how many field trips the group will take during the year and how often their child will miss classes.

Storytelling Club Application/Permission Form

Your son/daughter has expressed an interest in joining the storytelling club.

Storytellers meet after school once a week to learn, practice, and enjoy the art of STORYTELLING. Throughout the year, we will share our stories with students at other schools, senior citizens, preschoolers, and others.

Meetings are held on [_____] at [_____] at [_____]. Being a good storyteller requires commitment, practice, and attendance at meetings. Students who attend meetings regularly will be given priority in participating on field trips and performances.

Please sign the attached permission slip and return it to the club sponsor. In addition, this form will serve as a blanket agreement giving your permission for the student's participation in all field trips taken throughout the school year. Prior to each outing, your storyteller will be given a letter notifying you of the upcoming event.

Parents are always welcome and encouraged to join us on our field trips.

The first meeting of the storytelling club will be held on [_____]. If you have any questions, please feel free to call me at any time.

Group leader's name:

Sponsoring organization:

Phone number:

- -

My son/daughter, _____. Grade _____, has my permission to join the storytelling club. I understand that the meetings will be held on [day of the week] from [time] at [location] beginning [date].

My son/daughter also has my permission to ride the school bus or van and miss classes to participate in any field trips the storytelling club may take during the school year. (Students are expected to make up any schoolwork they have missed.

Parent's signature: _____

Today's date: _____

Phone number(s):_____
          (Daytime)   Evening

Figure 1.1. Sample application/permission form.

Things to Consider When Recruiting Members

- How will you alert students as to the time and place of your meetings?
  - Announcements over the public address system
  - Cable TV or televised announcements
  - Flyers, posters, mailings
- What kind of storytelling demonstration works best for you?
  - Telling stories yourself
  - Hiring a professional
  - Inviting storytellers from a local guild or story league
  - Training a few student storytellers
- What opportunities will you create to describe the program and what you are trying to accomplish?
- What incentives will you offer to members who bring a friend to the first few meetings?
- How will you make parents aware of the program?
- Have you included all of the important information needed on the permission slips?
  - Parent or guardian's signature
  - Daytime and evening telephone numbers in case of emergency
  - Indication of whether their child will be picked up or has permission to walk home after the meeting
  - Permission to attend all field trips and performances throughout the year
  - Date, time, and place of first meeting

Organizing the Space

How you prepare your storytelling space is almost as important as what you do in it. Circles work well for some activities but are not the best arrangement for telling stories. Many young people have difficulty making eye contact. In a circle, they not only have to think about gestures, facial expression, and voice, but where to look, and their backs ultimately face some of the listeners.

If you are meeting in a classroom, desks should be facing the front of the room so that everyone is looking at the storyteller. In a library or room with tables, a "U" shape works well, with the open part of the U being the performance space. Students should have freedom to move around and change or rearrange seats to suit the activity; but when someone is talking or telling a story, all other activity must stop and attention should be focused on the storyteller. This will minimize distractions, encourage "eye contact," and generate appropriate audience etiquette.

As often as possible, insist that your young storytellers stand in the performance space or in front of the room to talk or tell. This will help them become comfortable speaking in front of a group. The audience that causes the most anxiety is an audience of one's peers. Creating a specific telling space will help shy students who don't seem to have much to say and encourage more outgoing students to focus on exactly what they want to say without dominating the class.

Things to Consider When Arranging Your Space

- Is the room available on a regular basis?
- Can the furniture be rearranged easily?
- Do you need to notify the custodial staff to assist with room setup?
- Where is the best place for the "performance space"?
- Is the room large enough for the group without being overly large?
- Is the atmosphere comfortable?

Gathering Supplies

Each activity in a storytelling group has its own set of materials and supplies that are needed to carry it out, but there are a few basic supplies to gather ahead of time and have on hand for every meeting. Although not essential, having access to a copy machine is invaluable. Photocopies of stories are easier to work with than books, and they can be cut, pasted, marked, and written on. Many of the activities require copies for each student or team of students, and you will need copies of application forms, permission slips, and other necessary forms. If you do not have a free or inexpensive copy machine available, find the copy store or office supply store nearest your meeting place. Inquire about their prices and plan ahead. Many copy stores offer discounts for greater quantities.

A stopwatch or timer, a bell or whistle, and golf pencils are useful tools to have on hand. A timer is used in several ways. Many of the activities included in this book set time limits for carrying out the various steps or stages. Using a bell or whistle not only signals the end of the activity but can be used to call the group back together again. Timing stories is also important. Most beginning youth storytellers are comfortable with stories between five and ten minutes. Younger students may find that three minutes is about the maximum they can handle, at least in the beginning. Timing is especially important when you are given a certain time to fill. If you have a half-hour or forty-five minute program, you must know how many stories will fit into that time limit.

Many of the activities require writing, and most likely your students won't bring anything to write with to the meeting. We have found that a box of golf pencils, which you can purchase in most office supply stores, is a great resource to have on hand. They are inexpensive and packed 144 to the box.

Other supplies to consider are notebooks for attendance and record keeping. For the first few meetings, nametags are helpful, enabling you and your students to call each other by name without hesitation. If you get a box of one hundred or more ahead of time, extra nametags can be used for field trips and performances. A clipboard is helpful to keep track of checklists, as is a box for holding supplies, activity sheets, and other necessary items. If you are using someone else's room for meetings, you will need a box, cart, or closet where you can store your materials from week to week. A bookcase or cart with wheels might be considered a luxury but is a nice thing to have to keep your storytelling books easily accessible to your members. They can be purchased from a library supply company. Ask your school or public librarian to help you find a company with reasonable prices.

Supplies to Consider for Meetings

- Chalkboard or flipchart

- Name tags

- Access to a copy machine

- Timer or stopwatch

- Bell or whistle

- Golf pencils

- Book cart

- Attendance book, other note books

- Clipboard

- Boxes, carts, closet for books, supplies, props, and so forth

Laying the groundwork for your club is extremely important to help ensure a smooth beginning to your storytelling group or troupe. The more thorough your preparations, the better organized you will be and the more confident you will feel as you hold that all-important first meeting. With goals and objectives in mind, recruiting methods ready to be implemented, and space and supplies in hand, you are ready to welcome young people into your meetings. Continue to plan and organize as you nurture your young charges and establish a week-by-week schedule and activities.

Chapter 2

Let the Meetings Begin

Creating a Safe Environment

It is extremely important that you establish an environment where all members are accepted and where everyone is free to try without fear of disapproval or ridicule if they fail or make mistakes. A storytelling club is no place for competition. Storytellers need to understand that although everyone comes into the group with different talents and abilities, they are all here to learn the art of storytelling, to improve their skills, and to do their very best. Members should be applauded for taking risks and succeeding in their efforts. If everyone feels safe, your group will form a tight bond. They will be each other's strongest advocates and supporters.

Students need to understand the difference between a compliment, criticism, and a put-down. Compliments and criticism are ways of improving the teller's story or performance. By ensuring that praise is always given first before suggestions for improvement, the teller will benefit from the advice. Criticism must come from wanting to help the teller improve, even if the suggestion is not taken. A "put-down" attacks the teller. It can be as general as, "That story stinks!" or as specific as "You look silly when you tell that story." Instead of talking about the story or the growth of the teller, a put-down is meant to be hurtful and should never be allowed. The adult leader should model appropriate feedback and praise students for giving positive, constructive suggestions. In the chapter on coaching (Chapter 5), we give specific instructions on how to create a safe environment for helping young storytellers improve their stories and performance.

Sometimes there may be members who are too shy to speak up or who are willing to let the stronger more vocal people take over. There may be members who have great need to show off and dominate discussions and opinions. Remind students that all opinions are valid and that everyone needs to participate. Using activities such as "Rotation Station," described in Chapter 4, will help your group find ways to support and encourage each other.

Establishing Rules

Discipline or classroom management is something you need to consider. By its very nature, a storytelling club or group has a more casual feel to it than a regular classroom. There are many times when students work in small groups, and there are many opportunities for sharing and discussion, but sometimes you will have to keep a firm hold on the group, so things do not get out of hand. How you manage your group will depend largely on how much order and structure you need to feel confident that students are listening to you and will come back to order when you call. It is also important for the safety and well-being of the students to have a place where they feel comfortable and where they know the rules.

As a group leader, you need to evaluate your own classroom management style. Establish in your own mind how much noise and disruption you are willing to tolerate. Although you want everyone to have fun, it needs to be fun for you, too. Students should understand what behavior you are willing to tolerate and what you consider out of line.

It is vital that you establish rules for performances, whether in the classroom or on stage, whether for sharing the outcome of a game or telling a story. Stress the importance of helping one another and being a good audience. Older students are able to work with you to develop rules. With younger students, it's a good idea to set the ground rules and expectations—but not too many and not too long. Choose the most important rules and emphasize them. Work with your group to elicit rules for appropriate behavior, such as the following:

When Someone Is in the Performance Space, Members of the Audience Should

- Stay in their seats.
- Give their undivided attention to the storyteller.
- Listen without comment or interruption.
- Applaud when appropriate.

Establish ground rules for attendance and participation, too. Students should know why they are telling. If the goal is to perform, have a specific performance location in mind, whether it is in the school gym or the auditorium in a performance for parents or in a local preschool or a senior center. If members know where they are going, they will pay attention to deadlines. Remember, to put on the best performance possible, only students who have rehearsed their stories should be allowed to tell.

Attendance is important, but flexibility is the key. Kids today are involved with many competing activities. Allow some absences as long as students can still prepare for performances. If students miss three or four meetings in a row, check with them to see if they are still interested in the group. Sometimes they just need to know they are missed, or perhaps they simply need help finding a ride home after the meetings. No matter what, always allow students to drop out without losing face, especially if the excuse seems to be a weak one. Next year when friends or circumstances change, they may join again and become your most devoted members.

Tip for the Adult Leader: *With high school students you can designate officers' positions. Voices of Illusion has a student business meeting at which we have, among other positions, a person to call any member who has missed a number of meetings. We also have two co-chairs who oversee daily meetings, handle some booking questions, and give daily schedules. This involves the young people and gives them a sense of ownership and responsibility toward the group, while alleviating some of the leader's workload. —Kevin*

Things to Consider When Establishing Rules

- How can we help each other succeed?

- What is appropriate audience behavior?

- How can the group encourage everyone to participate?

- What are the consequences for someone who chooses to disrupt meetings?

- Should members be allowed to perform if they haven't attended meetings?

Structuring the Meetings

Structure your meetings in a logical sequence and keep the format consistent. The meetings should flow from one activity to another. This way your tellers will know what to expect each week. There will be less confusion, and if they miss a week or two, they will fit right back in. It's important to allow for some unstructured time, usually at the beginning or end of the meeting, so that your students will know each other better and bond as a community. A consistent opening and closing helps to frame the meeting and set the tone for what you are trying to accomplish.

Beginning storytellers need to hear stories as often as possible. Therefore, you need to provide a story listening experience every week, whether you do the telling or invite a guest to tell stories. Members also need activities and games to help them learn to tell stories and hone their skills. The following meeting format listed has worked well for us.

Social Time

As students arrive and sign in, allow your tellers some free time to socialize. This not only helps kids become acquainted with each other, especially if they come from other schools or different grade levels, but it gives you time to chat with kids one-on-one. If meetings take place after school or last longer than an hour, it is a good idea to have refreshments or allow students to bring snacks. Make it simple and unobtrusive, and make it clear that the munching stops once the meeting begins and it's time to get down to business.

Opening

It is often difficult to end the sociability and proceed with the business at hand. You want everyone to feel relaxed and ready to enjoy the work ahead. Just as the Pledge of Allegiance or the "Star-Spangled Banner" signals the opening of a civic meeting or ball game, using a beginning protocol brings everyone to attention. It may be as simple as calling the group to order with a clap of the hands or ringing a bell and saying, "The meeting will now begin"; it may be as complex as lighting a candle and playing a particular piece of music or reciting a special poem. Consider using the "Storyteller's Pledge" found in the introduction. Shel Silverstein's "If You Are a Dreamer," from his book of poetry *Where the Sidewalk Ends* (Harper & Row, 1974) is a wonderful poem to welcome participation, or you may use song or a favorite poem that one of your students has created. (If you like the idea of using a candle but are concerned about the safety issue, try a hurricane lamp or purchase an electric or a battery-operated holiday candle.) Call and response also works well. In Haiti, storytellers call out "Cric?" (pronounced "creek") when they have a story to tell. Audience members answer back "Crac!" (pronounced "crack") when they want the storyteller to begin.

Other options include choosing a different member each week to open the meeting by telling a brief story or anecdote. If you have a small group or the luxury of a longer meeting time, let members relate how stories or storytelling was part of their life that week. Try posting a "topic of the week" on the chalkboard or flip chart and letting members give a brief response (e.g., what is your favorite color, fairy tale, song, school subject, food, or holiday and why? Describe your favorite room, pet, or possession. Tell about one of your earliest memories, favorite school experience, or embarrassing moments).

After you've called the meeting to order, give the outline or schedule for the day. Let participants know approximately how much time will be spent on each activity. Review what was accomplished at the last meeting especially for the students who were absent.

Story

Include at least one story that you or one of the more experienced members tells. This usually works better at the beginning of the meeting rather than trying to squeeze it in at the end. Your new tellers in particular need to hear stories. They not only learn what is expected of them, but they learn to appreciate and enjoy the art of storytelling as well. Focus on simple, easy-to-learn stories that students may choose to tell for their own performance later. If you are new to storytelling yourself, enlist local tellers and learn to tell stories right along with your kids. If you have difficulty obtaining live storytellers, consider using some of excellent videocassettes, audio cassettes, and compact disks that feature nationally known storytellers. (Suggestions are listed in Chapter 9, "Resources.")

Tip for the Adult Leader: *For the first couple of meetings, I like to "stock" the audience. I always have three or four students tell a prepared story at each meeting. This way I don't leave it to chance that stories will be told. Making a good first impression at initial meetings ensures the longevity of the group.* —Kevin

Case in Point: *Justin heard me tell Joseph Bruchac's "Turtle Makes War on Men" from his book* Iroquois Stories *(Crossing Press, 1985). He liked it so well that he checked the book out of the library and learned one of the other stories in the book. My story of how Michigan got its unusual shape intrigued Brandon, so he learned the story and told it in his own way, which gave me a new perspective on it.* —Judy

Feedback

Whether you tell a story, engage a guest storyteller, or show a storytelling video, encourage your students to look for storytelling techniques while they enjoy the story. After the telling, allow the group to discuss techniques and give feedback. This will reinforce the strategies you are trying to teach. Young people can be perceptive and honest, especially in voicing their opinion about what they liked and disliked. There is nothing like having students teach the teacher!

When you encourage, you model the framework for the feedback they will receive when they tell their stories. Comments and suggestions should be voiced in a positive manner with suggestions given only if the teller requests them.

Things to Consider When Giving Feedback

- Are any questions about the story?
- Are there parts of the story that require more information?
- What parts of the story worked well?
- Describe the story's strong or weak points.
- Comment on the use of voice, pacing, facial expression, gestures, and eye contact.

Case in Point: *I told a personal story about my parents coming to America during World War II. My Talespinners liked the parts that made them laugh, but they also let me know that calling my parents by their first names was confusing to them. When I told them the story about my twelfth birthday, I had forgotten that I told it the year before. Rikki said it was better the second time, but he also let me know which long descriptions I could leave out.* —Judy

---

Activity

To make the meetings fun while strengthening storytelling skills, each meeting should contain at least one cooperative activity. In the beginning, concentrate on games that build community while helping to develop the skills needed to tell stories. As the year progresses, plan lessons that will help the tellers learn their stories and strengthen their delivery skills. After the group's first performance, provide a variety of activities designed to improve skills and help them to create new stories. Even if the club meets mainly to swap stories, a well-chosen activity will add variety to your meetings and can help your young people improve the quality of their stories as well as their presentation.

If your group is large, it is especially important to make sure that no one is left out. Young people learn best when they are actively engaged. Even with a small group, it is impossible to attend constantly to each student's needs. Plan plenty of partner or small-group activities that will keep everyone involved. It is helpful both for class management as well as improving students' skills to break the larger class into groups of twos, threes, or fours. Small groups foster community building. When they help one another, young people feel important—they feel they are being heard. Helping others also serves to reinforce the skills they have learned. Club members should practice telling their stories in small groups first to receive feedback and suggestions in a less threatening and less public format. Rearrange the groups often. Do not let the same friends work together all the time. Create a mentor system to encourage experienced or more proficient tellers to work with newer, less outgoing members of the group.

Calling the Class Back to Order

Choose a way to allow students to know when an activity is over and it's time to come together again as a group. Ring a bell, flick the lights on and off, or clap, but use the same method each time so students will come to recognize the signal.

Reflection

Allow time at the end of each meeting to bring everyone together to talk about what they have learned and to reflect on what worked well. Verbalizing what they've experienced helps members reinforce the skills they are developing. This also creates an opportunity to remind club members of what they need to prepare for the next meeting before they leave.

Things to Consider When Evaluating an Activity

- What did we do?
- How did we do it?
- What did we learn from it?
- How are we going to use what we learned?
- How will this make us better storytellers?

Closing

The closing protocol is equally as important as setting the right tone for the opening of the meeting. Relaxing with deep breathing or guided meditation, blowing out the candle, forming a circle and singing or playing a song or reciting a poem keeps the group together until the end and leaves everyone with a sense of completion.

Choosing a Name for Your Group

With a new storytelling group or club, spend part of the first few meetings choosing a name for the club. Incorporate the name of your school, library, or sponsoring organization, and make sure it is something you can live with for a long time. Keep in mind your goals for the group. Is storytelling performance a goal? Then you may want an exotic name or one with special pizzazz. Are your meetings primarily to swap tales among yourselves? Then consider a name with "story circle" or "story swappers" in it. Voting on the name gives students ownership from the get go. Be creative and have fun with the naming process.

During your first few meetings, brainstorm a list of names. Have students vote on their favorites, keeping in mind what they would like the name of the group to convey and what are the goals of the group. Unless there is a clear favorite, postpone the final vote until the second or third meeting so everyone will have time to think about it. Be sure the name is one that you as the leader can live with as well.

Story Tellers, Talespinners, Story Spinners, Story Weavers, and Tale Tellers are popular names. If these names are too ordinary for your group, we've come across a number of interesting and unique names: Off-the-Page Storytellers, The Polar Expressions, Freedom Train Student Storytellers, and Story Stagers. Kevin's high school troupe is called *The Voices of Illusion.* At one point, they considered calling themselves *The Voices of Allusion,* but decided that *Illusion* was a more appropriate description of their work.

Consider designing a logo that can be placed on publicity materials, T-shirts, hats, or vests. This will give your group a recognizable identity that can be used when performing and will give your members an extra sense of belonging. Use the group's talents in creating a logo. Perhaps there is a member with graphics experience or special artistic ability, or you can enlist the help of the art teacher or computer tech.

Things to Consider When Choosing a Name for the Group

- Does the name incorporate the name of the school, library, or organization?
- Does the name reflect the goal of the group?
- Can you "live" with the name for a long time?
- Is the name simple and clear enough, or will you have to explain it each time you use it?

Establishing a Schedule

When starting out, it is helpful to create lesson plans or agendas for several meetings in advance. (As examples, we have included two club-meeting schedules; see Figure 2.3.) Having a sense of defined parameters and expectations will give you confidence and alleviate uncertainty. Adjustments can be made along the way, but an agenda will keep you focused on what you want to accomplish with your young tellers.

These outlines are meant to serve as part of a continuum. The first is based on ten one-hour to hour-and-half weekly meetings that lead to a performance. The second condenses the process into six weeks. Continued meetings will develop and improve presentation skills and help build a stronger community. Additional meetings provide time for choosing stories, coaching sessions, and practicing for future performances.

First Meeting Agenda

The first meeting is perhaps the most important. You want to begin on the right foot and set the tone for future meetings. You want participants to know what happens at the meetings and what is expected of them. Begin by introducing yourself; explain why you started a storytelling club and what you hope to accomplish. Share an anecdote or funny story about yourself. Perhaps you got yourself out of trouble or were able to talk your way out of a difficult situation by telling a story. Or perhaps there was a special person in your life, a grandparent or teacher, who told you stories. Let your students know how or why you became interested in becoming a storyteller and why you want to help them become storytellers as well.

Your students may not know what a storytelling group is or does. Let them know that a storytelling club or group is a place to make new friends, but it is also a place to work and learn. It is not a class and they will not receive grades, but the benefits include recognition, applause, self-confidence, new skills, and appreciation. They will be expected to work on their own but also to help, encourage, and support each other. Spend some time discussing the goals and benefits of storytelling and ask students to contribute to the list, writing their comments on the chalkboard or flip chart. At a future meeting, you can refer back to the list, prioritize the goals and set group objectives. It is also important to communicate the rules at the first meeting. Write them on the board or use a handout and discuss them with participants.

Be sure to allow time for the students to introduce themselves, giving their name, grade, and other pertinent information, as well as telling the group why they joined and what they hope to get out of being a member of a storytelling club. Perhaps they could also relate something special or unique about themselves (e.g., what musical instrument they play, contests they have won, a time their picture was in the newspaper, where they were born, how many siblings they have). Include an icebreaker or community-building activity so that the students get to know each other and begin feeling comfortable with one another.

Prepare a story ahead of time to tell to the group. Let them experience what storytelling looks and sounds like. We have included a brief story called "Filling the Room" that you may wish to use. After the story, ask the students if they have any questions.

Filling the Room

There once was a farmer who owned a farmhouse, a barn, and a small piece of land. He had three children. The farmer was getting on in years, and before he died, he wanted to leave the farm to one of his children. Since the farm was small, he did not want to divide the property between the three children. So he decided to leave the farm to the child that would make the best use of it.

One day, he called his children to him and said, "I am getting on in years and will not live forever. I want to leave this farm to whichever one of you will make best use of it. To the others, I will leave a small sum of money to help you get started on your life's journey."

"I have devised a contest to help me decide who shall get the farm. I will give each of you a few coins to take to the market place. There you shall purchase something that will fill this room. Whoever makes best use of the money and fills the room the longest will inherit the farm."

And so the farmer gave a handful of coins to each one of his children. The oldest son took his coins and went to the marketplace, where he purchased several large bags of feathers. He brought his purchase home and opened all of the windows in his father's room. Then he opened the bags of feathers and threw them into the air. The draft from the windows blew the feathers around and around and filled the room for an hour. But, eventually the winds outside the windows died down and the feathers settled to the floor, leaving the floor covered with only a few of inches of feathers.

The second son went to the marketplace with his coins and purchased some matches and a candle. When he reached his father's house. He closed windows and lit the candle. For several hours the candle burned brightly, filling the room with light and warmth. But, eventually the candle burned down to a puddle of wax and the flame went out, leaving the room cold and dark.

Now, the youngest child took her coins and put them in her pocket. She did not go to the marketplace. Instead, she went to the homes of her friends and asked them all to come back with her to her father's house. When the girl's friends arrived, they sat down in her father's room. She invited her father to sit in the chair of honor and gave him back his coins. Then the farmer's daughter began to tell a story. When she was finished, one of her friends told another story. Soon another friend began to play a guitar and they all sang songs and another friend danced. Hour after hour, the farmer's daughter and her friends danced, sang, and told stories, filling the room with music and words.

And when the night was over, and the first light of morning began to creep over the horizon, the farmer called his children to him. "When I die," he said, "I shall leave the farm to my daughter, for she spent not a penny but filled the room with joy and laughter and friendship that not only filled this room but can fill a lifetime."

And so it was. The farmer gave his sons a small sum of money to begin their lives' journey. The oldest son became a doctor, and he healed the sick. The second son became an engineer, and he built magnificent buildings. To his daughter, the farmer left his farm. She worked the farm and made it prosperous. And every night friends came over and sang and danced and told stories.

Figure 2.1. Story: "Filling the Room," retold by Judy Sima.

Sample First Meeting Agenda

I. Social time

- Fill out name tags.

- Sign in or take attendance.

II. Opening

- Call the meeting to order, light a candle, recite a poem, and welcome everyone.

- Introduce yourself to the group and give them your background.

III. Tell a story to the group: Choose one of your favorites or tell the story featured in Figure 2.1, "Filling the Room."

IV. Game or Activity: Choose one of the activities from "Getting Ready to Tell," described in Chapter 3, or choose one of your own. ("Hello Bingo," "Storytelling's Scavenger Hunt," or "Meet My Friend" work well.) These engaging activities are designed to help you and the members get to know each other.

V. Discussion topics

A. *Why tell stories?* Possible answers:

- You feel good, and it makes others feel good, too.

- You gain self-confidence and overcome the fear of speaking in front of a group.

- It is fun.

- You make friends and go on fieldtrips.

- It improves your performance in school—memory, vocabulary, expressing yourself, getting organized.

- You get to share the oral tradition, the oldest form of communication.

B. *What are the goals of our group? State your goals and elicit suggestions from the group.* Possible answers:

- To learn to tell stories

- To tell stories that we've learned to a variety of audiences

- To become comfortable speaking in front of a group

- To become familiar with many kinds of stories

- To make friends

- To have fun

C. *What are the leader's expectations of group members?*

- Storytelling club is for serious storytellers. Have fun, but the primary purpose is to learn stories to share with others.

- That means attending meetings, staying on task, supporting one another, and practicing at home.

- Supporting each other means giving positive feedback, encouraging each other. There are no "bests" in our story club, just each teller getting better and doing his or her best.

- Being a good storyteller means being a good listener—listen to the adult leader, to other members, to guest storytellers. Everyone listens when someone is in the "storytelling place."
- When on a fieldtrip or performing, remember that you are ambassadors for your school, library, or sponsoring organization. Be on your best behavior.

  D. What happens at meetings?
  - Socialize and sign in.
  - Listen to stories.
  - Participate in partner, small-group, or whole-group activities.
  - Choose stories to tell.
  - Receive individual or group coaching.
  - Learn group chants and stories.
  - Practice stories; give each other feedback.
  - Prepare for performances—microphone techniques, introductions, and so on.
  - Reflect and discuss our experiences to improve.

  E. What are the rules?
  - Attend meetings. Let the adult leader know when you are going to be absent.
  - Get snacks ahead of time, go to the bathroom, and so on.
  - No wandering the halls.
  - Stories must be rehearsed before they are performed.
  - No put-downs. State suggestions in a positive manner.
  - When someone is in the performance space, stay in your seat, listen, do not interrupt or make comments, applaud when the performer is finished.
  - After the meeting, leave the room the way you found it.

VI. Choose a name for the group.

VII. Reflection: This can be done at the end of the meeting or as an introduction to each member.
  - Why did you join the storytelling group?
  - What do you expect achieve?
  - How do you think storytelling will help you?
  - What can you do to help make this a good experience for yourself and others?

VII. Closing
  - Form a circle or, from their seats, encourage members to express what they liked or learned from the day's meeting.
  - As the adult leader, comment on what was accomplished or learned and what you hope to accomplish at the next meeting.
  - Remind everyone of the day and time of the next meeting.
  - Blow out the candle, sing a song, recite a poem, and so on.

Figure 2.2. Sample first meeting agenda.

Meeting Formats

Figure 2.3 are two sample schedules for club meetings. Although the agenda or format remains the same from week to week, new stories and activities are added each week to build skills that will prepare students for their first performance. The first schedule is based on ten weekly meetings of one-hour to an hour-and-a-half. Additional mini-meetings may be needed for choosing stories, coaching sessions, or practicing for the performance, depending on the size of your group.

Maybe you don't have ten weeks, or you and your young tellers are anxious to take the show on the road. The second schedule provides a condensed outline to prepare students for performing more quickly. This will place greater responsibility on your students. Much of the searching for a story to tell and practicing will have to be done on their own time. Increasing the length of meetings to an hour-and-a-half to two hours a week will enable you to make the most of activities and practice time. As in the ten-week format, a story should be told at every meeting, whether by you, a guest storyteller, or on videotape of a professional teller, and meetings should end with a reflection on what was learned.

Following the Performance

Take notes during the performance so that you can praise your storytellers for what they did well. Immediately after the performance, or as soon as is practical, find time to talk about what went right and what might need to be changed or improved upon for the next performance. Have the students evaluate their own telling:

- What did I like about my performance?

- What am I going to work on for the next performance?

- How did the performance go as a whole?

- What went well?

- What could be improved for the next performance?

Use subsequent meetings for choosing new stories, working on tandem stories, building and strengthening skills, creating their own stories (see additional activities in Chapter 4), and, of course, preparing for more performances.

Ten Terrific Weeks (and Beyond) to Telling Time

Please note: * indicates that the form, reproducible, story, or activity is included in this book.

Week 1. *Focus:* Introductions and meeting structure

Purpose: To introduce group leader and members to one another. To make students aware of the purpose of storytelling and the goals of the group. To familiarize students with the structure of the meetings and rules.

- Opening (take attendance or sign in, light a candle, welcome members, call members to order)
- Story: told by leader, experienced member, or guest storyteller
- Sample First Meeting Agenda* (Figure 2.2)
- Reflection
- Closing

Week 2. *Focus:* Introduction of story genres and opportunity to speak in front of the group

Purpose: To help students develop an awareness of different literature and folklore genres. To encourage students to keep a record of the stories they read for future storytelling. To give students an opportunity to speak in front of the group and to help students to get to know a little bit about each other.

- Opening
- Story: tell one of your favorites or invite a guest storyteller
- Hand out and discuss Storytellers Bingo* (Chapter 3: Figures 3.1, 3.2, 3.3)
- Activity: I Am, I Can,* or Meet My Friend* (Chapter 3)
- Reflection
- Closing

Week 3. *Focus:* Learning and retelling a story

Purpose: To enable students to learn a story that can be retold easily and to demonstrate the effectiveness of collaboration when learning to tell a story. To motivate students to achieve various levels of expertise.

- Story: "The Tailor"* (Chapter 3: Figure 3.6) or a story of your choosing
- Activity: Partner Storytelling:* retelling "The Tailor" to partners (Chapter 3)
- Introduce Levels of Achievement: Circle of Excellence* (Chapter 6: Figures 6.1, 6.2)

Week 4. *Focus:* Selecting stories to tell

Purpose: To initiate the story learning process. To guide students in selecting stories that they will enjoy learning and telling.

- Begin story learning process: Introduce Sima's Six Quick Steps to Storytelling Success* (Chapter 3: Figure 3.7)
- Activity: Step 1. Choose It:* Begin to choose stories to tell (Chapter 3)
- Activity: Step 2. Read It:* Read story aloud to a partner (Chapter 3)

Week 5. *Focus:* Story structure and retelling stories in students' own words.

Purpose: To help students learn stories by understanding sequence and the importance of telling stories in their own words.

- Story: "Wilfrid Gordon McDonald Partridge" by Mem Fox (Kane Miller, 1985) or a story of your choosing

- Continue choosing stories and reading them aloud to a partner (Chapter 3)
- Activity: Step 3. Picture It:* Draw the sequence of the story using a Storyboard* or map the story using the Storytelling Map* (Chapter 3: Figures 3.8, 3.9)

Week 6. *Focus:* Guiding imaginations and practice

Purpose: To help students use their imaginations to improve the learning and telling of their stories. To provide an opportunity for students to practice telling their stories to members of the group.

- Activity: Step 4. Imagine It:* Guided visualization or imagining (Chapter 4)
- Activity: Step 5. Practice It:* Practice telling the story to a partner (Chapter 4)
- Teach the group a chant or story: "Jazzy Three Bears"* (Chapter 7: Figure 7.4)

Week 7. *Focus:* Identifying skills and practice

Purpose: To make students aware of the skills important to a good storytelling performance and enable them to acquire those skills.

- Activity: Rotation Station* (Chapter 4)
    - Positive ways to give feedback
    - How to support each other
    - What makes a story interesting to listen to
- Continue practice telling stories to a partner
- Practice group chant or story

Week 8. *Focus:* Improving and practicing stories

Purpose: To help students remember their stories and to recognize the parts of the story that needs more practice.

- Story: "Natural Habits" from *Thirty-Three Multicultural Tales to Tell* by Pleasant DeSpain (August House, 1993) or a story of your choosing
- Introduce: Storyteller's Feedback Form* (Chapter 4: Figure 3.10)
- Model coaching strategies by having students give you feedback on one of your stories (Chapter 5)
- Activity: Virginia Reel* telling (Chapter 4)

Week 9. *Focus:* Preparation for performance

Purpose: To help students become comfortable telling their stories in a performance mode. To begin preparations for performing the stories they have learned.

- Activity: Step 6. Tell It:* Choose volunteers to tell their story in front of entire group (Chapter 3)
- Begin preparations for performance: Field Trip Checklist* (Chapter 7: Figure 7.1)
- Practice Warm-Up Exercises* (Chapter 7)

Week 10. *Focus:* Final preparations for performance

Purpose: To prepare students for storytelling performance

- Make final preparations for performance.
- Practice group chant
- Final telling to group using a microphone: Using a Microphone* (Chapter 7)
- Choose a master of ceremonies and determine the order of the performance
- Establish rules for performance or field trip : "Rules of the Road"* (Chapter 7)

Figure 2.3. Ten-week meeting format.

Six-Week Step-Up Schedule:
A complete storytelling course in just six meetings

Please note: * indicates that the form, reproducible, story, or activity is included in this book.

Week 1. *Focus:* Introductions, meeting structure, story genres

> *Purpose:* To introduce group leader and members to one another. To make students aware of the purpose of storytelling and the goals of the group. To familiarize students with the structure of the meetings and the rules. To help students develop an awareness of different literature and folklore genres. To encourage students to keep a record of the stories they read for future storytelling.

- Opening
- Story: Filling the Room* (Figure 2.1) or a story of your choice.
- See Sample First Meeting Agenda* (Figure 2.2)
- Hand out and discuss Storytellers Bingo* (Chapter 3: Figures 3.1, 3.2, 3.3)
- Reflection
- Closing

Week 2. *Focus:* Group support, creating tellable stories

> *Purpose:* To help students take familiar tales and make them their own by adding their own ideas. To encourage students to work together to create stories involving audience participation. To provide students with a format for telling stories.

- Story: A retelling of an Aesop's fable (or one from another source)
- Activity: Bare Bones Fables* (Chapter 4: Figure 4.3) or Five Times Three*—Audience Participation (Chapter 4: Figure 4.4)

Week 3. *Focus:* Choosing stories to tell

> *Purpose:* To initiate the story learning process. To guide students in selecting stories that they will enjoy learning and telling.

- Begin story learning process: Introduce Sima's Six Quick Steps to Storytelling Success* (Chapter 3: Figure 3.7)
- Activity: Step 1. Choose It:* Begin to choose stories to tell (Chapter 3)
- Activity: Step 2. Read It:* Read story aloud to a partner (Chapter 3)
- On your own: Choose a story to tell

Week 4. *Focus:* Learning story sequence. Telling stories in tellers' own words.

> *Purpose:* To help students learn stories by understanding sequence and the importance of telling stories in their own words.

- Activity: Step 3. Picture It:* Draw the sequence of the story using a Storyboard* (Chapter 3: Figure 3.8) or map the story using the Storytelling Map.* (Chapter 3: Figure 3.9)

- Activity: Step 5. Practice It:* Tell story to a partner (Chapter 3)

- On your own: practice telling stories at home

Week 5. *Focus:* Feedback and practice telling stories

Purpose: To allow students to become comfortable telling their story in a performance mode. To guide students into giving appropriate feedback.

- Model coaching strategies by having students give you feedback on one of your stories (Chapter 5)

- Activity: Step 6. Tell It:* Tell story to the group (Chapter 3)

- Introduce: Storyteller's Feedback Form* (Chapter 3: Figure 3.10)

Week 6. *Focus:* Preparation for performance

Purpose: To prepare students for field trip for performance.

- Preparations for performance: Field Trip/Performance Checklist* (Chapter 7: Figure 7.1)

- Final telling to group or individual coaching

- Choose order of performance

Figure 2.4. Six-week meeting format.

Section II

Growing Your Storytelling Group

It is important to keep meetings lively, enjoyable, and productive both for you and your young tellers. Storytelling games and activities are a major part of what makes storytelling groups and troupes "fun." They are also useful tools for helping young people become better storytellers. As you work with your students from week to week, you may find that they will only practice their own story and listen to others practice their stories for so long before they become bored. The games and skills included in this section have the dual purpose of improving your students' stories and performance while keeping interest and motivation high.

These storytelling games and activities are used in all stages of story learning from standing comfortably in front of a group, to learning the story, to improving performance and delivery. They can be used prior to having students choose stories to tell as well as later on when the group tires of listening to each other practice. As a way of organizing the activities, they are grouped together into four sections. Chapter 3 includes "Getting Ready to Tell Stories" and "The Story Learning Process." Chapter 4 includes "Building and Strengthening Storytelling Skills" and "Creating New Stories." Each activity contains the following:

1. **Purpose:** This section states the goal or objective of the activity—what you can expect the students to be able to do or what you want them to accomplish by completing the activity.

2. **Supplies:** Any materials or supplies needed to carry out the activity will be given here.

3. **Directions for the Activity:** This section gives the teacher or adult leader a summary of the activity and step-by-step instructions for preparing and implementing the activity successfully. Reproducible game sheets and special forms are included where needed. Special considerations or ways of adapting the activity to different ages are noted. Whenever possible, the teacher or coach should demonstrate or model the activity and allow time for questions to ensure that the young people understand what is expected of them. By participating in the activity, you continue to model how the activity is done, and it allows you to describe your experience as a way of stimulating discussion after the lesson is completed.

4. **Examples:** Examples and anecdotes from our own experiences are included to clarify the process.

5. **Reflections:** It is important that the group leader reserve time for closure, reviewing and reflecting on what the students have learned. This section gives specific discussion questions to use after completing the activity. When students verbalize what they experienced, it reinforces the skills you are trying to teach. It is also a good time for you to restate what you expected them to get out of the activity and if there is any homework or information needed to prepare for the next meeting.

In addition to the specific questions given at the end of each activity, reflections should include the following:

- What did we do?

- How did we do it?

- What did we learn from it?

- What are we going to do with it?

- How will it improve our storytelling?

Tip for the Leader: *It is helpful to use a stopwatch or timer for many of these activities. This ensures that each student gets equal time to participate and will help keep the students focused and on task. Use a bell or whistle to signify the end of the activity or when it is time to switch partners to help create a gamelike environment.*

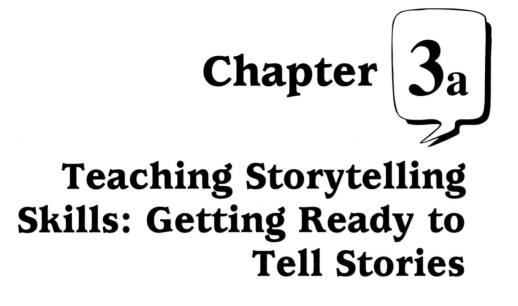

Chapter 3a

Teaching Storytelling Skills: Getting Ready to Tell Stories

The first few meetings of your storytelling group or troupe should be spent becoming acquainted with one another. As they participate in the games and activities listed in this section, club members learn to describe, enjoy, and perhaps laugh at their experience, and they become better at expressing themselves. As they bond as a group, each member develops a sense of belonging. You will want to do some of these activities right at the beginning and save others for later. These exercises enable your students to think in terms of "story." They will begin to see the elements of what makes a good story and realize that everyone has a story to tell and that their own personal experiences can be considered in terms of a story. They will become attentive listeners, and when their parents and grandparents speak of old times, they will listen with a greater appreciation.

Storytellers' Bingo

(Adapted with permission from Donna Boudreau)

Purpose: To help students develop an awareness of different literature and folklore genres. To encourage students to keep a record of the stories they read for future storytelling.

Supplies:

- Storytellers' Bingo (Figure 3.1) and Story Record (Figure 3.2) for every participant
- Storytellers' Bingo Category Definitions (Figure 3.3)
- Inexpensive prizes, such as bookmarks, pencils, book covers, and candy bars for the prize box
- Larger prizes such at gift certificates, paperback books, or posters

This game will encourage your club members to read and become familiar with many types of stories from all over the world, as well as with stories written by well-known authors. It is especially useful for those wishing to strengthen students' reading and speaking skills. If you do not have access to many books, make arrangements with the school or public library in your area to set aside books for your kids to check out. Purchase prizes ahead of time to have on hand when students complete a BINGO.

Directions for Storytellers' Bingo

1. Reproduce copies of the Storytellers' Bingo (Figure 3.1) and Story Record (Figure 3.2) forms for each member of the storytelling group.

2. Using the descriptions and examples in the Storytellers' Bingo Category Definitions (Figure 3.3), discuss the various types of stories that students will be required to read (e.g., Myth, King Midas or Hercules; African Folktale, The Cow-tail Switch; Tall Tale, Pecos Bill or Paul Bunyan; Fable, The Lion and the Mouse)

3. Tell students where they will be able to find books to read in order to complete the Storytellers' Bingo and Story Record. (In most libraries, fairy tales and folklore can be found in the Dewey Decimal number beginning with 398; mythology begins with 291 and 292. Literary stories can be found in the fiction, story collection, or picture book sections.)

4. Purchase small prizes such as pencils, bookmarks, candy bars, or notepads to reward students for every five stories read and larger prizes such as a paperback book, poster, or gift certificate to a bookstore when students have read one story from each of the twenty-five categories.

5. Direct club members to

   • Read at least one or two stories a week from different categories.

   • Write the name of the story, the title, and the page numbers of the book where the story is written on the Story Record sheet.

   • Write a one- or two-sentence description or plot summary of the story so the story can be remembered.

   • Indicate whether they would like to tell the story.

   • Place an "X" in the box on the Storytellers' Bingo sheet that best fits the story's category after reading a story. A story may fit more than one category, but a different story must be read for each square.

   • Use the definitions given in the Storytellers' Bingo Category Definitions and the descriptions in the books to decide where a story fits on the Bingo Board.

   • Choose a prize from the prize box when a BINGO is reached. A BINGO consists of five stories that have been read in a row vertically, horizontally, or diagonally.

   • Collect a gift certificate or special prize after all twenty-five types of stories have been read.

Example: Donna Boudreau, a youth services librarian in Plymouth, Michigan, created this activity to use with her storytelling club, the Off the Page Story Tellers. Meeting once a month, Donna found that this game helped her students grow in the art of telling stories and appreciating folk literature. When a student read five stories completing a Bingo row, she gave them a small prize, such as a bookmark or pencil. When they read one story from each Bingo square, they received a gift certificate to a local bookstore.

Reflection: What kinds of stories did you find the most interesting? How were the stories you read similar to each other? How were they different? What helped you decide which stories you would like to learn so that you can tell them?

Storytellers' Bingo

Myth 1	Native American Tale 2	Folktale from Africa 3	Celtic Folktale 4	Legend 5
Fairy Tale 6	Riddle Story 7	Tall Tale 8	Nature Story 9	Folktale from North America 10
Trickster Tale 11	Fable 12	Folktale Variant 13	Triumphant Tale 14	Ghost Story or Scary Story 15
Folktale from the Middle East 16	Literary Story 17	Circular or Cumulative Tale 18	Animal Tale 19	Folktale from Western Europe 20
Folktale from Asia 21	Folktale from Eastern Europe 22	Folktale from Central or South America 23	Humorous Tale 24	Pourquoi or How & Why Tale 25

Directions

1. Choose a box and read a story from the genre or category listed.

2. Put an "X" in the box and record the category, title, source, page numbers, and summary of the story on your Story Record sheet.

3. Answer the question, "Is this a story you would like to tell?" Yes or No.

4. Use the definitions given in the Storytellers' Bingo Category Definitions and the descriptions in the books to help you decide where a story fits on the Bingo Board. In most libraries, fairy tales and folklore can be found in the Dewey Decimal number beginning with 398, mythology begins with 291 and 292. Literary stories can be found in the fiction, story collection, or picture book sections. A story may fit more than one category, but you must read a different story for each square.

5. When you have read a BINGO (five stories in a row vertically, horizontally, or diagonally), you may choose a prize from the prize box.

6. Put an "X" in the squares below when you have completed a BINGO.

7. When you have read one story from each of the twenty-five types of stories you will receive a gift certificate or special prize.

1st Bingo	2nd Bingo	3rd Bingo	4th Bingo	5th Bingo

Figure 3.1. Storyteller's Bingo.

Story Record

Your name: _____

1. Bingo category: _____

    Name of the story:

    Source of the story:

    Page numbers:

    Summary:

    Is this a story you would like to tell?

2. Bingo category: _____

    Name of the story:

    Source of the story:

    Page numbers:

    Summary:

    Is this a story you would like to tell?

3. Bingo category: _____

    Name of the story:

    Source of the story:

    Page numbers:

    Summary:

    Is this a story you would like to tell?

4. Bingo category: _____

    Name of the story:

    Source of the story:

    Page numbers:

    Summary:

    Is this a story you would like to tell?

5. Bingo category: _____

    Name of the story:

    Source of the story:

    Page numbers:

    Summary:

    Is this a story you would like to tell?

Figure 3.2. Story Record sheet.

Storytellers' Bingo Category Definitions

Use the definitions given below and the descriptions in the books to help you decide where a story fits on the Bingo board. In most libraries fairy tales and folklore will be found with the Dewey Decimal Classification Number beginning 398, mythology begins with 291 and 292. Literary stories will be found in the fiction, story collection, and picture book sections. A story may fit more than one category, but you must read a different story for each square. A brief description of the stories given as examples may be found in the Bibliography in the back of this book.

1. A **myth** is a story that attempts to explain an event in nature or a specific belief or cultural practice. Many myths are related to religion and depict the actions of godlike beings.

   Examples: "The Weaving Contest: The Story of Arachne and Minerva" from *Favorite Greek Myths* by Mary Pope Osborne and "Echo and Narcissus" from *Wisdom Tales From Around the World* by Heather Forest.

2. A **Native American tale** comes from an Indian tribe in North America. There may be tribal customs that say when the story may be used for storytelling.

   Examples: "Turtle Races Bear" from *Iroquois Stories: Heroes and Heroines* by Joseph Bruchac and "Grandmother Spider Steals the Fire" from *Race with Buffalo and Other Native American Stories for Young Readers* by Richard and Judy Dockery Young.

3. A **folktale from Africa** comes from cultures living on the continent of Africa, such as the Ashanti people of Ghana, the Yoruba people of Nigeria, and the countries of Angola, Ethiopia, and Kenya.

   Examples: "The Cow-tail Switch" from *The Cow-tail Switch and Other West African Stories* by Harold Courlander and "The Lion's Whiskers" from *Thirty-Three Multicultural Tales to Tell* by Pleasant DeSpain.

4. A **Celtic folktale** comes from the countries of England, Ireland, Scotland, or Wales.

   Examples: "The Three Sillies" from *English Fairy Tales* by Joseph Jacobs and "The Mermaid and the Selkie" from *The Celtic Breeze: Stories of the Otherworld from Scotland, Ireland, and Wales* by Heather McNeil.

5. A **legend** is a story about people, places, or events that have some basis in historical fact, but the stories have been retold so often and the incidents are exaggerated to such a degree that it is usually impossible to prove they actually happened. Examples include tales about Robin Hood, Johnny Appleseed, and King Arthur.

   Examples: "Beowulf: The Fight with Grendel" from *The Firebringer and Other Great Stories* by Louis Untermeyer and "The Legend of William Tell" from *Medieval Tales That Kids Can Tell* by Lorna MacDonald Czarnota.

6. A **fairy tale** is story that includes magic, an enchantment, or other supernatural elements that are clearly imaginary. It does not necessarily contain fairies but may include such fairy folk as little people, pixies, elves, leprechauns, giants, and witches, as well as brave and timid, good and evil people.

   Examples: *The Old Woman Who Lived in a Vinegar Bottle* (Wales) by Margaret Read MacDonald and "Janet and Tamlin" (Scotland) from *Tatterhood and Other Tales* by Ethel Johnston Phelps.

7. A **riddle story** presents a mystery or a problem the audience is invited to solve before the answer is told.

   Examples: "Three Rosebushes" from *Stories to Solve* by George Shannon and "The Magic Seed" from *The Cow of No Color: Riddle Stories and Justice Tales from Around the World* by Nina Jaffe and Steve Zeitlin.

8. A **tall tale** involves characters that are larger than life and incidents that are extremely exaggerated. These stories evolved out of the American frontier experience. Although they may be remotely based on actual happenings, great exaggeration gives these stories their name. Tales of Paul Bunyan, Mike Fink, and Pecos Bill are examples.

   Examples: "Sally Ann Thunder Ann Whirlwind Crockett Meets Mike Fink, Snappin' Turkle" by Caron Lee Cohen from *From Sea to Shining Sea* by Amy Cohn and "Paul Bunyan" from *American Tall Tales* by Mary Pope Osborne.

9. A **nature story** may be about the seasons or attempt to explain something in the natural world.

   Examples: "Nanabozho Brings the Seasons" from *Earth Tales from Around the World* by Michael Caduto and "Guara Devi Saves the Trees" (India) from *Spinning Tales Weaving Hope: Stories of Peace, Justice & the Environment* by Ed Brody.

10. A **folktale from North America** comes from Canada, the United States, or Mexico.

    Examples: *Wiley and the Hairy Man* by Molly Garrett Bang and "La Llorona and The Wailing Woman" (Mexico) from *Magic Moments* by Olga Loya.

11. A **trickster tale** usually involves animals like Anansi or Coyote who sometimes simply get into mischief and sometimes play a trick to solve a problem. Occasionally the trick is on the trickster.

    Examples: "Why Anansi Owns Every Story" from *Trickster Tales: Forty Folk Stories from Around the World* by Josepha Sherman and *Anansi and the Moss Covered Rock* by Eric A. Kimmel.

12. A **fable** is a story in which the main characters are usually animals behaving like people. It always teaches a moral or lesson, which is usually clearly stated at the end.

    Examples: "The Camel Dances" from *Fables* by Arnold Lobel and *The Tortoise and the Hare* by Janet Stevens.

13. A **folktale variant** is a different version of a familiar folk or fairy tale that comes from other countries and cultures. There are more than seven hundred versions of "Cinderella" from countries all over the world.

    Examples: *Lon Po Po: A Red-Riding Hood Story from China* by Ed Young and "Ashenputtel" (Germany) from *Cinderella* by Judy Sierra.

14. The **triumphant tale** theme happens when the weaker or smaller character wins through wisdom or cleverness. A classic example is "The Tortoise and the Hare."

    Examples: "How Brother Rabbit Fooled Whale and Elephant" from *Children Tell Stories* by Martha Hamilton and Mitch Weiss and *Tops and Bottoms* by Janet Stevens.

15. A **ghost or scary story** usually contains supernatural or ghostly characters. The story may be imaginary or based on an actual occurrence. Scary stories sometimes contain a "jump" that startles or surprises the audience.

Examples: "Aaron Kelly's Bones" from *Scary Stories to Tell in the Dark* by Alvin Schwartz and "Mary Culhane and the Dead Man" from *The Goblins Giggle* by Molly Bang.

16. A **folktale from the Middle East** comes from the countries of Saudi Arabia, Iraq, Iran, Israel, Jordan, India, Pakistan, Syria, Turkey, Afghanistan, Morocco, Algeria, Libya, and Egypt.

    Examples: *The Three Princes* by Eric A. Kimmel and "Dispute in Sign Language" (Israel) from *Favorite Folktales from Around the World* by Jane Yolen.

17. A **literary story** is written purely from an author's imagination. These stories are often difficult to tell because they rely on the special way the author uses words. Often the stories are considered classic, such as *Rutabaga Stories* by Carl Sandburg or *Just So Stories* by Rudyard Kipling; however most modern picture books fit into this category as well.

    Examples: "Come Again in the Spring" from *Richard Kennedy: Collected Stories* and *Where the Wild Things Are* by Maurice Sendak.

18. A **circular tale** starts and ends with the same situation. A **cumulative tale** builds incident upon incident until a surprise occurs at the end.

    Examples: *The Greatest of All* by Eric A. Kimmel and *The Stonecutter* by Gerald McDermott.
    Examples: *The Fat Cat* by Jack Kent and "The Enormous Turnip" from *Putting the World in a Nutshell: The Art of the Formula Tale* by Sheila Daily.

19. An **animal tale** uses animals as the main characters. They often are examples of human behavior.

    Examples: "Why Alligator Hates Dog" from *Cajun Folktales* by J.J. Reneaux, "Why the Giraffe Has a Long Neck" from *When Hippo Was Hairy and Other Tales from Africa* by Nick Greaves, and "A Tiger by the Tail" from *A Tiger by the Tale and Other Tales from the Heart of Korea* by Linda Soon Curry.

20. A **folktale from Western Europe** comes from countries such as France, Germany, Switzerland, Belgium, Italy, The Netherlands, Norway, Denmark, Sweden, Greece, Austria, Spain, or Portugal.

    Examples: "Magic Mill" (Norway) from *Wonder Tales from Around the World* by Heather Forest and "Stone Soup" (Belgium) from *Multicultural Folktales: Stories to Tell Young Children* by Judy Sierra and Robert Kaminski.

21. A **folktale from Asia** comes from countries such as China, Korea, Japan, Vietnam, Nepal, India, Tibet, Philippines, Malaysia, Thailand, Cambodia, Laos, and Indonesia.

    Examples: "The Crane Maiden" from *Mysterious Tales of Japan* by Rafe Martin and "Li Chi Slays the Dragon" (China) from *Not One Damsel in Distress* by Jane Yolen.

22. A **folktale from Eastern Europe** comes from countries such as Russia, Poland, Ukraine, Romania, Hungry, Bulgaria, Bosnia, Croatia, and the Czech Republic.

    Examples: "The Fool of the World and the Flying Ship" (Russia) from *Best Loved Folktales of the World* by Joanna Cole, "About the Hedgehog Who Became Prince" from *Favorite Fairy Tales Told in Poland* by Virginia Haviland, and "Old Dog Sirko" from *The Magic Egg and Other Tales from Ukraine* by Barbara J. Suwyn.

23. **A folktale from Central or South America** comes from the countries of Cuba, Haiti, Guatemala, Nicaragua, Cost Rica, Honduras, Brazil, Venezuela, Peru, Ecuador, Colombia, Paraguay, Uruguay, Argentina, Bolivia, and Chile.

    Examples: "Owl" from *The Magic Orange Tree and Other Haitian Folktales* by Diane Wolkstein and "Why Beetle Is Beautiful" (Brazil) from *The Emerald Lizard* by Pleasant DeSpain.

24. **Humorous stories** often include exaggerated situations and characters called sillies and numskulls.

    Examples: "The Wise Fools of Gotham" from *Noodlehead Stories: World Tales That Kids Can Tell* by Martha Hamilton and Mitch Weiss, *Obedient Jack* by Paul Galdone, and "The Holmolaiset Build a House" from *Story Medicine: Multicultural Tales of Healing and Transformation* by Norma Livo.

25. **Pourquoi (how and why) tales** explain the origin of certain characteristics of animals or the reason for some scientific phenomena. *Why the Bear Has a Stumpy Tale* or *Why the Sun and Moon Live in the Sky* are examples of how and why stories.

    Examples: Rainbow Crow by Nancy VanLaan and "How the Rabbit Lost Its Tail" by Len Cabral from *Len Cabral's Storytelling Book.*

Figure 3.3. Bingo category definitions.

Storytelling Scavenger Hunt

(Adapted with permission from an activity by Mary Hamilton and Cynthia Changaris)

Purpose: To enable students to express personal experiences in story form. To enable students to recognize the story from other people's experiences.

Supplies:

- Storytelling Scavenger Hunt (Figure 3.4) game sheet for every participant

- Pencils

By encouraging students to talk and interact while moving around, this engaging activity helps students to get to know one another quickly. It also helps them begin thinking about personal experiences in terms of "story." Storytelling Scavenger Hunt is an enjoyable icebreaker to use when bringing students together from different schools or clubs for a Youth Storyteller's Exchange (see Chapter 7). It can also be used as a group activity during a Family Storytelling Night or when your group tells stories to senior citizens.

All participants are given their own game sheet and collect their own answers. As participants move around the room, have them respond to the story prompts and sign each other's game sheet. Keep the game going as long as there seems to be interest.

After completing the game, have everyone take a seat. Choose volunteers to share something interesting that they learned about someone else in the group. Ask questions to bring out the "stories." Usually, there will be one or more people who can do something unusual with their body—such as wiggling their ears, touching their tongue to their nose, or doing the splits; get them to demonstrate for the group. When the students tell each others' stories, it encourages listening as well as telling. When you as the leader become involved in the Scavenger Hunt, you can initiate the discussion by first telling what you learned about someone in the group.

The Scavenger Hunt prompts listed on the reproducible form are only suggestions. Add or subtract questions or develop new ones depending upon the age, ability, and experience of the group. When working with an intergenerational group, be sure to add an "historic" perspective. Tell about …

- Where you were and what you were doing when you learned that Pearl Harbor had been bombed, that President Kennedy or Martin Luther King had been shot, that the *Challenger or Columbia* exploded, that Princess Diana had died, or that the World Trade Center had collapsed. (For additional story prompts, see Donald Davis, *Telling Your Own Stories,* August House, 1993.)

- A favorite game you played when you were young

- A favorite taste, smell, or sound

- A favorite teacher, librarian, camp counselor, or minister who made a difference in your life

- Something you lost and found years later

- How you met your wife or husband

- About the house or street where you grew up

- A time when something you thought was true turned out to be a lie

- Something you did that you hoped your parents would never find out about

Directions for Storytelling Scavenger Hunt

1. Give each participant a Storytelling Scavenger Hunt (Figure 3.4) game sheet and a pencil.

2. Direct participants to

   • Move around the room.

   • Ask one of the other participants to show, do, or tell them about one of the story prompts listed on the game sheet.

   • After they have told their story, tell or do one in return. (It does not have to relate to the same Scavenger Hunt question.)

   • Before moving on, participants sign each other's game sheet.

   • More than one person may answer the same question, but each person may only sign the game sheet once.

   • Try to get at least one signature for each question.

3. After completing the game, have everyone take a seat.

4. Choose volunteers to share something interesting or unusual that they learned about someone else in the group.

5. Ask if there is someone who really wants to share something that he or she told someone else that wasn't already mentioned.

Example: Ashorina related that her "interesting experience with an animal" was that she taught her African gray parrot to dance. For the prompt, "tell something your mother always says," Brian related that his mother always says, "If you can't say something nice about someone, don't say anything at all." For the prompt "show something unusual you can do with your body," we've had everything from Darnell who could do splits and Kimberly who could fold her tongue in thirds, to Andrea, Audrey, and Amanda's elderly grandfather who could lift his leg and tuck his foot behind his ear while standing. —Judy

Reflections: How are our experiences like stories? How can telling stories about ourselves help us to get to know each other better? What kinds of questions can we ask to encourage someone to tell their "story?" What makes someone's personal experience story interesting to listen to?

Storytelling Scavenger Hunt

Directions to Players

As you walk around the room, ask someone to show, do, or tell you about one of the things listed below. When he or she has completed the activity, have that person sign your sheet of paper. Each person may only sign one time.

Now you must tell, show, or do one of the activities in return, then sign your name on that person's paper. Share only what you are willing to share and have fun!

Find Someone Who Will Tell or Show You

1. A jump-rope rhyme, a nursery rhyme, a poem, or sing a favorite song or commercial

2. About something his or her mom, dad, aunt, uncle, grandma, grandpa, brother, or sister (or other friend or relative) always says

3. About an interesting experience with an animal

4. About a favorite secret hiding place

5. About a time he or she cooked something that didn't turn out

6. About the time he or she was lost or scared

7. About an award, contest, trophy, or medal he or she won

8. Something funny or unusual that he or she can do with their body

9. About the best or worst day he or she ever had in school

10. About a place he or she used to live but doesn't live there any more

Figure 3.4. Storytelling Scavenger Hunt.

Hello Bingo

Purpose: To build community. To help students recognize the commonalties and uniqueness of each member.

Supplies:

- Hello Bingo (Figure 3.5) form for each participant
- Pencils

This icebreaker takes less time than the Scavenger Hunt and is an excellent vehicle for building community. Encourage participants to take time to tell their experiences and to listen to others. The goal is not to finish first but to collect the most stories. Participants must have every box signed before calling out "Bingo." Play the game along with your students and make suggestions in the form of a short story or anecdote to motivate them to share what they found.

Directions for Hello Bingo

1. Reproduce and give each participant a copy of the Hello Bingo (Figure 3.5) sheet.

2. Direct participants to

   - Write their names in the Bingo box in the upper-left-hand corner of the game sheet. This is a "free" square.

   - Find people who fit the criteria in each Bingo box while moving around the room.

   - Initial or sign their names in the appropriate box. Each person may only sign one box.

   - After every square has been filled with other students' signatures, call out "Bingo."

3. Remind students to listen to each others' stories before signing their name in the box.

4. When most of the participants have completed their Bingo sheet, have them return to their seats.

5. Ask the students the following questions: (Have participants tell each others' stories before answering the questions for themselves.)

   - Did anyone learn something interesting about someone else in the group?

   - Who had something in common with another person in the group? How many of you have a birthday in January, February, March, and so on?

   - What musical instruments do you play?

   - What other countries or states have you lived in?

   - Who speaks another language?

Example: Jeremy and Ashley found they had both broken their arms falling off their bike. Over the years, we learned that a number of Talespinners could speak Arabic. Farzana spoke Bengali, and Jackie spoke Portuguese. Other Talespinners could speak Spanish. Many students had brothers and sister who had been in Talespinners and had encouraged them to join. Some students even had parents who had been part of our parent storytelling group. —Judy

Reflections: How are our experiences like stories? How can telling stories about ourselves help us to get to know each other better? How is telling a story about someone else different from telling a story about yourself?

Hello Bingo

Directions:

   Sign your name in the upper left-hand square. Walk around the room and get aquainted. Find someone who can answer "yes" to one of the squares. Write his or her name in the square. Besides his or her name, write the answer in one or two words. (Example: broken baone? "arm") A person may only put his or her name in one square. When you've filled the entire sheet, yell, "Bingo!"

Find someone who ...

Sign your name here!	Who speaks another language	Has a pet	Has lived in another state or country
Writes poetry	Plays a musical instrument	Has spoken on stage with a microphine	Plays the same sport as you
Was born on a holiday	Is good in math	Has had a picture in the newspaper	Has won a contest
Was born the same month as you	Has a special hobby	Likes to dance	Has had a broken bone

Figure 3.5. Hello Bingo.

Meet My Friend

Purpose: To encourage students to learn about each other by listening and repeating what was heard to the rest of the group. To enable students to express themselves by relating a short anecdote or story.

Supplies:

- Bell or whistle

- Watch or clock to time activity

This is a good activity to break down barriers between young people and helps them get to know one another. You may have students of different ages or who come from different schools. This activity stimulates conversation between students who do not know each other well and encourages listening and thinking about what makes a good story. As participants relate what they have learned from their partner, they become more comfortable speaking in front of the group as well as expressing themselves in story form. If you are planning to bring your storytelling group together with another one for a Youth Storytelling Exchange (see Chapter 7), this activity works extremely well to introduce groups of students who don't know each other. Have each club develop the questions and interview topics ahead of time such as

- What would we like to know about the other students?

- What would we like them to know about us?

- What kinds of questions will encourage stories rather than short, simple answers?

Other suggested questions are given in the directions that follow.

Directions for Meet My Friend

1. With your students, brainstorm questions that will help them get to know one another better.

2. As students call out ideas, write the topics and questions on the chalkboard. Let them know that all answers are acceptable; there are no wrong answers.

3. Encourage questions that require a brief story or anecdote as well as one- or two-word answers. Ask participants to pick out questions that will elicit the most interesting answers.

4. *Topics that work well*: favorite color, food, TV show, sport, book, or school subject; family birth order

5. *Questions that encourage longer answers*:

    • What does your bedroom look like?

    • Did you ever break a bone?

    • What is the best or worst thing about being the oldest/youngest/middle child in your family?

    • Tell me about a time you were lost.

    • What was your most embarrassing moment?

    • What kind of pet do you have? How did you get your pet? What kind of things does it do? How did you choose your pet's name?

    • What is the best or worst birthday/holiday/family vacation you have ever had?

6. Next, divide the group into partners who do not know each other.

7. Instruct participants to ask questions that will elicit stories, but they should not add their own comments or experiences.

8. After five or ten minutes, ring a bell or blow a whistle and have the partners switch roles.

9. After both partners have had a chance to be interviewed, give them another few minutes to clarify answers or to respond to something that was said. Allow the conversation to continue as long as the students seem to be learning about one another.

10. Ask for volunteers to introduce their partners to the rest of the group. Have volunteers stand as they introduce them.

11. Remind students not to interrupt or make corrections while the introductions are being made. After everyone has had a chance to introduce his or her new "friend," allow the group to ask questions of the interviewer or the person who was interviewed.

Example: Kim and Derek found they had the same pets, including two dogs, a cat, and a hermit crab. We learned that Jill broke a finger in gym, and Brandi broke her arm falling off her bike. Almost everyone loved pizza, spaghetti, McDonald's hamburgers, and candy, but only Ryan loved dill pickles. —Judy

Reflection: What made it easy or difficult to introduce your partner? Why is it important to listen to someone when they speak? How did this activity help you to get to know other members of the group? Is it easier to tell about yourself or someone else?

I Am, I Can, I Like, I Hope

Purpose: To give students the opportunity to speak in front of an audience and to help students get to know a little bit about each member of the group.

It is sometimes difficult to get to know all of your students, especially in the beginning. This activity not only helps everyone get to know each other better, but you may quickly see who are your "naturals," your leaders, and those who may need the most help. This exercise encourages your students to overcome their shyness and reluctance to speak in front of a group. For some of them, it may be the first time they have been in front of an audience of peers. They have an opportunity to experience what it is like to be the focus of attention when they talk about themselves. It also allows them the opportunity to bask in the glow of appreciative applause.

As in most of the activities, you, as the adult leader, initially demonstrate the activity, modeling what is expected of the young people. Remind participants that all eyes are to be on the speaker and that they are not to interrupt or make comments while the storyteller is in front of the group. Students are always allowed to "pass," but encourage them to take a turn later. When you go around the room student by student, there is less chance of leaving someone out. It eliminates commotion and time wasted as they vie for being next.

Directions for I Am, I Can, I Like, I Hope

1. Ask for a volunteer, or choose a student if no one volunteers, to stand in front of the group or in the storytelling space

2. Direct the volunteer to

   • Walk to the front of the group and pause to look over the members of the audience before starting.

   • Then complete the following sentences:

      My name is …
      I am …
      I can …
      I like …
      I hope …

   • When finished, remain in front of the group until the applause has died down.

3. Direct the audience to remember the following:

   • Give full attention to the speaker.

   • There is to be no talking, comments, or interruptions.

   • Give each speaker an enthusiastic round of applause when he or she is finished speaking.

Example: We learned that eighth-grader Nicole had a part as one of the children in the upcoming high school musical, *The King and I*. We also learned that she wanted to be an writer and an actress and that she liked to tell stories. We learned that Adam has two older sisters who had been in Talespinners, and he learned to tell their stories. We learned that he likes basketball, football, hockey, baseball, playing an instrument, reading, drawing, and riding his bike. He hopes to be a journalist or a hockey player. —Judy

Reflections: How did it feel standing in front of the group and talking about yourself? How did the applause make you feel? Is it easier to talk about yourself or someone else? What would make it easier to stand in front of the group next time? As an audience, how can we help the people who are telling us about themselves?

Academy Awards Acceptance Speech

Purpose: To help students feel comfortable in standing in front of an audience, ad libbing, and acting spontaneously.

Supplies:

- An old sports trophy

- Videotape of actual Academy Award acceptance speeches (optional)

This impromptu activity encourages students to think on their feet. It gets everyone involved from the most outgoing to the shyest. As in the previous exercise, it allows students the opportunity to stand up in front of their peers and experience applause. While everyone in the room is staring at them, they have to think of something appropriate to say.

If you have the opportunity, you might videotape some actual acceptance speeches from television and show them to your group. Otherwise, simply demonstrating an acceptance speech for them is fine. As the game progresses, you may find that the speeches get longer and more involved. Make cue cards for yourself for the more unusual awards, for example, "best writer of a foreign film about the United States," "best director of a science fiction film about a space monster," "best voice of a cartoon character."

Directions for Academy Awards Acceptance Speech

1. Begin by calling for volunteers. (It is also fun to make it a surprise, as it would be in the real Academy Awards. When calling up a student, announce, "And the winner for Best Actor is … Johnny Jones!" or "And the winner for the Best Director is … Sally Smith!" or "the winner for the Best Makeup Artist is … Sammy Johnson.")

2. Hand the trophy to the students as they come to the front of the room to make their acceptance speech.

3. Direct the students to

   - Show some exaggerated emotion (e.g., surprise, happiness, disbelief)

   - Walk to the front of the room and accept the trophy

   - Give a short speech thanking those who have helped or inspired them and why it is such a great honor to be the winner

   - Wait for the applause to die down before taking their seats

4. Direct audience to give an enthusiastic round of applause when the "winner" finishes speaking

---

Example: And the winner for the best actress in a supporting role is: Jennifer. "Oh I can't tell you how much this award means to me. My mother will be so proud. She's been taking me to acting lessons, voice lessons, and auditions since I was five years old. I'd like to thank the cast, the director, my fourth-grade teacher, and my plastic surgeon, who gave me this beautiful nose. I would especially like to thank all of my loyal fans for buying tickets and coming to see all my movies. I will put this Oscar in my living room so anyone who comes to my house will see how great I am!"

Reflections: How did it feel to stand up in front of the group? What made it scary? What would help make it easier?

"Me" Story Bags

Purpose: To enable students to learn more about each other. To encourage students to find stories about their names. To encourage students to relate stories involving objects that are important to them.

Supplies:

- Small- to medium-sized paper bag for each participant
- Paints or crayons to decorate bag
- Markers
- Five or six personal items to place in the bag

This wonderful introductory activity not only provides an opportunity for the members of the group to get to know each other better, it also helps them realize what makes them alike and different from one another. Your young storytellers are also encouraged to ask their parents for their family stories. If students are sharing their bags in small groups, you'll want to be sure that the larger group hears some of the interesting stories. Ask if anyone learned something interesting about someone in his or her group. Have them tell each other's stories first before asking if anyone really wants to share something from their bag that they think the rest of the group would like to know. It is important for the teacher or group leader to model this activity for the group, not only to show how it is done, but also so that everyone can get to know you.

Objects That Work Well

- The mouthpiece of a musical instrument (students tell how they came to play it)
- Photos of students' family or pets (students describe what was happening when the picture was taken)
- A souvenir from a trip (students elaborate on a story about anything funny or interesting that happened on that trip)
- A book from a favorite author (students explain why that author is a favorite)
- An award, medal, trophy, or certificate (students describe how they earned it)
- A special toy or object (students reveal who gave it to them and why)

This pre-storytelling activity also can be used successfully when bringing students together from different clubs or schools for a Youth Storytelling Exchange (see Chapter 7). In this case, seat the students in groups of six or eight and have them share their bags as they go around the table. This gives everyone an opportunity to talk and share without having to think up topics of conversation with kids they don't know. After everyone has had ample time to reveal the contents of their "Me" Bag, call the group together. Ask if anyone would like to tell something interesting that they learned about someone at their table. They will be amazed how much they have in common with other young people, even if they are different ages or come from different social, economic, or ethnic backgrounds.

Directions for "Me" Story Bags

1. Most of the preparation for this activity must be done by participants outside the meeting.

2. Direct students to

    *   Find five or six objects that tell something special about them. Try to find objects that have a story associated with them.

    *   Look at all the things in their bedrooms and around the house. Think about what they like to do, what they are good at, awards they've won, and their favorite books, sports, hobbies, and music.

    *   Find a paper or gift bag large enough to hold the special objects.

    *   Write their full names in big letters on the outside of the bag.

    *   Decorate the bag with favorite colors, cartoons, sports stars, stickers, and so forth.

    *   Ask their parents to tell them the story behind their names. Why was the name chosen? Who were they named after? Are there any unusual circumstances surrounding their births or naming?

    *   Bring your "Me" bag to the next storytelling meeting.

    *   Be ready to tell why the objects are special and why they put them in the bag. Think of a brief story associated with each item.

    *   Students should not bring anything that is breakable or valuable to the meeting.

3. At the meeting, divide participants into small groups to share the contents of their bags or call for volunteers to share contents in front of the entire group, telling the stories behind the objects and the story of their name.

Example: We learned that Renee, whose family came from Iraq, had so many male middle names that she couldn't remember them all. In her family, children have the middle name of their father, grandfather, great grandfather, and so on. We also learned that Lisa had a brown belt in karate. (She became a karate instructor when she graduated high school.) Over the years, we found that everyone had collections, such as Beanie Babies, troll dolls, and key chain ornaments. We also learned that although we all like to listen to music, we have many different favorites depending on our tastes. —Judy

Reflections: How do objects help tell stories about us? What makes a personal-experience story interesting to listen to? What did you learn about yourself as you collected objects and asked about your name story?

Partner Storytelling

Purpose: To learn how to tell a specific story. To demonstrate the effectiveness of collaboration when learning a story.

Supplies:

- Whistle or bell

- Repetitive story such as *"The Tailor"* (Figure 3.6)

This exercise gives everyone the opportunity to learn at least one story quickly. Before the meeting ends, tell your students that their homework assignment is to tell the story to someone else at least two or three more times before the next meeting. After telling a story three times, it becomes familiar and comfortable, and it begins to be "your story." The more times a story is repeated, the easier it is to tell and the better it sounds. You will find that some of your student tellers will want to embellish the story and tell it in their own way.

With younger storytellers, you may wish to repeat this activity for the first few meetings using a different story each time. In this way each student will be able to tell two, three, or more stories. It is also helpful to have them take turns retelling the story one at a time in front of the class in addition to retelling the story to a partner. For additional reinforcement, have each student fold a sheet of paper into eight sections and draw little pictures in each square representing events in the sequence of the story, adding a few words or a sentence to describe each picture. The paper can then be folded up again and put in students' pockets so they will be able to refer to it as they retell the story to their parents.

Tell simple repetitive or cumulative stories to the group. Participation stories work well or use, for example, "The Tailor" (Figure 3.6). This type of story encourages or requires the audience to become involved by saying a phrase, making a sound or repeating an action at the appropriate time in the story. Sometimes storytellers tell the audience exactly what motions to perform and what to say. Other times, the audience gets the idea after a few repetitions and spontaneously joins in without formal directions.

In addition to "The Tailor," we have included a number of repetitive stories in the bibliography, such as *The Three Billy Goats Gruff* by Janet Stevens (Harcourt Brace, 1987), *Anansi and the Moss Covered Rock* (Holiday House, 1988) or *The Greatest of All* (Holiday House, 1991) by Eric A. Kimmel, *The Fat Cat* by Jack Kent (Scholastic, 1971), *The Little Old Lady Who Was Not Afraid of Anything* by Linda Williams (HarperCollins, 1986). See also, Sheila Dailey's *Putting the World in a Nutshell: The Art of the Formula Tale* (Wilson, 1994), which gives many examples of circle stories, cumulative tales, chain story, and others.

A Word of Caution: Storytellers, both student and adult, should obtain permission from the author or publisher to tell copyrighted stories in paid performances. Telling copyrighted material will be covered in greater detail Chapter 7.

Directions for Partner Storytelling

1. Tell a short, repetitive, or cumulative story (or use a video or audio cassette). Remind participants ahead of time to listen carefully because they are going to have to tell the story to someone else.

2. After you have told the story, review the sequence with your group, checking that everyone understood the story.

3. Next, divide the class into pairs.

4. Instruct one partner to begin retelling the story just the way he or she heard you tell it. Partner number one continues telling the tale until you give a signal by blowing a whistle, clapping your hands, or simply calling out "change!"

5. Next, instruct partner number two to continue telling the story from where partner number one left off, again telling the story as he or she heard you tell it.

6. The partners are to continue telling the story, switching each time they hear the signal to change or until they have told the entire story.

7. It is helpful if you initiate the Partner Storytelling activity by repeating the first few lines of the story to "jump start" the students into a successful retelling. After all the pairs have finished, repeat the last few lines of the story. (The beginning and the end of a story are the most difficult part of a story to remember.)

8. Allow enough time after the activity is completed to talk about what was learned by retelling the story to a partner. Discuss how good storytelling includes some of the things you observed such as eye contact, gestures, cooperation between teller and listener, facial expressions, enthusiasm, and fun.

Example: I have found that many times Talespinners want to use "The Tailor" as their performance piece. They tend to add and adapt my version to suit their personality and style. The variations are endless. Bernie made the Tailor a motorcycle buff that cut his leather coat down to a leather button. —Judy

Reflections: What made the story easier to tell? What made it more difficult? How did you help one another remember? How can we help each other learn to tell a story better? How important was eye contact, gesture, and facial expression in making the story more enjoyable or interesting to listen to?

The Tailor

Almost all storytellers have this story in their repertoires in some form or another. Originally, it came from a Jewish folk song from Eastern Europe. This is the version I've developed after many years of telling it. —Judy

There once was a little old tailor who made wonderful clothes. He made dresses for the ladies and suits for the men. He made skirts for the girls and pants for the boys. He was such a good tailor that he even made clothes for the Czar. He was a very busy tailor and never had time to make clothes for himself. One day he said, "Enough! I'm going to make myself a brand new coat!"

He did not have time to shop for any new fabric, so he took pieces of material from the clothes he'd made for everyone else. He took purple velvet from the robe of the Czar, red taffeta from the Czarina's gown, blue denim from a little boy's pants, yellow linen from a little girl's dress, and green wool from the mayor's new suit. The tailor laid out all of the pieces of fabric on a table, and he began to cut. (*Make a cutting sound with your mouth and tongue. Use your fingers to show a scissors cutting.*)

Then he stitched it up on a sewing machine. (*Make a sewing machine sound. Put your fists together with your thumbs sticking up to show the fabric being pushed through the sewing machine.*)

Finally, he used a needle and a thread to stitch it all together, and then he tied it off with a knot. (*Make a sound of a needle going through fabric. Use the fingers of one hand to stitch up the fingers of the other. Make a big popping sound for the knot. Use hand motions to show the knot being tied.*)

The tailor put on the coat. It was a very beautiful coat. It had a red pocket and a blue pocket. It had green and yellow buttons and a purple collar. It was so beautiful, that he wore it here. (*Make a sweeping circular motion from the back to the front with your right arm.*) He wore there. (*Make a sweeping circular motion from the back to the front with your left arm.*) He wore it everywhere. (*Make a sweeping circular motion from the front to the back using both arms going in the opposite direction.*)

He wore it and he wore it and he wore it and he wore it until the coat was all worn out! (*Use both hands rolling over each other—he wore it and he wore it—then spread your hands apart—he wore it out.*)

At least he thought it was all worn out. The red pocket was torn, and he lost one of the green buttons. But when he took it off and looked at it, he saw there was just enough good material left to make a jacket. So he took his scissors and he cut. Then he stitched it up on the sewing machine. Finally, he used a needle and a thread to stitch it all together and then he tied it off with a knot. (*Repeat above motions.*)

The tailor put the jacket on. It was a very beautiful jacket. It had a red pocket and a blue pocket, green and yellow buttons, and a purple collar. It was so beautiful that he wore it here. He wore it there. He wore it everywhere. He wore it and he wore it and he wore it and he wore it until the jacket was all worn out. (*Repeat above motions.*)

At least he thought it was all worn out. The blue pocket was torn. He lost one of the yellow buttons, and the purple collar was frayed. But when he took it off and looked at it—when he really, really looked at it—he saw he had just enough good material left to made a vest.

So he took out his scissors and he cut … (*Repeat all of the above.*)

The tailor put on the vest. It was a very beautiful vest. It had a red pocket and a blue pocket, green and yellow buttons, and a purple collar. It was so beautiful that he wore it here. He wore it there. He wore it everywhere. He wore it and he wore it and he wore it until the vest was all worn out … (*Repeat the motions.*)

At least he thought it was all worn out. The red and blue pockets were hanging by a thread. He lost another green button and another yellow button and the purple collar was a mess. But when he took it off and looked at it—when he really, really looked at it—he saw there was just enough good material left to make a tie.

So he took out his scissors and he cut … (*Repeat all of the above*)

The tailor put on the tie. It was a very beautiful tie. It was red and blue and green and yellow and purple. It was so beautiful that he wore it here. He wore it there. He wore it everywhere. He wore it and he wore it and he wore it and he wore it until the tie was all worn out.

At least he thought it was all worn out. There were mustard stains and catsup stains. There were coffee stains and chocolate stains and it smelled like pickle juice. —Oooh, disgusting! But when he took it off and looked at it, he saw there was just enough material left to make a button out of it. So he took out his scissors and he cut and so on.

He put the button on his shirt. It was a very beautiful button. It was so beautiful that he wore it here. He wore it there … and so on.

But when he took it off and looked at it. When he really, really looked at it, he saw there was just enough material left, just enough good material left to make up a story about it.

And it was a very beautiful story. It was so beautiful that he told it here. He told it there. He told it everywhere. He told it and he told and he told it and he told it. The tailor told the story to me, and that is why I am telling the story to you. And because it's a story, it's never all—worn—out!

Figure 3.6. Story: "The Tailor," retold by Judy Sima.

Hot Seat

(Adapted with permission from an activity by Finley Stewart)

Purpose: To broaden students' understanding of how stories change from teller to teller. To help students realize the importance of listening while learning a story. To improve listening skills.

You will find that your young people will want to play this storytelling game again and again because it is so much fun. Have the students work together to build the story, or have them tell the story in a round robin with each person adding on to what was told before. The fun and enjoyment comes from the changes the story makes as it evolves from one storyteller to the next. Many young people will want to "blow up" or kill off the characters in a violent fashion. Insist that they end the story peacefully. To save time, make up a story yourself or use the story given in the example following the directions to this activity.

Directions for Hot Seat

1. Before you begin the activity, explain that some of the group will be story creators, some will be tellers, and the rest will be the audience.

2. Send three or four volunteers out of the room. They will be called back one at a time as the game progresses.

3. Next, choose three to five other students from the remaining group to create a story. The story should be relatively short and have a beginning, a middle, and an end. The story does not have to make sense—in fact, the sillier the better.

4. Choose a member of the audience or have one of the story "creators" act as the first storyteller.

5. Bring one of the volunteers back into the room and have them sit in a chair in the front of the room and give the following directions:

    • You are sitting in the "Hot Seat." (The audience responds with, "Sssssss" to signify a sizzling hot seat.)

    • Listen carefully to the story you are about to hear. You must retell the story exactly as you heard it to the next volunteer who returns to the room.

    • You may not interrupt or ask questions.

    • There are to be no comments or interruptions from the audience

6. After the directions are given, have the first storyteller tell the story to the volunteer in the hot seat.

7. When the story is completed, bring another volunteer back into the room and tell him or her to sit in the hot seat. The first volunteer then becomes the new storyteller. The process is repeated with each volunteer.

Example: Here is one of my silly stories: Once there was an old man that lived in an old haunted house by the side of the sea. He had four orange cats, two blue Sheep Dogs, and one green crow whose name was Hiccup. One day the old man went for a swim in the ocean and found an octopus inside an old sunken ship. He took the octopus home and kept it in his bathtub. No one wanted to stay in his house because every time they took a bath, the octopus would spray black ink, and the person taking the bath would get dirtier than he was before.

People liked to visit the old man because he had a magic apple tree that grew in the middle of his living room. Instead of apples, the tree grew peaches and plums. The peaches would take you anywhere you wanted to go. The plums would give you anything you wanted. You just had to be careful not to wish to go somewhere while biting into a plum or wish to have something you wanted while you were eating a peach.

One day when the man was going for a swim in the ocean, the octopus got loose from the bathtub and made its way to the living room. It used all of its eight arms to take the peaches and plums off the apple tree and fed them to the dogs, the cat, and the crow. After the animals had eaten all the fruit, the old man came home and found that the cat had turned into a pineapple, one sheep dog had turned into a cow, the other sheep dog turned into a hot dog, and the green crow was flying around the room singing "Jingle Bells."

That didn't worry the old man; he just sent out invitations and invited all of his friends to a Halloween party. And he lived happily ever after. —*Judy*

Reflections: How did the story change? How did it stay the same? What made it easier to remember? Why do you think the story changed with each teller? How important is it that everyone tells a story exactly the same way?

Toy Stories

Purpose: To stimulate the use of imagination in creating stories. To encourage students to use their own words when telling a story. To build and strengthen storytelling skills.

Supplies:

- Small toys or objects

- Bag or box for storage

There are a number of activities you can do based around toys, trinkets, and other objects. This activity, its variations, and the two following are designed to encourage students to use their imagination and to tell stories in their own words. All of the exercises involve gathering objects ahead of time. Begin by collecting toys from fast-food restaurants, cereal boxes, dollhouses, junk drawers, dollar stores, and so on. Small objects work best and are easy to store, but you may wish to use larger toys with younger students. Keep all of the objects in a brightly colored gift bag or box.

Sample objects: Rubber insects, plastic zoo animals, farm animals and dinosaurs, sunglasses, a toothbrush, a compass, a comb and brush, a mirror, a little book, a spongy star, a troll doll, a plastic airplane, several Hot Wheels cars, a plastic skeleton, a balloon, a fan, plastic space creatures, an eyeball ring, a globe pencil sharpener, a whistle, chopsticks, a plastic matador, a fake diamond ring, a spoon, a watch, a sheriff's badge, a "smile" button, a plastic Easter egg, plastic vegetables and food, a kazoo, a baby bottle, plastic scissors

---

Directions for Toy Stories

1. Have the students form a circle, then dump the contents of the bag onto the floor in the middle of the circle.

2. Direct the students to select one of the toys or objects from the middle of the floor.

3. Going around the circle, have students take turns answering one or more of the following questions:

    - Why did you pick this object?

    - How is the object like you?

    - How does this object tell something special about you?

    - How does this object remind you of something that happened to you?

    - How could you use this object in a new or unusual way?

4. After everyone has had a turn to answer, tell students to place the objects back into the middle of the circle and select a new one.

5. Proceeding around the circle a second time, direct students to tell something magical or fantastical that they would like to do with the object or to answer the following question: What story does the object remind you of?

Example: Jill picks a pair of glasses because to her they are magic glasses that allow her to see into the future. Johnny chooses a plastic horse because he likes to run. Leah chooses the rubber star because she would keep it in her pocket and always have it to wish upon.

Variation 1

Divide the students into groups of three or four. Using the toys they have selected, have each group make up a story using all of objects. Have the students practice the story and present it to the rest of the group. They may tell the story as a group or choose one person to tell it for the group.

Example: With an elephant, a pair of sunglasses, and an airplane—the students can tell a story of how a talented baby elephant was discovered in Africa singing rock-and-roll songs. Everyone was so amazed at the elephant's voice that they bought the elephant a ticket and sent him by airplane to Hollywood, where he became a famous rap star. The elephant was so famous that he had to wear sunglasses to disguise himself when he went out in public.

Variation 2

Sitting in a circle, one student begins telling a story. It may be a well-known folktale or fairy tale, or it can be a story that he or she creates. The first student tells the story for a few minutes, incorporating the object. The next person continues the story from where the first person left off, incorporating the toy that he or she selected. The story continues around the circle until everyone has had a chance to add to the story using his or her object.

Example: With a rabbit's foot, a spider, a pair of sneakers, and a harmonica, the students come up with the following tale: Sally begins: "Once upon a time, there were three bears, a Papa Bear who liked to keep a rabbit's foot in his pocket because it gave him good luck." Joey continues: "Besides Papa Bear, there was a Mama Bear and a Baby Bear who looked like a giant spider because that's what he liked to eat." Karen adds: "One day Mama Bear made some porridge in an old pair of sneakers. When she brought it to the table, it was much too hot, so the Three Bears decided to go for a walk in the forest." Jerry tells: "While they walked, Papa Bear played his harmonica while Mama Bear and Baby Bear sang along."

Variation 3 (Watch-ma-call-its and Thing-a-ma-bobs)

Collect tools or parts of equipment that are unusual looking and unfamiliar. In small groups or alone, have students make up a story of how these objects were found and how they were used. With older students, have them put the unusual objects into a historical context.

Example: When Johnny Appleseed found this thing-a-ma-bob, he used it to dig holes to plant his apple seeds in. He also found it useful for cutting up apples and wild vegetables to eat for his supper. This watch-ma-call-it was used as a tool by artisans in the Middle Ages to fashion armor for King Arthur's knights. A squire always kept one in his pack in case his master's armor needed repair.

Reflection: How did choosing a toy help you to think of a story idea? What made it easier or more difficult to make up a story in a group? What can we do to make working in a group better and more productive? How does "telling" a story in a group differ from "acting out" a story?

Magic Key

Purpose: To encourage students' use of imagination in creating a story. To help them use their own words to tell a story with a beginning, middle, and ending.

Supplies:

- Keys of all shapes and sizes

Collect a variety of different keys—house keys, skeleton keys, car keys, tiny suitcase or diary keys. The more varied the sizes and shapes, the better. Put them all in a box.

Directions for Magic Key

1. Tell the group that they are going to create a brief story about a magic key with a beginning, a middle, and an ending.

2. Have the students form a circle.

3. Give the box to one of the students. Have the student pick one of the keys.

4. Tell the student to use his or her imagination to create an impromptu story that answers the following questions:

   - Where did you find the key?

   - What does the key unlock?

   - What did you find once the lock was opened?

   - What did you do about it?

Example: Rima found her magic key in a Cracker Jacks box. She took it outside where she unlocked the pirate's chest that was sitting in the middle of the pumpkin patch. When she opened the chest, inside she found gold coins and jewels. She kept some of the jewels and had them made into rings and necklaces. Then Rima bought a new car with some of the gold coins and gave the rest to a homeless shelter so the people living there could buy a new house.

Reflections: How does your imagination help you to create a story? What was the hardest part about making up a story about a key? Why is it important to have a good beginning, middle, and ending to your story?

Chain or Circle Storytelling

Purpose: To encourage students to listen attentively to one another to develop a cohesive story. To encourage students to use their own words in telling a story. To encourage students to analyze the characteristics that make a story interesting.

Supplies:

- A ball of yarn made up of many colors

- A colorful stick or Nerf ball

This activity begins with students sitting in a circle. Each person adds a little to the story as it is passed around the circle. The story may meander in different directions, but it should flow seamlessly from one person to the next. While someone is adding to the story, everyone else listens. There are no interruptions or comments, and everyone looks at the storyteller. Always give students the right to "pass" if they cannot or are unwilling to contribute. Stories told could be simply a nonsensical fantasy or adventure tale that the participants make up as they go along, or they can be a tale based on a historical event such as the American Revolution, or a science concept such as the water cycle or food chain. This activity also works well when retelling a familiar story or one that you are trying to teach. The variations are endless.

With younger children, circle storytelling is a good way to see if they can retell familiar stories such as "Goldilocks and the Three Bears," "Little Red Riding Hood," or "Sleeping Beauty." You can also to do a circle telling instead of a partner telling to help kids remember a story you are trying to teach them. For example, one person begins telling "The Tailor," (Figure 3.6) continuing it for a minute or two and passing it along to the next person in the circle.

Sometimes it is helpful to pass around an object that signals the speaker's turn and gives students an opportunity to add to the story when the object is passed to each individual; a bean bag, a colorful "story stick," or a Nerf ball works well. The ball or story stick is tossed or passed from the storyteller to the next person in the circle or to whoever wants to continue the story.

Directions for Chain or Circle Storytelling

1. Have students gather in a circle.

2. Instruct students to make up a story, beginning "Once upon a time…." They continue telling the story for a minute or two, and then turn the story over to the next student in the circle.

3. Have the next storyteller continue telling the story from where the previous student left off, telling the story for a little while before handing it off to someone else in the circle.

4. Remind participants to

   - Listen to the speaker ahead of them.

   - Continue telling the story, repeating the last sentence of the previous teller before adding a new part to the story.

   - The story must make sense.

   - Tellers may not shoot, bomb, or blow up any of the characters.

5. The last person in the circle must bring the story to a conclusion.

6. *Variation using a ball of yarn*: Tie long strips of different-colored yarn together and roll them into a ball.

7. As each storyteller adds to the story, he or she unrolls the ball of yarn until coming to a knot or new color. Then the ball of yarn is passed to the next storyteller, who continues the story. The ball of yarn may be passed to the next person sitting in the circle or to someone across the circle.

8. As the ball of yarn crisscrosses the circle, the yarn becomes a web, signifying how a story can be woven from different threads.

Example: At a workshop with California storyteller David Novak, we used the water cycle as the framework for a circle story in which each teller picked up the tale and carried it further. We began with an imaginary drop of water and traced its journey into the different forms that water can take and the places water can be found.

The first teller began, "Once there was a little drop of water that lived in a hot water heater. One day someone turned on the hot water, and the little drop of water felt himself moving around and swimming out of the water heater, up the pipes into a teakettle. At first he just sat there, warm and cozy among the other warm drops of water, but eventually he felt himself getting hotter and hotter. He started bumping the other drops of water. The more he tried to sit still, the more he bumped until he felt himself getting lighter and lighter."

The next teller continued, "Suddenly, he felt so light that he floated to the top of the teakettle and rushed out in white, wet fog. He could hear a terrible, high-pitched whistle as he moved out of the teakettle. He could feel himself getting lighter and lighter until he floated up to the ceiling." The next teller continued, "When he hit the cold ceiling, he felt himself getting heavier and heavier until he dropped back down to the floor in a puddle with other cold drops of water. He sat there for a while until a dog came and lapped him up." —Judy

Reflections: Why was it important to listen to each person telling the story? What helped you to think of what to say next or add to the story?

Chapter 3b

Teaching Storytelling Skills: The Story Learning Process

Young people learn in different ways. Some are visual learners and learn best by visualizing or imagining pictures in their minds. Others are able to construct meaning by listening and hearing the words being repeated over and over again. Still others learn best if they can write, doodle, draw pictures, or simply keep moving around as they work and study.

In helping young people become storytellers, you will find that almost all of them will eventually find a method of learning stories that works best for them. Some are naturals and will be able to tell stories well with little effort; others have to work harder and practice more, and still others will need to be nurtured and encouraged for longer periods of time. When you take everyone through the same story learning process, you will find that students make their own adaptations. *Sima's Six Quick Steps for Storytelling Success* (Figure 3.7) encompasses most students' learning styles—visual, auditory, and kinesthetic. As your young storytellers learn new stories, they will capitalize and focus on the steps that work best for them.

Whatever their learning style, encourage students to learn their story "by heart" rather than by rote. By heart, we mean that the intent, tone, plot, direction, and integrity of the story are internalized and maintained, but the words come from the teller. Discourage students from memorizing their stories. The more the story is internalized, imagined, and felt, the easier it is to remember and the less likely the storyteller will get stuck on a word or phrase and forget it. A story learned by heart sounds less stilted and more genuine. It is told in the student's language and words rather than with those of the adult author who wrote the book. Using one's own words allows the teller to focus on the audience rather than on the text of the story.

Sima's Six Quick Steps to Storytelling Success

There are only a few parts of a story that should be memorized word for word—the first few sentences, the ending sentences, and any repetitive phrases that are important to keep the meaning or the flow of the story. This, too, may be in the student's own words. They should memorize the opening so they will know exactly how to begin, giving them security, confidence, and a sense of the direction of the story. Once those first couple of lines are delivered, the rest of the story usually tumbles out easily.

Knowing exactly how the story is going to end is equally important. You do not want your young tellers to be fumbling around for a way to get out of the story. Memorizing the end of the story will help students tie it up in a nice, neat package, ending with self-assurance. When confident of the ending, the teller drops his or her voice on the last word or two so the audience will know when to clap. Some students may rush the ending and swallow the last few words, but insist that your students deliver the last sentence with the same sense of purpose as the first.

Encourage students to use their own words to tell the story unless it is absolutely essential to the understanding of the story. It is imperative that students memorize repetitive phrases or certain lines in the story. What would "Jack and the Beanstalk" be without, "Fee fi fo fum, I smell the blood of an Englishman." In the English folktale, "Mr. Fox," the lines, "Be bold, be bold, but not too bold, lest your heart's blood runs cold," captures the eerie feeling and sense of foreboding in the story. Memorizing repetitive phrases or special lines also give students an opportunity to add repetitive gestures and invite the audience to join in. In "The Tailor" (Figure 3.6), the words "He wore it here. He wore it there. He wore it everywhere," encourages the audience to participate in the story without having to be told.

Figure 3.7. Sima's Six Quick Steps to Storytelling Success.

Sima's Six Quick Steps to Storytelling Success

Step 1. Choose It: Choosing a Story to Tell

Purpose: To guide students in selecting a story that they will enjoy learning and telling.
Supplies:

- Picture books with strong story lines

- Books of storytelling collections

- Photocopies of good stories

Prior to selecting stories to tell, students should become familiar with what storytelling looks and sounds like. Tell them stories often, especially during the first few meetings. Expose your group to many different kinds of stories—folktales, literary tales, historical and personal stories, participation stories, and more. If you are new to storytelling, find storytellers in your community who are willing to come to your meetings. Some tellers require payment, but others may be willing to come as a service and pass on the tradition to your young people. Audio- and videotapes are available that can be shared with your group. We have listed a number of them in the bibliography, along with several Web sites and organizations where you may find storytellers willing to come to your meetings.

After listening to many stories and doing numerous "Getting Ready to Tell" (Chapter 3) activities, it is time to start choosing stories to tell. Don't rush this important first step. You want your tellers to find a story they really enjoy because they will be working and living with it for a long time.

> **From Our Experience:** *I ran into Laura years after she graduated from Talespinners and was working her way through college as a bartender. She proudly revealed to me that she told the stories she learned in middle school to her customers!* —Judy

Young people come with different learning styles and interests, with different levels of motivation and sophistication; they will get the job done at different speeds. Some kids will come knowing exactly what story they want to tell; others will seem to take forever to find the right story and then may continually change their minds. Some of your young tellers will look for a short easy story so they won't have to work so hard. Others will choose a long complicated story because it intrigues them or it allows them to remain on stage longer. When planning, aim for the middle ground. Assume that it will take most students some time to make a decision.

Provide many choices of stories, from easy to difficult, from one-page stories photocopied from a collection to tales found in picture books. Some of your students may want to tell the stories you have told them, so have printed copies available for them to learn. For students with reading difficulties, make audio- and videotapes available for them to use instead of books. For students with special needs and learning problems, let them work with a strong teller to learn a tandem story. There are many suggested stories for two or more tellers listed in the Storytelling Resources (Section IV). If you are working with younger students, have the entire group retell several stories you have told them before they choose a story of their own.

Begin to build a storytelling collection geared to the ages and abilities of your students. If money is a problem, you might have your troupe tell stories at a local bookstore in exchange for a gift certificate that covers the costs of some folktale collections or picture books. Ask club members to bring old picture books from home that they enjoyed listening to when they were younger. Ask the local elementary school to send discarded picture and folktale books your way. Visit used book sales at the public library. Have a fund-raiser or ask your school parent group for money to help start your storytelling collection. See Chapters 7 and 9 for additional suggestions.

A Word of Caution When Considering a Story from a Well-Loved Picture Book

Picture books are generally thirty-two pages long, and often the stories are enriched with extra descriptions and details to fill all those pages. For beginning storytellers, a picture book may be too long or have too many details. Sometimes the opposite is true. There might not be enough words because pictures are used to show action and description. Inexperienced storytellers may have difficulty filling in enough details to make the story understood. Often the pictures themselves get in the way of learning the story. Photocopy or have students copy just the words and encourage them to formulate their own pictures in their imaginations. Find similar stories without pictures in folktale or story collections. If all else fails, suggest that they choose an alternate story when the picture book story isn't coming together as a complete piece.

Allow students plenty of time to read, listen, and talk with each other. Let them take the stories home to reread and think about, but give them deadlines, say, two or three weeks to find a story, although their "final" choice may still change. Having a goal in mind is especially helpful in establishing deadlines. If they know their first performance is in six weeks, they must determine their choice quickly to be ready to tell.

Knowing ahead of time where the stories will be told may help students make appropriate choices. For example, if your first field trip is going to be to the local preschool, Head Start program, or kindergarten class, encourage students to choose short, lively stories with lots of repetition and uncomplicated plots. Stories with repetition and audience participation also work well for young elementary-school-age children and are enjoyable to learn and perform. If you are inviting parents or a group of senior citizens to listen to the group's stories, the tales they choose can be longer and contain intricate plots. Story length may not be a problem for adult audiences, but students should be aware that longer stories are more difficult to learn. If you have a large club, you might have to limit the length of the stories chosen by members so everyone has a chance to tell.

Remind tellers that the most important factor in choosing a story to tell is choosing a story that they really like. The story they choose must stand the test of time. Will they still like the story after they have worked with it and told it many times? Help students to analyze exactly what aspect of the story appeals to them (e.g., humor, the culture or country in which the story originates, the repetition, having heard someone else tell the story, the funny ending, etc.) Getting to know your students over the weeks of meeting with them will help you suggest certain stories to them. Refer to the list of resources in Section IV for suggestions of stories that are appropriate for all levels of storytelling expertise.

Directions for Choosing Stories to Tell

1. Tell, show videos, or play audiotapes of many different kinds of stories.

2. Help students select a story that is right for them (from stories you have photocopied in advance or from picture books and folklore collections) by asking the following questions:

    - What do you like about the story?

    - Is the story too short, too long, or just the right length?

    - Will you have to add details or cut out parts of the story?

    - Will you be able to live with the story for a long time?

    - What kind of audiences will enjoy the story?

Example: Jackie came from Brazil, and David was born in India. They both chose stories from their countries of origin. Jim May's *Boo Baby Girl Meets the Ghost of Mable's Gable* (Brotherstone, 1992) is a perennial favorite. Even before the book was published, Talespinners passed this story down from one teller to the next ever since Jim May visited our school in 1987. Adam chose to tell a Japanese tale, "Roly Poly Rice Ball" because his sister Diana told it when she was a Talespinner. Latress and Tiffany chose "The Southpaw" by Judith Viorst (from *Free to Be, You and Me* McGraw Hill, 1974) because they could tell the story together. Justin heard me tell a story from Joseph Bruchac's book, *Iroquois Stories* (Crossing Press, 1985). After checking out the book and reading all of the stories, he chose to learn "Battle with the Snakes." Ellen chose *Stephanie's Ponytail* by Robert Munsch (Annick Press, 1996) because she could use her hair as a prop. Caleb chose Helen Lester's *Tacky the Penguin* (Houghton Mifflin, 1998) because he feels he's just like Tacky—"an odd bird, but very nice to have around." —Judy

Reflections: What makes a good story? Why are you drawn to some stories rather than others? Why is it important to choose a story you like?

Step 2. Read It: Reading the Story Aloud

Purpose: To help students understand that hearing how a story sounds helps them to choose the story they want to tell.

Hearing the story read orally will give students an idea of how it will sound when told. Encourage them to read with expression, changing voices to make the characters come alive. Reading a story silently to oneself is different from hearing it read aloud. When students read a story silently, they are reading for meaning. When the story is read aloud, they read. When the story is read aloud, they read for language, understanding, and appreciation. As they read aloud, they will notice if the structure of the sentences is comfortable for them. They will see the possibility of different characterization. And, most importantly, they will realize whether they like the story well enough to tell it.

Directions for Reading Stories Aloud

1. Have students work with a partner or in groups of three.

2. As students select books or stories they want to tell, have students read them aloud to their partners.

3. Direct students to take the story home and read it aloud to someone.

4. Ask students to answer the following questions after they have read the story aloud three times:

    - Does the story make sense to you?

    - Do you still like the story and want to learn to tell it?

    - Is the story a comfortable length?

    - Will you be able to retell the story in your own words?

    - What changes will you make?

    - Are there parts you want to memorize?

Example: Two storytelling coaches from elementary schools with many disadvantaged and at-risk students emphasized the importance of this step. "Repeated reading" is a current instructional strategy for enabling students to increase reading comprehension. Many of their club members were struggling readers. Reading their stories aloud gave them a credible purpose for reading it over and over again, with storytelling as a strong motivator. Over the course of the semester, the reading achievement of all the tellers improved, along with their confidence and self-esteem. When the students later told their stories to younger children in the school, they were admired and revered as "the Storytellers." In addition, the younger students were anxious to read the books that contained the original retold stories for themselves.

Reflections: How does reading a story aloud help you to choose the story you want to tell? Why should you read the story aloud more than one time? How does reading a story aloud help you in learning to tell the story?

Step 3. Picture It: Drawing, Outlining, or Mapping the Story

Purpose: To help students learn stories by understanding sequence. To enable students to view stories as a series of pictures or events and tell the story in their own words.

Supplies:

- Storyboard (Figure 3.8) and Storytelling Map (Figure 3.9) forms

- Pencils

This activity is designed to help students understand that stories are a sequence of events with a beginning, a middle, and an end. The process encourages beginning storytellers to use their own words rather than the words found in books to retell stories and to begin using images to help them remember the sequence of a story. Work through the mapping or outlining process with your group using a familiar folktale or a story that you have told before letting the students try it on their own. Storyboards (Figure 3.8) work better with younger storytellers, while Storytelling Maps (Figure 3.9) are more appropriate for older students.

A method, similar to the Storyboard, to use with young tellers is to have them simply fold a sheet of 8 $\frac{1}{2}$ x 11 paper into eight sections. With this kind of story map, students can draw more detailed pictures to outline the sequence of events, writing simple phrases or sentences underneath pictures to describe the action. The more details they include, the more they will embellish. The name of the story, author, country of origin, and opening and closing lines must also be written down. The paper can then be refolded into a small rectangle, then taken home and used to learn the story.

Directions for Mapping the Story

1. Duplicate a Storyboard (Figure 3.8) or Storytelling Map (Figure 3.9) for each student.

2. At the top of the page, have students write

   - Their name
   - The title of their story
   - The author's name
   - The story's country or culture of origin

3. Have students record the first few opening lines and the last two or three lines of the story exactly as they plan to say them. This may be written in their own words or taken directly from the printed page. These are the lines the student commits to memory.

4. For the six sequence sections, instruct students to do the following:

   - Draw the important parts of the story using simple pictures or stick figures.
   - Use one or two sections for the beginning, three or four sections for the middle, and one or two sections for the ending.
   - Use the back of the sheet if necessary.
   - Write a sentence or several short phrases describing what is happening in each picture.
   - List repetitive phrases or important lines, gestures, or other things that they think are important.

Reflections: How did this exercise help you to see the important events in the story? How will the story map help you to learn the story by heart? What is the importance of memorizing the first few lines and the last few lines?

Storyboard

Directions:
Draw a picture and write a sentence or several phrases to describe the main events in the story in order that they happen. Use you Storyboard to help you remember the story.

Name of the story:_____ **Author/Country:** _____

Opening lines: _____

Sequence 1	2	3
4	5	6

Closing lines: _____

Things to remember: _____

Figure: 3.8. Storyboard.

Storytelling Map

Directions:
   Fill in the blanks. Write the main events in the story in the order that they happen. Use this Storytelling Map to help you remember the story.

Name of the story: _____

Author or country of origin:
Settings:
Characters:
Summary:
Opening lines:
Sequence:
Closing lines of the story:
Things to remember: **Gestures:** **Words to memorize:**

Figure 3.9. Storytelling map.

Step 4. Imagine It: Visualizing or Imagining the Story

Purpose: To help students use their imaginations and to improve the learning and telling of their stories.

This is perhaps the most important step of the entire story learning process. The more time spent "imagining," the better the storyteller will remember the story and the more details the teller will include. A teller might stumble and lose his or her place, but if coached effectively, students will think of the picture and describe images or visualizations. They will be able to continue telling the story without a hitch. If the telling seems flat or lacks detail, remind students to visualize the characters and setting and help the audience "see" the picture.

The story coach or teacher guides the tellers through the imagining process after they have successfully completed their storytelling map or storyboard. Repeating this exercise more than once helps students visualize the characters as well as the story sequence of events. Tell students to try the exercise again at home while they are learning the story. If they have difficulty getting from one part of the story to the next or if they are getting stuck on a certain part, encourage your storytellers to imagine the story happening on TV with the sound turned off. Then replay it with the dialogue and the voices of the characters inside their head. "Play" or "pretend" the story as if they were making it up.

After completing the guided imagining, allow plenty of time to discuss students' visualization and feelings. Some students will have very clear, Technicolor pictures and can describe the images in great detail. Others will need to be prodded. Some students are able to develop the setting and characters more easily as they describe them aloud. If they have difficulty expressing what they saw in their imagination, talk the students through the process. Ask questions to bring out descriptions.

If you have a large storytelling club and cannot assist every student, have them break into partners or groups of three. Allow several minutes for one partner to describe what he or she imagined, then switch. Listeners should not interrupt the description process, but it may be helpful to have them ask questions when the teller is finished. Having a timer is useful for ensuring an equal and prescribed amount of time for each partner.

Directions for Visualizing or Imagining the Story

Read the following directions slowly, allowing time for students to relax and become familiar with the process. Add some of your own descriptions and ideas.

- Remove everything from your desks and from your hands.

- Sit with your feet flat on the floor, your hands in your lap, and your back and shoulders straight.

- Close your eyes or look down in your lap.

- Relax, take a deep breath in through your nose, and let it out slowly through your mouth. Repeat this several times.

- Gently and quietly shake your hands, shrug you shoulders, roll your head, and rotate your feet.

- Relax. Breathe deeply. Push everything out of your mind.

- Now imagine the setting where your story takes place. Is it in a forest or a castle or a cottage or meadow or a town? Imagine yourself in the middle of the setting where your story takes place.

- In your imagination, look at the ground, the sky or ceiling, the walls or trees. See yourself looking all around you. What do you see? Notice the colors and textures.

- Try and feel the temperature. Is it hot, cold, windy, or calm? Breathe in through your nose. What can you smell?

- Have your main character walk into your setting and stand. Look carefully at your main character. How tall is the character? If it is an animal, does it have human characteristics? If it is a person, is the character young or old? What is he or she wearing?

- Look at the expression on the character's face. Is it happy, sad, fearful, curious? Have your character turn around slowly, looking at the setting. Does its expression change? Try to feel what the character is feeling.

- Now have another character in the story walk into the setting. Have the two characters face each other. Notice which one is bigger, older, stronger. Notice their expressions as they look at each other. Try to feel what each character is feeling. Have the two characters walk around each other.

- Slowly have the second character walk out of the setting.

- Have your first character look around one more time. Now have the first character slowly walk out of the setting.

- See yourself one last time in the setting. Is there something you didn't see the first time?

- When you are ready, slowly bring yourself back and open your eyes. Sit quietly until everyone is back in the room.

Reflections: How will imagining your story help you to remember the story? How will it make your story better? How will it keep you from forgetting the story when you are telling it?

Step 5. Practice It: Rehearsing the Story

Purpose: To help students remember their story and recognize the parts of the story that need additional practice.

As they practice and learn their stories, it is important for students to hear themselves say the story aloud and to know which parts come easily and which need more work. Telling aloud begins to fix the story in their minds. It also gives students an opportunity to use voices and gestures.

Give beginning storytellers many opportunities to practice with a partner or in small groups of three or four. Encourage them to practice telling their story aloud to themselves at home or to a younger brother or sister, cousin, pet, or even a stuffed animal. Remind students to refer to the Storytelling Map or Storyboard to recall the story's sequence and parts. They may need to go back to the original written version but only to add more detail and information to the map.

While students may not be willing to do this activity over and over again, it will get everyone involved at the same time. It helps new tellers overcome their nervousness once they know they can tell the story from beginning to end without faltering too much. This is also a good time to use activities such as the Virginia Reel and Exaggeration Station (see Chapter 4: Advanced Activities).

Directions for Rehearsing the Story

1. Have students spread themselves around the room and stand facing the walls. If possible, there should be at least two arm lengths between students.

2. Direct students to tell their story aloud to the walls or bookcases:

   • On the first try, students speak in a normal speaking voice so they do not distract their neighbors.

   • On the second try, students concentrate on using gestures and a different voice for each character.

   • When they have completed the second telling, turn around and wait until everyone is finished. They may retell the story in a whisper for a third time while waiting for the others to finish.

3. Next, have students find a partner and take turns telling the story to their partners. Partners must not interrupt but may ask questions or offer suggestions after both students have finished their telling.

Reflections: How did these two activities help you to learn your story? Why is it important to practice telling your story aloud? How was it helpful to tell your story to a partner? How can we help each other practice? Why is it important to practice telling your story over and over again?

Step 6. Tell It: Telling the Story to an Audience

Purpose: To allow students to become comfortable telling their story in a performance mode. To guide students into giving appropriate feedback. To develop an understanding of appropriate behavior for members of an audience.

Supplies:

   • Storyteller's Feedback Form (Figure 3.10)

When most of your storytellers feel confident that they have learned their story, it is time for them to tell their story standing up in front of the entire group. It is also time for the group to evaluate progress and to lend support by giving their attention to the storyteller.

Establish rules for audience behavior when tellers present stories in front of the entire group. Many of today's children learn audience skills by going to sporting events or rock concerts. Even at school-sponsored concerts, children and family members often talk and move around. By establishing guidelines young people learn expectations for audience behavior when listening to a live performer.

You may wish to determine the rules together. State the rules in a positive form. What does a good audience member look like? What rules would make it easier for people to tell their stories?

With younger students, have them practice what a good audience looks like and put the rules on the chalkboard or on a poster board.

Things to Consider When Establishing Audience Guidelines

While someone is in the performance space, members of the audience should

- Remain seated
- Give undivided attention to the storyteller
- Listen without comment or interruption
- Applaud when appropriate

As they perform for the group, many young storytellers display grammatical or physical idiosyncrasies in telling their story. Rather than correct or criticize each student, tell the entire group ahead of time to watch for certain common performance mistakes. Let the students point out the problems. Then discuss why they are distracting to the audience and detract from the story:

Things to Consider When Discussing Common Performance Mistakes

- Chewing gum while telling a story
- Telling the story in one continuous sentence, connecting the parts by saying, "and so, and so"
- Saying, "he goes" instead of "he said" or "he says"
- Using pronouns instead of the character's name so that the audience becomes confused as to what is happening to whom. Encourage your storytellers to use the character's name or description as often as possible instead of "he," "she," or "they"
- Rocking back and forth or from side to side; pointless pacing
- Playing with clothing, tugging at shirts, hitching up pants
- Touching or playing with hair, tucking long hair behind the ears
- Racing through the telling
- Speaking too softly
- "Swallowing" or rushing the end of the story

A good time for the rest of the group to comment on the performance is after an enthusiastic round of applause and before the youngster returns to his or her seat. Ask the performer if he or she would like feedback. The student should always have control over whether he or she wants suggestions to improve the story. For first-time storytellers, having the experience of telling a story from beginning to end in front of an audience is usually sufficient. Have members of the audience tell what parts of the story they liked best.

Giving feedback should always be a supportive and encouraging process. If a student chooses not to receive suggestions, the group leader or teacher should comment on what was done well. While members of the audience usually have good suggestions, the storyteller will look to you, the adult leader, for praise and suggestions. Point out what was done well. Try to find something positive for every teller, even if it is simply that he or she told the story from beginning to end.

In addition to audience feedback and the feedback of the adult leader, it is helpful to have each storyteller evaluate his or her own performance. For students new to storytelling, have them state what they liked about their performance. For more experienced tellers, have them also evaluate what they think could be improved. Keep it upbeat and positive.

Things to Consider When Giving Feedback

- The storytellers have the right to choose whether they want feedback.

- Positive comments are to be given before suggestions for improvement.

- Storytellers should evaluate their own performance.

- The adult leader's comments should be given last.

Use The Storyteller's Feedback Form (Figure 3.10) to help the group focus on what to evaluate when storytellers are telling their stories. Additional suggestions for coaching youth tellers may be found in Chapter 5, "Encouraging and Coaching the Youth Storyteller."

Directions for Telling Stories to an Audience

1. Establish or review rules of good audience behavior with the group. such as:

   Good audience members

   - Listen attentively to the storyteller.

   - Keep their eyes on the speaker.

   - Keep hands in their laps or resting quietly on the table.

   - Lean their body slightly forward toward the teller.

   - Nod or smile encouragingly when the teller says something they appreciate or with which they agree.

   - Do not make comments or interrupt.

   - Clap politely when the story is over.

2. Discuss, demonstrate, or role-play common performance mistakes.

3. Discuss how to evaluate and give feedback for stories that are told.

4. Call for volunteers to tell their story in front of the group.

5. After the story is told

   - Elicit positive comments on the content and presentation of the story from the rest of the group.

   - Ask the storyteller to tell what he or she liked best about his or her own performance.

   - Ask if the storyteller would like suggestions from the audience.

   - Allow audience to give their suggestions for improvement of story or presentation.

   - Give your own positive comments and suggestions for improvement.

Reflections: How did telling your story in front of the group make you feel? What made it easier? What made it more difficult? What does a good listener do? What kind of feedback was the most helpful?

Storyteller's Feedback

Directions: When the storyteller has finished, write down two things you liked about the story. Then write down something you think might make the story better. Do the same thing for the story you told.

Group Evaluation: Complete the sentences below for each teller. Two positive comments must be given before suggestions for improvement.

1. The thing I liked best about your story was …

2. The part I could visualize best was …

3. I liked your gestures when you …

4. I liked how you used your voice when you …

5. I liked your facial expressions when you…

Other Things to Comment On

Opening or closing

Eye contact

Building of suspense

Setting the mood

Use of different voices

Use of language

Preparation

Talking speed

Name of Storyteller:_____

Things I liked: _____

_____

_____

_____

Suggestions for improvement: _____

_____

_____

Storytellers Self-Evaluation (Complete the following sentences)

Title of my story: _____

Things I liked best about my story and storytelling: _____

_____

Things I would like to work on and improve: _____

_____

_____

Figure 3.10. Storyteller's feedback form.

The beginning weeks of a storytelling club are the most important, and they can be the most fun. The new tellers are eager to participate, learn, and experience. Take your time and do not rush the processes detailed in the "Getting Ready to Tell" and "Story Learning" sections. Both provide the strong foundation needed to prepare students for telling stories in front of an audience. Once they have chosen the stories they wish to tell and then practiced telling them, your young charges are ready to hone their skills. Practicing and rehearsing can be long and tedious, but the activities that follow in the next chapter will help keep interest and enthusiasm high.

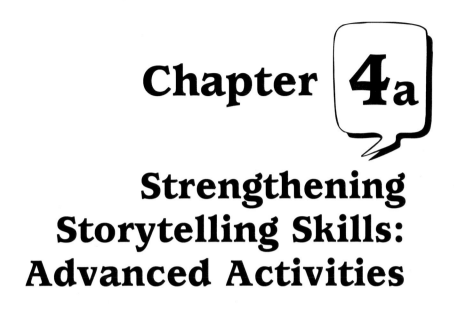

Chapter 4a

Strengthening Storytelling Skills: Advanced Activities

By now all of your budding storytellers have a story to tell. They've practiced and told their story in front of the group at least once. So far, so good. They are now willing to listen to each other's story one more time, but don't push your luck! Now is the time to schedule a field trip or performance to hold their interest. Continue practicing in small groups. If possible, bring in one or two adults to coach your students individually or in small groups while you work with the remaining tellers (see Chapter 5, "Encouraging and Coaching the Youth Storyteller").

You will find that some of your young people want to tell their story in front of the group every time you ask for a volunteer, while others never volunteer. Students quickly tire listening to each other tell the same stories over and over again. Some kids do not practice on their own without the help of their peers. The activities in this section are designed to make sure that all students are participating, practicing, and improving while maintaining high interest. These games and activities will increase students' competence in evaluating themselves and others and generate dialogue and description, gestures, and genuine emotion.

Rotation Station

Purpose: To encourage students to actively support each other. To enable students to verbalize or name the skills important and necessary for a good storytelling performance.

Supplies:

- Sheets of butcher block paper, poster board, or flip chart paper

- Crayons or markers in various colors

- Masking tape
- Whistle and timer

This activity works well after most of the tellers have learned their first story and are ready to tell it in front of the group. It helps set the stage for how club members will support each other and what they will look for in their own storytelling performance. As the needs of the group change, repeat the exercise using different prompts, or post the same questions at a later date and compare how their ideas have changed.

Always keep the questions positive. With younger students, discuss what it means to "brainstorm." Encourage them to generate as many answers to the questions as they can. No wrong answers exist. Although some answers may be silly and others out in left field, both good and bad answers will help students to evaluate the most important responses.

Sample Questions:

- How can we encourage one another?
- How can we help each other succeed?
- What is respectful storytelling club behavior?
- What does respectful audience behavior look like?
- How does good listening help the storyteller?
- What does good listening look like?
- How can we improve our storytelling?
- What makes a story interesting?
- What techniques are helpful in learning and remembering a story?
- What performance mistakes should we try to avoid?
- What are some tips to help remember a story?

Directions for Rotation Station

1. Determine questions ahead of time and write them on sheets of butcher paper or poster board.

2. Tape question sheets on the walls around the classroom.

3. Divide group into teams of three to five students and give each group a different colored marker or crayon.

4. Send one team to each of the posted questions. Make sure there are enough stations so that all teams are involved at the same time.

5. Use a timer and a whistle and set a time limit of two to three minutes per question.

6. Direct teams to

   - Chose a secretary to record answers. When the game starts, have each team write down as many answers or ideas as possible that answer the question.

   - All team members must stay with their teammates.

- The teams write all the ideas they can think of. There are no wrong answers.

- When the whistle blows, teams move on to the next question.

- Each suggestion may be written only once. Do not repeat any of the other teams' answers.

7. After every team has had a chance to add ideas to all of the stations, take the sheets off the wall and give one question to each team to evaluate.

8. Direct the teams to

- Read all of the suggestions aloud to each other.

- Add any points that may have been missed.

- As a team, decide which answers are the best or most important.

- Underline or put an asterisk next to three or four of the best suggestions.

- Choose one representative to report the teams' conclusions to the rest of the class.

Example: This activity was quite helpful when one of the Talespinners was being overly critical and picking on some of the younger, less proficient members of the club. The group was becoming polarized, and some of the kids didn't want to come to meetings anymore. What began as a negative experience turned positive as the group found ways to encourage and help one another. The offending Talespinner and the other members were able to use their own words and ideas to build community and to support one another. —Judy

Reflections: How did working together help you to think of ways to answer the questions? Why is it important for group members to support each other? How did this activity help you to think of ways to improve your storytelling?

Virginia Reel

(Adapted with permission from an activity by Cynthia Changaris)

Purpose: To provide opportunities to practice telling stories while enabling students to actively listen to one another's stories and make suggestions for improvement.

Supplies:

- Whistle and timer

A difficult task for any leader is to maintain interest in practicing stories consistently and continually once students believe they have mastered their tales. Until students realize the value of practicing, they consider it "boring." Although most students resist practicing at home, it is critical if the telling is to improve. This activity involves pairs of storytellers alternating back and forth to tell their story and listen to their partner's story. It can be used to review and strengthen a variety of storytelling skills such as rehearsing stories, adding description, telling personal stories, making up dialogue, or using gestures. At times, it might get noisy and distracting, but you'll find that everyone is participating and having a good time. Participants are either telling or actively listening and watching.

Often this activity often evolves into being the best session for peer coaching. As one student focuses on another and really listens, suggestions are given and changes to the telling are made, thereby improving the story. Those shy students who rarely volunteer and perhaps never feel they are ready to tell in front of the group will tell their story to one or two people. They will listen to suggestions because these ideas are given one-on-one. When listeners are expected to respond, they tend to listen carefully. The listeners' stories improve, too, because they either like what they see and hear or feel they can do a better job.

Directions for Virginia Reel

1. Have participants form two lines. Arranged facing each other, they may stand in two parallel lines or be seated in two parallel rows of chairs. Leave a space of one or two arm lengths from side to side between participants.

2. Using a timer or a stopwatch, have all participants in one of the lines begin telling their stories to those facing them in the other line. Call "switch" or blow your whistle after two or three minutes.

3. Have the students in the second line tell their stories. Blow the whistle again after two minutes and have the first partners continue telling their stories from the last stopping point.

4. Continue going back and forth until all pairs have finished telling their stories to each other. If the partners finish early, they may make comments or ask each other questions when their turn comes.

5. Remind the students who are listening to

   • Listen without interrupting.

   • Encourage their partners by using good eye contact.

   • Tell their partners two things they liked about their stories.

   • Give their partners one suggestion that they think could make the story better.

6. Next, have the student seated at the head of one of the lines walk to the end of the line while everyone else in the line moves up one position.

7. Repeat the activity several times, so that students tell their story to different partners.

8. Remind students that if they liked their old partner's suggestions, they should add them to their new telling.

Example: Jason, a shy quiet student, found that his listening partner laughed when he used a high-pitched voice for the princess in the story. He received another laugh when he told the story to his second listening partner. His second partner encouraged him to act like a girl when using the princess's voice, so Jason batted his eyelids and clasped his hands near his chest and received an even bigger laugh. He later used the voice and gestures in his telling and always received a laugh from the audience. —Judy

Reflections: Why is it important to practice telling your story over and over again? How does telling your story to a partner help you to remember and improve your story? What does a good listener do? How can we help each other remember and improve our stories?

Exaggeration Station

Purpose: To help students feel comfortable using gestures while telling stories. To encourage the use of meaningful gestures.

Supplies:

• Whistle and timer

Kids love this variation of the Virginia Reel. It initiates awareness of gestures during telling. This activity also loosens them up and helps them to feel comfortable with their hands and bodies. Students begin to think about which gestures are meaningful and help the story along and which gestures detract from the story.

Directions for Exaggeration Station

1. Before giving directions, demonstrate how exaggerated gestures look, for example, by flinging your arms from side to side or wildly above your head.

2. As in the Virginia Reel, have the participants stand facing each other in two lines. Spread them out as far as possible from side to side while keeping the two lines straight.

3. Using a timer or stopwatch, have the participants in one line begin telling their story to the person facing them. Instruct those students telling stories to use greatly exaggerated hand and body motions.

4. Call "switch" or blow your whistle after two or three minutes and have students in the second line tell their story using greatly exaggerated hand and body motions.

5. When the time expires, have the student seated at the head of one line walk to the end of it while everyone else in the line moves up one position.

6. Next, have students tell their story to their new partner using greatly exaggerated facial expressions to emphasize meaning.

7. Call "switch" or blow your whistle after two or three minutes and have students in the second line tell their story using exaggerated facial expressions.

8. Move the line again and switch partners a third time and have students "tell" their stories again, this time without words, using only gestures and facial expressions to express meaning.

Example: Robyn found that using exaggerated gestures improved her telling of *Anansi and the Moss Covered Rock*, by Eric A. Kimmel (Holiday House, 1988) and it also encouraged the audience to join in with the story. Josh usually told his story in an almost monotone voice with his hands stiffly at his sides. After this activity, not only did his gestures improve, but his voice became more varied and interesting. He found he could make his audience laugh if he exaggerated his gestures even more. —Judy

Variation: Another good way to do this activity is to have the students tell their stories in gibberish or numbers using facial expressions, gestures, and tone of voice to carry the meaning. Repeat the activity again, having them tell their stories in slow motion or with great speed. The more times they tell their stories, the more they improve.

Reflections: What did you learn by telling your stories with exaggerated gestures? How do you think using gestures will improve your storytelling? Why are facial expressions important in conveying the story's meaning? What kinds of gestures help the story move along? What kinds of gestures detract from the story?

All Hands Down

Purpose: To improve students' use of eye contact when telling stories.
Supplies:

- Index cards with the names of nursery rhymes and popular songs.

More often than not, young people feel inhibited or intimidated when making eye contact. This activity employs the use of nursery rhymes or song lyrics to help students feel comfortable looking directly at the audience. Adults sometimes instruct students to "look at the tops of people's heads," but this is not the same as good eye contact. Looking directly into the eyes and faces of the audience gives storytellers instant feedback. When they tell to preschoolers, eye contact will keep the little ones engaged and focused. With adult audiences, students will see the approval, encouragement, and enjoyment in their eyes. Eye contact is the major difference between reading or acting and storytelling. This one feature of storytelling makes it the confidence-building experience that students enjoy. Eye contact encourages and motivates most storytellers, even more than appreciative applause.

Directions for All Hands Down

1. Ask for a volunteer or choose one student to come to the front of the room or performance space.

2. Tell the volunteer to

   - Think of a nursery rhyme or song lyric he or she knows well and can say in class (e.g., "Jack and Jill," "Humpty Dumpty," "Mary Had a Little Lamb," "My Bonnie Lies over the Ocean," "On Top of Spaghetti," or "Rudolf the Red-Nosed Reindeer").

   - Recite a nursery rhyme or sing the lyrics of a favorite song while looking at each person in the audience directly in the eyes.

3. Direct remaining participants to raise their hands when the recitation begins.

4. Tell the volunteer to

   - Keep looking at each person's eyes until each participant in the audience puts his or her hand down.

   - Continue singing or reciting until all hands are down.

5. Instruct the members of the audience to

   - Keep their hands high in the air.

   - Put their hands down when they notice that the volunteer is giving them good eye contact by looking directly into their eyes.

   - Clap enthusiastically when the volunteer has "all hands down."

---

6. If your students have trouble with nursery rhymes, use index cards or post a list to help them recall familiar titles.

7. Continue the activity until everyone has had a chance to achieve "All hands down." Encourage students to use different rhymes or songs.

Example: Ashley was extremely shy. When practicing her stories, she would look down at her feet or off to the side of the audience. After repeating "Jack and Jill ran up the hill" about ten times, giving direct eye contact to each Voices of Illusion member, Ashley not only felt more comfortable looking at her audience, but found that she could make her audience laugh at her gestures and expression. —Kevin

Reflections: How did looking everyone in the eye make you feel? Why is eye contact important when telling a story? What can you do to overcome nervousness about using eye contact?

Emotions Circle

Purpose: To enable students to improve characterization in their storytelling.
Supplies

• Index cards with types of emotions and feelings written on them

• Index cards with character types

Many young tellers rush through their telling as they concentrate on the words of their story, leaving the characters lifeless and uninteresting. This activity will help students bring their characters to life by practicing feelings and emotions. Before you begin the activity, discuss what makes a character in a story "real" or lifelike. What does it mean to "be" the character rather than just tell about the character? How can you get inside a character's feelings? How can you differentiate each character in the story without saying, "He said. She said."

With younger students, discuss different kinds of feelings and emotions before you begin the exercise. Put only the emotions students understand on the index cards and give the same emotion to several students. Begin by demonstrating a specific emotion yourself.

Emotions and feelings that can be printed on index cards: Shy, disgusted, awestruck, impressed, remorseful, lost, forgetful, frustrated, vengeful, shocked, affectionate, suspicious, wicked, stubborn, romantic, annoyed, bored, concentrating, happy go lucky, sympathetic, perplexed, angry, cautious, relieved, envious, guilty, embarrassed, grouchy, innocent, stuck up, sly, lonely, crazy, goofy, curious, overwhelmed, sneaky, dreamy, love struck, shifty, careful, excited, indecisive, exhausted, indifferent, tired, hungry, spooky, disappointed, confused, eager, hesitant, irritated, cranky, sleepy, happy, sad, devastated.

Sample characters for applying emotions: dragon, old man, witch, eagle, young woman, mother, cranky baby, baby learning to walk, juggler, soldier, preacher, teacher, bad guy, cowboy, clown, large animal, small creature.

Directions for Emotions Circle

1. Have participants sit in a circle.

2. Give each participant an index card with an emotion written on it.

3. Direct students to

    • Think about the emotion on their index cards.

    • Think about a character that might experience this feeling or a situation that might cause it.

    • When their turn comes, students begin acting out that emotion with movements and facial expressions while sitting.

    • Next, they stand up and walk around the circle, using as few words as possible to express the emotion.

    • Students continue using the emotion until they are ready to choose someone to take their place.

    • The students choose someone else in the circle to act out their emotion by taking their seat.

    • Reveal the feeling that was on the index card and the situation before the next actor takes a turn.

4. After everyone has had a turn, collect the cards, shuffle them up, and pass them out again.

5. Have the participants repeat the activity, this time as a specific character type. Allow students to think of their own character or pass a second card with a different character type written on each card.

6. Repeat the activity a third time having participants use dialogue to demonstrate the emotion.

Example: Kim's card said "dreamy," and that suited her perfectly. She raised her head and practically floated around the circle until she came to Brian. Before she tapped Brian on the shoulder, she told us she was thinking about the lead singer from her favorite rock group. Brian looked at everyone with shifty eyes and a sly grin before he got up and slunk across the circle, looking back over his shoulder. His card said "wicked" and he was thinking of a character from a horror movie. —Judy

Reflections: Why does using emotion help to make your story better? How do emotions or feelings make characters seem more real or lifelike?

Pass the Mask

Purpose: To encourage use of facial expression that brings story characters to life.

This activity uses pantomime. Like the previous activity, it helps students make their characters more lifelike and real. For this exercise, students choose their own emotions or feelings to demonstrate. Discuss or brainstorm feelings and emotions ahead of time or list some on the board to give kids ideas. Talk about how one can show emotion without using words. As in other activities, the adult leader should begin the activity or demonstrate how to do the activity.

Directions for Pass the Mask

1. Have participants sit in a circle.

2. Tell students that this will be a pantomime activity. They are not to talk during the activity.

3. Explain that you have an invisible magic box in front of you containing many different masks. The box may change size, shape or how it opens, but inside the box are many masks showing different kinds of emotions.

4. Direct students to

    • Pass the "box" around the circle.

    • Pretend to open the box, take out a mask, and put it on.

    • Show everyone in the circle what the mask looks like by demonstrating an emotion or feeling.

    • Create an emotion or chose from the ones listed on the board. Each emotion may only be used once.

    • After everyone sees the "mask," remove the mask slowly and place it back in the box.

    • Close the box and pass it to the next person.

5. Pass the box around again. This time instruct students to

    • Take out an imaginary costume and put it on.

    • Demonstrate a simple activity such as combing hair, drinking a glass of water, bouncing a ball, or eating a bowl of soup as the character who would wear the costume.

Example: Damien slowly opened the imaginary box and began rummaging around throwing out one pretend mask after another, until he found what he was looking for. Demonstrating the feeling of hunger, he held one hand open, palm up; with the other he carefully fed himself from the imaginary plate. We could tell he was eating spaghetti when he took a big breath through a round mouth, then pretended to use his shirt to wipe his face and clean up the imaginary sauce that splattered all over. He even reached over and wiped some off the kids sitting next to him. Then he patted his stomach and gave us a contented smile. —Judy

Reflections: How can our facial expressions make our stories better? How can gestures make our stories easier to understand?

Excuses, Excuses

(Adapted with permission from an activity created by Jean-Andrew Dickmann)

Purpose: To encourage students to use their imaginations in creating stories and situations. To strengthen students' abilities to tell stories in their own words.

Supplies

- Bean bag, ball, or plastic potato

This activity, like the ones that follow, is designed to give young storytellers experience in creating and using language. The more experience students have expressing themselves in a variety of situations and scenarios, the more they will transfer this ability into their own stories. The more they exercise and stretch their imaginations, the more they will use their imaginations to stretch and strengthen their storytelling.

In this exercise, you ask students to do something with which they may already be fairly accomplished—making excuses. You will try to channel and challenge that ability by giving participants specific situations to make up those creative excuses. Having a beanbag, ball, or even a plastic potato is useful in moving the activity along.

Some Sample Situations: Driving over the speed limit, forgetting homework, being late to school or work, breaking a valuable object, eating the last of something, not doing a specific chore, getting lost.

Directions for Excuses, Excuses

1. Have the class sit or stand in a circle.

2. Give students a situation or scenario (e.g., forgetting homework).

3. Instruct class to

    - Pass the bean bag around the circle.

    - Pretend it is a "hot potato." When students hold it, they want to get rid of it as quickly as possible.

    - When given the hot potato, students quickly think up an excuse to fit the situation before passing the potato on to the next student.

    - Make up a new excuse each time without repeating any of the previous ones.

4. Always allow participants the right to pass if they are stumped.

Example: Talespinners excel at this activity. Passing the bean bag, Renee forgot her homework because her little brother spilled orange juice all over it; Jenny forgot it was a school day and overslept; Joey tripped on the way to the bus and dropped his homework in a mud puddle; David said his gerbil got loose and ate it. —Judy

Reflections: How can a game like "Excuses, Excuses" help you to improve your own storytelling? Why is it important to be able to think up something to say quickly?

Tall Tale

(Adapted with permission from an activity by Jean-Andrew Dickmann)

Purpose: To encourage students to use their imaginations in creating stories and situations. To strengthen students' ability to tell stories in their own words.

Supplies

- Paper or plastic fan
- Glove or mitten

In this activity students pass a mitten or glove and a fan around the circle; one person gets the fan, the next gets the mitten. Explain to your group that a tall tale is a story that is so exaggerated that it couldn't possibly be true. Usually, it contains a character bigger than life who can do amazing things, such as Paul Bunyan and Pecos Bill. As students receive the mitten or the fan, they create a one-sentence story "starter," giving them the opportunity to craft a brief "tall tale."

As an example of a tall tale, read a story from Robert San Souci's *Cut from the Same Cloth: American Women of Myth, Legend, and Tall Tale* (Philomel, 1993) or Mary Pope Osborne's *American Tall Tales* (Knopf, 1991).

Directions for Tall Tale

1. Have participants sit in a circle.

2. Tell students to pass the mitten and the fan around the circle, skipping every other person (i.e. one person has the fan while the other has the mitten).

3. Direct students make up a "tall tale" or exaggerated end to the sentence:

   - If they receive the mitten, complete the sentence, "It was so cold that...." Give two examples.

   - If they receive the fan, complete the sentence, "It was so hot that...." Give two examples.

   - Students can make the examples as wild and crazy as they want but should not repeat anyone else's tall tale.

Example: First teller: "It was so hot that if you tossed an egg up in the air, it would come down hardboiled, and you could salt it from the sweat dripping down your forehead." Next teller: "It was so cold that whatever you said would freeze as soon as the words came out of your mouth, and you wouldn't be able to hear them until they melted in the spring." Next teller: "It was so hot that once the words melted, you still wouldn't be able to hear them because they would boil and become steam before they reached your ear.   All you would hear is, 'Sssssssss.' "

Reflections: What makes a "tall tale" enjoyable to listen to? How can exaggeration improve your story?

Good News–Bad News

Purpose: To encourage use of imagination in creating stories and situations. To strengthen students' abilities to tell stories in their own words.

This exercise helps students to become aware of conflict and tension in a story and to become accustom to audience response. As an example, read the book *Fortunately* (Aladdin, 1993) by Remy Charlip, to your students prior to engaging students in this exercise. In the story, a boy on his way to a party encounters some mishaps and near disasters but is saved in the nick of time only to encounter another calamity. Each event is prefaced by "Fortunately" or "Unfortunately."

Directions for Good News–Bad News

1. Have group members sit in a circle.

2. Begin the activity by discussing what makes an event or situation "fortunate" or "unfortunate," good news or bad news.

3. Tell the students that you will begin telling a story in which the main character embarks on a journey to an interesting or exciting place. Continue the story for two or three sentences until the character finds or does something fortunate or lucky.

4. Instruct the audience to respond by saying, "Oh, what good news!"

5. Continue the story until the character meets up with an unfortunate circumstance.

6. Instruct the audience to respond by saying, "Oh no, what bad news!"

7. Instruct members of the class to continue telling the story. As the story passes around the circle, alternate the character's adventures between fortunate and unfortunate, lucky and unlucky experiences, between good news and bad news.

8. After everyone in the circle has had a chance to add to the adventure, the last person completes the story by bringing the character to his or her final destination, when everyone in the circle says, "Oh what good news! Thank goodness!"

Example: First person: "A little boy was on this way to the store to buy some bread for his mother. Suddenly, he spotted a dollar on the sidewalk." The group responds, "Oh, what good news!" The next person continues, "But as soon as he bent down to pick up the dollar, a strong wind came and blew it up into a tree." Group responds, "Oh, no, what bad news." The next person continues: "The little boy was a good climber, and he climbed the tree and grabbed the dollar in his hand." Group responds, "Oh, what good news!" The next person continues, "But, as soon as the little boy grabbed the dollar, he lost his balance and fell out of the tree." Group responds, "Oh, no, what bad news!"

Variation: Retell a familiar fairy tale using the "Good News–Bad News" format.

Example: Once upon a time there were three bears who lived in a lovely cottage in the woods. "Oh, what good news!" The bears were always hungry, especially Baby Bear. "Oh, no, what bad news!" One day Mama Bear made some delicious porridge for breakfast and put some in each of their bowls. "Oh! What good news!" Papa Bear tasted the porridge and said, "This porridge is too hot." "Oh, no, what bad news!" So the Bears decided to go for a walk in the woods. The day was sunny and bright and Mama Bear sang a little song as they walked along. "Oh, what good news!" No sooner had they left the house, when a little girl name Goldilocks left her house by the edge of the woods and walked there. Her mother had warned her not to go into the woods because there were wild animals in the woods, but Goldilocks went anyway. "Oh, no, what bad news." ...

Reflection: How can creating good and bad situations for a character improve your own storytelling?

To Get or "Mother May I ..."

Purpose: To increase students' abilities to create dialogue.

Young people really enjoy this activity. They are able to do what they do best—beg and whine—and they can say "no" no matter what. By assigning different situations, students learn to create dialogue. Encourage tellers to use as much dialogue as possible, not simply "why" and "because I said so."

Some Situations You Can Use

- A teenage girl tries "to get" her mom to take her to the mall.
- A boy tries "to get" his mom to let him stay home from school.
- A little girl tries "to get" her father to buy her a dog for her birthday.
- An employee tries "to get" his boss to give him a raise.
- A girl tries "to get" her younger sister to go away when her boyfriend comes over.
- A salesperson tries "to get" a prospective customer to buy a used car.

Directions for To Get or "Mother May I"

1. Place two chairs in the front of the group.

2. Choose two students and have them sit side by side in the two chairs.

3. Tell the volunteers the following:

    - They will be given a role and a situation.
    - One of them must try to get the other to do something he or she doesn't want to do.
    - The second person must not give in and state a reason for refusing.
    - The student who is being asked must refuse no matter how ardent the plea.
    - There is to be no hitting and no name-calling.
    - Students should create dialogue. Do not say "why" or "because I said so."
    - When the students have run out of things to say, reverse the roles.

4. Assign a new situation or repeat the last one, choosing two new volunteers.

Example: Nicole promised to clean her room and make her own lunches "to get" her mom, Heidi, to take her to the mall for a new dress. Heidi refused saying, that she enjoyed making lunches and warned that Nicole had better clean her room or she wouldn't be going to the dance at all. Nicole threatened to run away from home, refused to do her homework. Heidi asked if Nicole wanted help packing. When that didn't work, Nicole tried to gain Heidi's sympathy by explaining that her old dress was torn, that no one wore that style anymore, and that three girls had the same dress when she wore it to the dance last time. Heidi said that the dress was perfectly good, that she paid a lot of money for it, and that she just bought it a few weeks ago.—Judy

Reflections: How does dialogue or conversations make a story more interesting? How can you use the dialogue between two people in a story told by one teller?

Drawing from a Description

Purpose: To encourage students to add detail to their descriptions of people, places, and things in their stories.

Supplies:

- Reproducible drawing forms, Figure of a House (4.1) and Figure of a Man (4.2)

- Blank sheets of paper

- Pencils

This activity encourages young tellers to pay attention to detail. The leader explains that if you want your audience to see the old man, the monster, or the beautiful princess in your story, you have to describe in detail how they appear in your mind. The better the description, the more likely the picture in the imagination of your listeners will match your own. Remind students that the goal is to see how well a picture can be created from someone else's description. If they "cheat" or look, it won't be as much fun.

Directions for Drawing from a Description

1. Divide the class in half.

2. Have half of the students sit at tables. Provide these students with a blank sheet of paper and a pencil.

3. Have the other half of the students sit back to back, directly behind the first group of students. (Separate the pairs of students as much as possible so they cannot hear or see the other pairs.) Provide these students with a copy of the reproducible, "Figure of a House" (Figure 4.1).

4. Instruct the students with the house to

   - Describe the picture in front of them.

   - Include size, shape, location on the paper, and as many details as possible.

   - Do not show the paper to their partner

5. Instruct the students with the blank pieces of paper to

   - Draw the picture that is being described to them.

   - Ask questions to clarify the details of the description.

   - Do not look at their partner's paper.

6. When the drawing is complete, compare the drawing with the actual figure.

7. Reverse roles, giving the second partner a blank piece of paper and giving the first partner a copy of the second reproducible, "Figure of a Man" (Figure 4.2).

8. Repeat the activity, but this time, the person doing the drawing may not ask any questions.

Example: Pictures tend to improve greatly the second time around as students realize they must be very specific: "You are going to draw a man, draw a circle for his head near the top of the paper. His right eye is closed and he has five eyelashes coming down from his eyelid. His left eye is open with a black pupil with a white center. He has five eyelashes coming out on top of his eyelid. His eyebrow is curved over his left eye and a straight line over his right eye.…

Variations:

- This activity can also be done with matching laminated-paper geometric shapes. Provide each pair of participants with matching shapes (e.g., one large rectangle, two medium squares, three small triangles, one large triangle, two medium circles, two long narrow rectangles). Have students sit facing each other with a barrier between them. One partner creates a figure or picture using the shapes and then tries to describe for the second partner how to create the same figure or shape by telling his or her partner how and where to place each shape.

- Although descriptions add vivid imagery to a story, sometimes these narrations can become too detailed and therefore boring. Try the activity using cartoons or simple pictures from greeting cards. Have the students see how little they can say to impart the essence or spirit of the picture.

Example: "You are going to create a house. Put the large rectangle in the middle of the paper horizontally. Put the large triangle on top of the rectangle for the roof. Put one of the long narrow rectangles on the right side of the roof going vertically.…"

Reflections: Why is it important to add detailed description to your stories? How does adding more description and detail make a character come alive for the listener? What kinds of descriptions create the best pictures in your imagination?

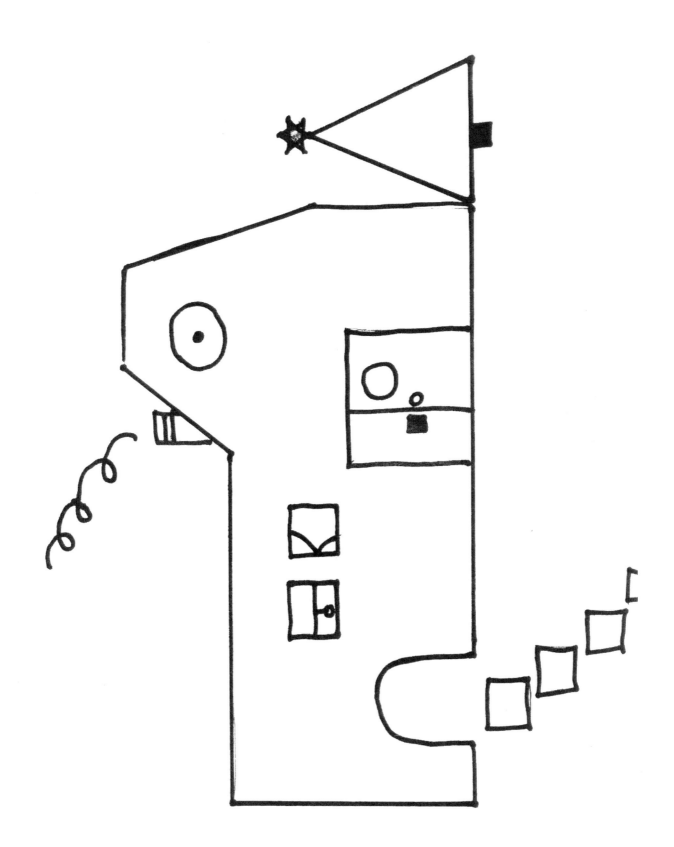

Figure 4.1. Figure of a house.

Figure 4.2. Figure of a man.

Chapter 4b

Strengthening Storytelling Skills: Activities for Adapting and Creating Stories

The activities in this section are designed to help young people create new stories using a variety of story prompts and simple frameworks. Some of the lessons help students develop their own version of familiar tales, while others encourage them look at their lives in terms of story. Even if your storytellers never perform the stories they create, they will become better at expressing themselves and retelling stories in their own words from the books that they've chosen. No longer will student storytellers rely on memorizing the author's words.

In helping youth storytellers adapt or create their own stories, it is important to first discuss the parts of a story and what makes a story interesting and exciting to hear. All stories have a beginning, a middle, and an end. They have a problem that must be resolved and brought to a satisfying conclusion. Good stories have interesting characters and usually a well-defined setting. Dialogue or conversations between characters make a story more interesting for listeners than merely describing the plot. Dialogue that is concise helps to move the story along. Have your students analyze some of the stories you have told or have seen on videotape and discuss what makes the story work. This is also a good time to discuss how facial expression, voice, and gestures improve the telling of a story.

Occasionally, a story coming from one of these activities can be shaped, honed, and developed into a tellable tale. However, unless you have had experience teaching youngsters how to write well-crafted stories, encourage your students to tell stories that can be found in books or on tape for performance purposes. Some young people rewrite and adapt stories well, but for the most part, creating a well-designed tellable tale from scratch without the benefit of coaching is something that is beyond the scope of many storytelling clubs or troupes. We have found that the stories students create on their own often lack the basic elements of a good, tellable tale. This is especially true of younger and inexperienced storytellers. Many times stories are made up on the spot or are simply uninteresting. Unless a storyteller is willing to spend time crafting an original story, the piece should not be told in a performance but rather kept within the confines of the meeting.

Some of the activities in Chapter 3, "Getting Ready to Tell," are also designed to help students create stories (see "Toy Stories" and "Magic Key"). Although the directions are given for small groups, you can take these one step further and encourage students to make up stories by themselves using the same prompts. (See Appendix for sample stories written by members of the Chatterton Talespinners and Voices of Illusion.)

Crafting Adapted and Original Stories for Performance

Developing original stories and preparing them for performance takes time and requires the leader to work one on one with students. Whenever young people ask to create their own stories, encourage them to do so only if you have ample time to assist in the process. Work with them to craft the story into a strong, tellable tale. Use the following guidelines when working with original, rewritten, adapted stories or with parodied stories.

- First and foremost, appreciate and honor the effort the student has put into the process. Find an area to praise and build from that point.

- Writing is a complement to telling and can be an effective way of building and remembering the story. But this should be done at a comfortable pace so the teller can grow from the experience. Many young people dislike and fear writing, which should be taken into consideration. If this is the case, encourage them to simply write down the beginning, ending, and main points of the story. Use the Storyboard (Figure 3.8) or Storytelling Map (Figure 3.9) to help with this process.

- Students usually have a plan in mind for their story, however they may not know the best direction to take to realize their ideas. By listening to the story, you can suggest various alternatives. Have the young person read aloud what he or she has written. Although the entire story does not have to be written down, it needs an audience for the shaping process.

- Help the storyteller craft the story from start to finish. Concentrate on "How should the story begin?" and "Why does the story end the way you have chosen?" Discuss the characters and their interaction with one another. Have the student pick out the "problem" and turning point or climax.

- Sometimes it is helpful for students to read or tell their story into a tape recorder. Hearing the story helps distance them from the process of writing and creating and make the teller more objective, especially if the story-creating process becomes stalled. Ask, "Does the story make sense to you?" "What problems do you see with the story?" "What seems to be missing?" "Does the story need more dialogue, character development, or a stronger conclusion?"

- Provide enough time for students to tell their stories over and over again. When storytellers are free to play with the story in practice sessions, they are able to observe the story in action. As much as rehearsal is useful to the stage actor, "play" time or a time to try various methods of telling is vital to the teller crafting an original story. Use other club members as sounding boards. Often they will add valuable comments and suggestions.

Bare Bones Fables

Purpose: To encourage students to develop stories from a skeletal outline. To help students take familiar tales and make them their own by adding their own ideas.

Supplies:

- Bare Bones Fables (Figure 4.3) reproducible

This activity is designed to help students retell stories in their own words by encouraging them to elaborate and add details, description, and characterization. Eight well-known fables that have been stripped down to their "bare bones" are included at the end of this activity. Most of the details have been eliminated, and only the bare essentials of the story are given.

Explain that a fable is a brief story that teaches a lesson. The lesson or moral is almost always given at the end of the story. Usually, the characters in a fable are animals that display human characteristics and personality traits. Read each Bare Bones Fable aloud to the class. If your tellers are already familiar with the tales, simply read the title and give a one-line description or summary. Have students raise their hands to indicate which story they would like to work on, and divide the class into groups of two, three, or four based on the story they have chosen. Working together, each group must create a retelling of the fable adding setting, details, description, dialogue, and a moral. Each group begins the activity by reading the Bare Bones Fable aloud so everyone within the group becomes familiar with the story

Emphasize that they are going to "tell" a group story. Discuss the difference between "telling" a story and "acting it out." In telling a group story, the group stands side by side facing the audience. The audience is told rather than shown what is happening in the story. The group may use a narrator to introduce the story and move it along while each person in the group tells his or her part as it comes up, or the group may divide the story equally between all members and each person tells a portion of it. Gestures and descriptions should be used rather than acting out the parts of the story. Encourage participants to use their own words but not to write anything down, otherwise it becomes a script.

There are two excellent resources you can use with your students to help them understand how one fable can be made into many stories. A story on *Storytelling World Magazine's* audiocassette, *Choices of Voices* (East Tennessee State University, 1995), "The Crow and the Pitcher," features eight storytellers telling their version of this well-known fable, including a literary retelling, a tandem retelling, a song, an Evangelical preacher's voice, a cute little voice, and a nagging mother's voice. The magazine that accompanies the tape contains the written form of each story. Young people also enjoy applying the same skills to well-known fairy tales such as "Goldilocks and the Three Bears," "The Three Little Pigs," " Jack and the Beanstalk," or "The Three Billy Goats Gruff."

Storyteller, David Novak's "The Ant and the Grasshopper (3X)" recorded on his audiocassette, *The Cookie Girl* (August House, 1993), is an excellent selection to play after the groups have told their stories. In this version, David retells the Aesop's fable three times with different endings and morals.

Several books containing Aesop fables are included in the bibliography, including *The Lion and the Mouse* by Doris Orgel (DK Publishers, 2001), *The Tortoise and the Hare* by Janet Stevens (Holiday House, 1984), *Aesop's Fables* by Jerry Pinkney (Seastar, 2000), and *Eric Carle's Treasury of Classic Stories for Children* (Orchard Books, 1996).

Directions for Bare Bones Fables

1. Read or tell an Aesop's fable and define "fable" for the class.

2. Give a copy of *Bare Bones Fables* (Figure 4.3) to each group and read each fable aloud to the class.

3. Allow students to choose which fable they would like to work on and then divide class into groups of three according to the fables they chose.

4. Discuss the difference between "telling" a story and "acting it out."

5. Direct students to

   • Reread the selected fable aloud within their groups.

   • Summarize the story in their own words.

   • Retell the story adding a setting, a description of the characters, and dialogue.

   • Add a moral or lesson at the end of story

   • Choose who is going to tell the story (it may be one or all of the members of the group).

   • Practice how they want to tell the story.

6. Call on each group to tell its fable to the rest of the class, reminding group members to

   • Face the audience when telling the fable.

   • Tell the story. Do not "act it out."

Example: After listening to the *Choices of Voices* tape and working together in a group, five Talespinners—Heidi, her sister Holly, Rachel, her sister Leah, and Emily—put together a "Crow and Pitcher Rap" in which each girl had a part. It became one of the highlights of our Family Storytelling Festival. —Judy

Reflections: How is telling a group story different than telling alone? How does working together help make the story better or worse? What things are important to remember when you are retelling a story? How is telling a story different from acting it out?

BARE BONES FABLES

A fable is a short story, usually about animals, that teaches a lesson. Often the lesson or "moral" is given at the end of the story. Retell one of the following stories in your own words adding description and dialogue. Be sure to add the moral to the end of the story.

The Tortoise and the Hare

A tortoise and hare were having an argument about which animal was the fastest. They made a date to race each other and settle the argument. When the race began, the hare took off like shot, and, in no time at all, he was far ahead of the tortoise. The hare was so confident he would win the race that he lay down under a tree and took a nap. Meanwhile, the tortoise kept plodding along, one foot in front of the other, slowly and steadily without stopping. After a long while, the tortoise passed the sleeping hare, who finally woke up when he heard the crowd cheering as the tortoise crossed the finish line.

The Crow and the Pitcher

A very thirsty crow came upon a tall pitcher that was half full of water. When the crow tried to take a drink, he found that his beak was too short to reach the water. While trying to decide what to do, the crow saw some pebbles lying nearby. He picked up the pebbles and, one by one, dropped the pebbles into the pitcher. Soon the level of the water rose almost to the top, and the crow was able to drink.

The Goose That Laid the Golden Egg

One day, a farmer went to collect eggs from his favorite goose and found that the goose had lain an egg of solid gold. Needless to say, the farmer was delighted. Every day after that, when the farmer went to collect the eggs, he found another egg of solid gold. Soon the farmer became rich. But after a while, he became greedy because the goose only laid one golden egg at a time. So the farmer killed the goose and found that there was not one single egg inside, and his precious goose was dead.

The Lion and the Mouse

Once there was a mighty lion that loved to roar. Whenever he roared all of the smaller animals in the jungle would run and hide. One day, a little mouse heard the lion's roar but decided not to run away. As soon as the lion fell asleep, the mouse crawled up on to the lion's nose. The lion woke up. "Please don't eat me," said the mouse. "If you spare my life, I might be able to save your life one day." The lion agreed to let the mouse go. Several days later, the lion became entangled in a hunter's net. When the mouse heard the lion roaring, he quickly came to the lion's aid and chewed a hole in the net large enough for the lion to escape.

The Fox and the Crow

There once was a crow who had stolen a piece of cheese. A hungry fox came along and saw the crow sitting on a branch of a tree. Determined to get the cheese away from the crow, the fox began to tell the crow how beautiful she was and what a beautiful voice she had. The fox begged the crow to sing for him. The crow was so flattered by the fox that she opened her beak and began to sing. As she did so, the cheese fell out of her mouth and into the waiting jaws of the fox.

The Milkmaid and Her Pail

A milkmaid was on her way to market carrying a pail full of milk on her head. As she walked along, she thought about all of the wonderful things she would buy with the money she was going to make when she sold the milk. First she was going to buy eggs. Then she was going to hatch them and sell the chickens. With the money she earned from selling the chickens, she would buy a beautiful new dress. All the young men would want to marry her because she looked so beautiful in the new dress, but she would only marry the mayor's son. She would toss her head and put her nose up in the air to all those other boys. As she thought about it, the milkmaid tossed her head and the pail fell down spilling the milk all over the ground.

The Ant and the Grasshopper

An ant was busily carrying bits of corn and wheat into her ant hole to store it for the coming winter months. A grasshopper sat nearby watching the ant. He was busy chirping and singing. "Why don't you stop and sing with me?" said the grasshopper to the ant. To which she replied, "I have no time to sing and play. I am storing food for the winter. You better do the same or you will have nothing to eat when the snow comes." The grasshopper ignored her warning and continued to sing. When winter came he had nothing to eat and no warm place to live.

The North Wind and the Sun

The North Wind and the Sun were having an argument as to which one of them was more powerful. Suddenly they saw a man walking along a road. He was wearing a warm cloak. They decided that whoever could make the man take off his cloak would be declared to be the strongest. The North Wind went first. He blew up a storm but the more he blew, the tighter the man pulled his cloak around himself. Finally the Wind gave up. Next was the Sun's turn and he began to shine down on the man. Soon the man became warm and then hot. He became so warm that he took off his cloak and carried it over his arm.

Figure 4.3. Bare Bones Fables.

Five Times Three: Audience Participation

(Adapted with permission from an activity by Tom McCabe)

Purpose: To encourage students to work together to create a story. To help students create stories that involves audience participation.

Supplies:

- Books of *Aesop's Fables* and other fable collections

- Photocopies of fables

- Five Times Three: Audience Participation form (Figure 4.5)

This is a wonderful activity to help students work cooperatively to create a story that is both tellable and that invites the audience to participate in the telling. Provide books and examples of Aesop and other fables. You may also refer to the Bare Bones Fables (Figure 4.3) from the previous activity. Other types of stories can be used, but fables work best because they are so brief.

With younger students, work through the exercise with the entire class before dividing them into smaller groups. Create the actions, movements, and sounds together or use the sample story at the end of this activity.

This technique is particularly effective for novice tellers because they do not have to stand by themselves in front of the group. They work as a team. If a teller is positively terrified, have the kneeling partners face the teller; when the teller gets nervous, simply have him or her tell the story to the partners. In this instance, when the partners get to the audience participation parts, they simply look over their shoulders at the audience and do the sounds and movements. Almost automatically, the audience will join in. Once their stories are perfected, teams can tell their story in front of an audience, taking turns being the teller or the supporting partners. The more they tell the story, the more confident the novice storytellers become.

Directions for Five Times Three

1. Provide books and examples of fables or other brief stories.

2. After students have become familiar with a number of different fables, divide students into groups of three.

3. Have each trio choose a fable to retell.

4. Provide each team with a copy of Five Times Three: Audience Participation (Figure 4.5).

5. Direct students to

    • Fill out their form by identifying the characters and the main problem that one or more of the characters has.

    • Reread the story aloud and pick out five words in the story that show action—that is, something the character(s) is doing—and write the actions on the form.

    • Create a movement or gesture to go along with each action and write them down. Each action should be from the waist up so they can be demonstrated from a sitting position (e.g., the lion roars: raise hands to look like claws; the mouse creeps: move fingers of both hands to demonstrate creeping; the crow flies: move arms up and down in a flapping motion).

    • Create a sound for each movement and write them down (e.g., the lion roars: "grrrrrr"; the mouse creeps: slowly say "creeeep, creeeep"; the crow flies: "swish, swish, swish." If they cannot think of a sound, have the team use the action word or verb.

    • Rehearse each movement, then rehearse each movement with its sound.

    • Find five places in the story where they can add each of the movements and sounds.

6. Using the formula, "five actions times three places," have teams retell their stories using five action-movement sounds three times within the story. This will create fifteen places in the story where the audience can participate. To get all fifteen actions into the story, the team may have to expand the tale and add additional episodes.

7. After the groups have practiced telling their fable, have them choose one member of the team to be the storyteller.

8. Have the storyteller face the audience while the two other partners kneel at the teller's feet facing at an angle half way between the teller and the audience.

9. Instruct the team as follows:

   • The teller tells the story while facing the audience.

   • Each time the teller comes to an action, the partners look at the audience and demonstrate the movement and sound that goes along with the action.

10. Direct the audience to join in with the gestures and sound.

11. Repeat the activity two more times or assign it for homework and have each member of the group come back with his or her own fable. The triads will then have three stories to tell. Each member of the team takes a turn being teller and assistant.

Example: "The Lion and the Mouse." Once upon a time there was a lion that loved to roar ("grrrrrr" and show claws). Not far from the lion's den, there lived a little mouse. He was afraid of the lion's roar ("ooooo"; sound scared, shiver, and hug the body). One day, as the lion went walking through the forest, he became very sleepy and began to yawn (yawn and stretch). The lion lay down, fell asleep, and started to snore (make snoring sound and put hands together under ear). The little mouse decided he was not going to be afraid of the lion any more ("ooooo" sound; scared, shiver, and hug the body). He walked up to the snoring, sleeping lion (snoring sound and hands together under ear) and climbed up on the lion's tail and haunches ("creep, creep, creep" and wiggle fingers to show climbing up). The lion kept on sleeping and snoring (snoring sound, hand under ear). He climbed up the lion's back and shoulders ("creep, creep, creep" and wiggle fingers) until he reached the lion's head. All of a sudden, the lion woke up. First he yawned (yawn and stretch), and then he roared ("grrrr" and show claws). He grabbed the little mouse and held him tight in his paws. "I'm going to eat you," said the lion. "Oh, please don't eat me," said the mouse. "One day, I may save your life." The lion laughed and said, "A little thing like you, save a big strong lion like me? I don't think so. That's impossible, but I will let you go this time. Don't let me catch you again, or I will surely eat you." The little mouse ran away from the lion. The next day, the lion was walking through the forest, and he stepped into a hunter's net. The net closed tight around the lion. He tried to get loose, but the more he struggled, the tighter the net became. The lion began to roar ("grrrr" and show claws). The little mouse heard the lion and said, "The lion must be in trouble. I will see if I can help him." When the little mouse saw the lion caught up in the hunter's net, he said, "Don't worry, Friend Lion, I will help you." So the little mouse climbed up the net ("creep, creep, creep," wiggle fingers) and began to chew a hole in the net. He chewed and chewed until there was a hole big enough for the lion to crawl out. "Thank you, my friend," said the lion, "You saved my life." The lion was very tired after his ordeal. First he yawned (yawn and stretch) and then he lay down, fell asleep, and began to snore (snoring sound and hands under ear). The little mouse went back to his hole and was never afraid ("oooo"; shiver and hug the body) of the lion again.

Reflection: How did working together in a group help you to make up a story? What made it easier? What made it more difficult? How can you use partners or friends to help you in creating a story to tell? How do adding sounds and gestures make a story more enjoyable to tell? How does adding participation make a story more enjoyable for an audience?

Five Times Three: Audience Participation

Directions

- Working in teams of three, pick a fable to retell.

- Read the fable aloud. List the characters.

- What problem or conflict are the characters having with each other or with something else?

- Reread the story. Find five verbs or actions

- Create a gesture or movement and a sound to accompany each action.

- Find fifteen places in the story where you can use the action, movement, and sound.

- Practice telling the fable using all fifteen actions, movements, and sounds.

Team members' names:

1. _____

2. _____

3. _____

Name of the fable: _____

List the characters: _____

_____

What is the story's problem? _____

_____

Five actions in the story	Five gestures or movements	Five sounds
1.		
2.		
3.		
4.		
5.		

Figure 4.4. Five Times Three: Audience Participation.

Telling Your Own Story

Purpose: To help students to think of events in their own lives in terms of story. To encourage students to tell personal anecdotes that are interesting for the listener.

Supplies:

- Whistle or bell

- Watch or timer

This activity uses a variety of story starters or prompts. The idea is for students to keep improving a simple story about themselves by telling it to different people. Have the group switch partners and retell their story three or four times. The story will improve each time it is told as tellers remember more details. Encourage the students to be good listeners because they may be called on to tell someone else's story. Remind them that eye contact is important for both the teller and the listener. Good listeners do not interrupt or make comments until the storyteller has finished telling their story.

At the conclusion of the activity, ask if anyone would like to tell one of the stories that he or she heard from someone else in the group. When students hear their own stories retold, they gain an awareness of what is important to someone else. They think about what they could have emphasized more or told more effectively so that the listener would have a deeper understanding of the story. Ask the kids to point to those tellers who had a particularly interesting story that everyone should hear and have those tellers share their story in front of the group. Discuss what happened to their story as they told it over and over again to different people. How did the story improve? What helped them to make the story better? What made the stories they heard interesting, funny, or memorable? Any number of prompts can be used. We have included a number that work well. For additional story topics, see Donald Davis's *Telling Your Own Stories* (August House, 1993).

Topics You Can Use

- Tell about a time you were lost or scared.

- Tell about a time that you cooked something that didn't turn out the way you had expected.

- Tell about how you lost your first tooth.

- Tell about an embarrassing moment.

- Tell about a trip that turned out to be a disaster.

- Tell about a blind date that turned out to be a disaster.

- Tell about something that someone in your family loves to tell about you.

- Tell about something funny, sad, or interesting that happened to someone in your family.

- Tell about an award, contest, or achievement that makes you proud.

- Tell about a secret hiding place.

- Tell about a place where you once lived.

- Tell about something you did that you hope your parents never find out about.

Directions for Telling Your Own Story

1.   Hand out the list of story prompts, or write them on the chalkboard or flip chart.

2.   Divide the group into pairs and have partners decide who is going to be the teller and who the listener.

3.   Use a timer and whistle to begin and end segments of the activity, allow three to four minutes per partner.

4.   Direct the tellers to

   • Choose one of the story prompts.

   • Relate an anecdote or experience based on the story prompt to the listener.

5.   Direct listeners to

   • Listen carefully to their partners.

   • Not to interrupt their partners.

   • When their partners have finished telling their stories, ask questions or comment on parts of the story that are not clear or that they do not understand.

   • Tell the partner what parts of the story they liked best.

6.   Have partners switch roles so that the listener has a turn to tell a story. Use a timer so that everyone has the same amount of time to tell and receive feedback.

7.   After each student has had a turn to tell, have the students find a different partner and tell the same story to a new partner.

8.   Have the group switch partners three or four times and retell their stories to a new partner.

Example: Kristen told how when she was a little girl, she made breakfast in bed for her mother on Mother's Day. The first time through, she told how she covered up the burnt toast with peanut butter and jelly and how she spilled the orange juice carrying the breakfast up the stairs. After answering her partner's questions, Kristen's subsequent tellings included her mother's reaction to the breakfast, the mess she left in the kitchen, and what she learned about making breakfast. Each telling became funnier and more exaggerated until one of her partners insisted that we all listen to Kristen's story. —Judy

Reflections: What makes a story interesting? How does repeated telling of a story help to improve it? How can we use a partner to improve our storytelling?

Personal Encounter with an Animal

(Adapted with permission from an activity created by Jean-Andrew Dickmann)

Purpose: To help students think of events in their own lives in terms of story. To encourage students to think of interesting ways to begin and end stories.

This activity is a variation of Telling Your Own Story but is done in a slightly different way using larger groups. Any number of topics or story prompts may be chosen, but most children can relate to an encounter with an animal. They may talk about a pet, a trip to the zoo or farm, or something highly unusual. With younger students, discuss the meaning of encounter and brainstorm examples (e.g., choosing a new pet, seeing an animal up close for the first time, a time an animal did something they did not expect).

Directions for Encounter with an Animal:

1. Break the group into small circles of four to six students.

2. Ask students to think of something unusual, funny, sad, or interesting that happened to them involving an animal that they would like to tell about. If necessary, brainstorm possible encounters.

3. Direct students to

    • First, think of a good opening sentence that will make people want to listen to the rest of the story. A good opening will grab the listener's attention and make them want to know more (e.g., "Once when I was little, I was chased by a ..." or "The best cat we ever had was ..." or "The last time I visited my Grandpa's farm ..." or "I was afraid of dogs until ...") .

    • Next, think of an interesting way to end the story. A good ending, such as what the students learned from their experiences, wraps up the story and brings it to a satisfying conclusion; other satisfying endings include how their life is different now, what warning would they give others in a similar situation (e.g., "and I never saw Patches again" or "Don't ever put your finger in a hole in a tree in the woods" or "I learned that a parakeet can be just as much fun as a dog") .

4. Have students take turns telling their stories as they go around the circle.

5. While a student tells a story, there are to be no interruptions, but students can make comments or ask questions once the story has ended.

6. After all participants have had a chance to tell their stories, ask one person from each group to retell one of the stories.

7. Have each group choose one person to tell his or her story to the rest of the class.

Example: Rikki, who was from India, told about a time a bull, attracted to Rikki's red backpack, chased him and his brother on their way home from school. Rikki began his story by telling how he obtained the new backpack and how much he liked it. He and his brother encountered the bull when they decided to take a new route home. He ended the story by saying that they never walked home that way again. Rikki's brother, David, told about going up a mountain to a temple and encountering monkeys who stole things from them. David began the story by telling us that monkeys are prevalent in the mountainous areas where his family had lived. He told us how he happened to be going to the temple with his family. He ended the story by saying how happy he was that in the United States, monkeys only live in the zoo. —Judy

Reflections: What makes a personal story easy to tell? How does a good beginning and a good ending improve a story? As a listener, what makes a story easier to understand and enjoy?

Point of View

Purpose: To help students think about the characters in the stories they tell. To encourage students to look at a familiar story from the point of view of various characters in the story.

Supplies:

- Index cards with fairy tale and nursery rhyme characters

The following activity takes well-known fairy tales and nursery rhymes and asks students to look at them in a new way. Before you begin the activity, discuss what "point of view" means. Use the example of how a teacher might describe an argument between two students and how the students involved in the argument might describe it. This is exactly what you are going to have them do in this activity.

An impartial narrator usually tells most folktales, fairy tales, and even literary stories. They don't often delve into the feelings or views of the characters. There are a number of books on the market that tell familiar fairy tales from a different perspective or from the point of view of a nontraditional character. One of the best known is Jon Scieszka's *The True Story of the Three Little Pigs* (Viking Press, 1989), told from the point of view of the wolf; "Abner T. Wolf, but you can call me Al," who just wanted to borrow a cup of sugar for his dear Granny's birthday cake. Not only is it a wonderful story to tell, it also helps students see that familiar story in a different light.

Fairy Tale and Nursery Rhyme Characters You Can Use

- Jack and Jill
- The prince and the forgotten fairy (Sleeping Beauty)
- Third little pig and the wolf
- The woodsman and the wolf (Red Riding Hood)
- Jack's mother and the giant's wife (Jack and the Beanstalk)
- Two of the king's men (Humpty Dumpty)
- Little Red Riding Hood's mother and grandmother
- Cinderella's stepsister and the prince
- Goldilock's mother and the mama bear
- The middle billy goat gruff and the troll
- Hansel and Gretel's father and the witch
- One of the dwarves and the prince (Snow White)
- The magic fish and the fisherman's wife

- Jack Sprat and his wife

- The oldest and the youngest child of the old woman who lived in a shoe

- Cinderella's fairy godmother and the prince's mother

- Little Miss Muffet and the spider

- Mary (who had a little lamb) and her teacher

Directions for Point of View

1. Divide the group into pairs.

2. Give each pair a card with the name of two characters from a well-known fairy tale or nursery rhyme.

3. Direct students to

   - First summarize the story or the rhyme so both partners have the same idea of what the story is about.

   - Then choose one of the characters. Before they begin, they should think how that character might have felt about the other characters in the story.

   - Partner 1: Retell the fairy tale or nursery tale to your partner from the "point of view" of that character.

   - Partner 2: Retell the story from the point of view of the other character.

   - Decide how best to tell the story to the rest of the group.

4. Allow time for each pair to share their work with the rest of the group. They can keep the stories separate or combine them in a dialogue. Many students will find it easier to tell the story in first person, but third person may be used as well.

5. Before the retelling begins, remind students that they are telling a story, not "acting it out." Teller should face the audience. Caution students not to contradict or argue with their partner but simply to tell the story from their character's point of view.

Example: For "Jack and Jill went up the hill to fetch a pail of water," Jill might complain that her brother is a real pain, always running and fooling around but because he's strong, she needed his help carrying the bucket of water. She told him to be careful, but as usual he got silly and tripped. Serves him right that he broke his crown. Jill managed to survive the tumble with only a few cuts and bruises. Jack might blame Jill for the accident; after all, he could have fetched the water all by himself, but with her nagging and complaining all the time, he wasn't watching where he was going. Actually, he thinks Jill tripped him and that's why he fell.

Reflections: How did the story change when a different character told it? How can you use "point of view" to improve your storytelling?

Variation*:* Divide the class into groups of three or four tellers. Have each group retell a familiar fairy tale in a modern setting or from one of the character's point of view. Review the traditional way the story is told with your students first.

Several fairy tale variants are listed in the bibliography at the end of the book. See *The Fourth Little Pig* (Steck-Vaughn, 1992) by Teresa Celsi, *The Cowboy and the Black-Eyed Pea* (Putnam, 1992) by Tony Johnson, *The Three Javelinas* (Northland Publishing, 1992) by Susan Lowell, *The Three Little Wolves and the Big Bad Pig* (McElderry, 1993) by Eugene Trivizas, and *Flossy & the Fox* (Scholastic, 1986) by Patricia McKissack.

Traditional Stories You Can Use

- Goldilocks and Three Bears
- Three Billy Goats Gruff
- Three Little Pigs
- Little Red Riding Hood
- Cinderella
- Snow White
- Sleeping Beauty
- Rapunzel
- Jack and the Beanstalk

Crazy Mixed-Up Fairy Tales

Purpose: To encourage students to build stories from dissimilar parts. To stimulate creative and original thinking.

Supplies:

- Five colors of copy or construction paper, cut into quarters
- Pencils

This activity works especially well with middle and high school students. It challenges students to use their creativity and their ability to work together.

Directions for Crazy Mixed-Up Fairy Tales

1. To begin, you will need five sheets of colored copy or construction paper, cut into quarters. Each color of paper represents a different topic.

2. Divide the class into groups of two, three, or four. Give one square of each color to each group.

3. Direct students to use a different color paper to write the following:

   - The name of a character from a favorite fairy tale (yellow paper)
   - The name of an exotic place (blue paper)
   - The name of a character from a different fairy tale (green paper)
   - A problem (pink paper)
   - A quest (white paper)

4. Collect all of the paper squares, then separate them by color and mix them up.

5. Have each group pick one card from each pile.

6. Direct each group to do the following (allow 10 to 15 minutes):

   • Create a story using each of the five elements.

   • Decide how to tell it and practice telling it.

   • Chose one person to tell the story or have each person in the group tell a part.

   • Then have each group tell its story for the rest of the class. For younger students, eliminate either the quest or the problem card.

Example: 1. (character) Cinderella. 2. (place) The North Pole. 3. (second character) Big Billy Goat Gruff. 4. (problem) A giant is eating all the crops and livestock. 5. (quest) To find the fountain of eternal youth. In the story, Cinderella is searching for the fountain of eternal youth, which lies somewhere near the North Pole. She sets off one day to find the fountain but can't find any food because a giant has eaten all the crops and there is nothing left to pack for her long journey. One day she meets up with the Big Billy Goat Gruff, who tracks down the giant and butts him back into the sky where he came from. The goat and Cinderella go off on the journey together; sometimes she rides on the goat's back, and sometimes she carries him until they arrive at the North Pole. There they find the fountain of eternal youth, which is frozen. They light a fire, melt the fountain, take a long drink, and they both live happily ever after.

Reflections: What was the most difficult part of creating the story? How can working in a group help improve the writing or telling of a story?

A Picture Is Worth a Thousand Words

Purpose: To encourage students to create a story from a picture or photograph. To help students understand story sequence.

Supplies:

   • Magazine pictures mounted on construction paper

This activity may be done in small groups or individually. Collect interesting and unusual pictures from old magazines, calendars, museum prints, or posters. Mount them on construction paper and laminate them. Spread pictures out on a table and have participants choose one that appeals to them. Students may work with one or several partners. They may each have a different picture, or they can work on a story together using the same picture. Younger students may only be able to describe what they are seeing in the picture, while older students may be able to pick out some unusual aspect of the picture to develop the story.

Directions for A Picture Is Worth a Thousand Words

1. Before beginning the activity, discuss story sequence.

    - All stories must have a good opening or beginning that catches listeners' attention, arouses curiosity, and entices them to listen to the rest of the story.

    - Most stories have a problem to be solved or a conflict to be resolved.

    - Stories contain a series of events that build to a climax in the middle and have a satisfying conclusion or ending.

2. Spread laminated pictures around the room and ask student to choose one that interests them.

3. After selecting a picture, instruct students to think about or decide the following:

    - What is happening in the picture?

    - What happened before the picture was taken?

    - What will happen next?

    - How will the story end?

    - How can you add dialogue to the story?

    - Create a good way to begin your story.

    - Create a satisfying way to end the story.

4. Direct students to build a story around the picture that they have chosen.

5. Remind students that a good story

    - Has a beginning, middle, and a satisfying conclusion that ties up the story and brings it to an end

    - Has well-defined, interesting characters and an intriguing setting

    - Has a conflict or problem that must be resolved

    - Has interesting dialogue in which the characters' conversations describe what is happening

6. Direct students to practice telling their stories to a partner. Remind partners to

    - Listen without interruption.

    - Ask questions about what is not clear.

    - Give suggestions to make the story better.

7. Require students to tell the improved stories to new partners before telling the story to the entire class.

8. Encourage students to tell the story first and then show the picture at the conclusion of the story.

Example: A picture of a peaceful seashore scene might evoke a story of an impending storm or a day at the beach collecting seashells or of finding a bottle with a message in it from a lost sailor. A photo of a little girl smelling a flower could evoke a story of a magical garden where wishes come true, of a lost princess, or of planting flowers at grandmother's house.

Variation: Have the students draw a picture—any picture. Collect the drawings and pass them out again, checking that each student has someone else's picture. Then have the students make up and tell a story inspired by the drawing. Show the drawing after the story is told. The kinds of stories generated by student artwork can be fascinating.

Reflections: What was easy and what was difficult about creating a story from a picture? How did the picture generate the beginning, middle, and end of a story? What makes story interesting or exciting to listen to? How is a story like a picture?

Storytelling activities, games, and exercises keep your meetings interesting and exciting while strengthening skills and preparing young tellers for performances. If meetings seem stale and interest is waning, take a break from practicing; try a new activity. Things will liven up again. Soon you'll be ready for that all-important first performance.

Chapter

Coaching: Guiding the Youth Storyteller

What Is Coaching?

As you begin to work with your students, they will look to you for support. They will seek your advice on topics such as, "How can I improve my storytelling skills?" "How do I shape my story?" and "How can I ease my stage fright?"

According to *Merriman-Webster's Dictionary,* to coach means "to instruct or direct." A preset definition comes to mind when we hear the word "coach." Images are conjured up of a basketball coach whose primary job is to work so the team can succeed. Coach can also mean a private trainer who works one-on-one with someone to instruct, model, or demonstrate a skill or talent. Unfortunately, we also have impressions of a coach as someone who berates members of the team and does "anything possible" to ensure a win. The coach in this case seems to place his or her goals and directions before that of the player.

A storytelling coach, unlike a basketball coach, is not concerned with scores, but with the overall development and performance of the student teller. This concern goes beyond that of a single game or even the season. It might include attitudes toward telling, the ability to create stories, or skills to work with others. An effective storytelling coach is concerned with everything involved with the telling experience, with the teller, the tale, and the audience.

A storytelling coach firmly believes that various audiences listening to the teller can help a student become a good storyteller. Experience is often the greatest teacher. Talent comes with time and telling. The coach holds firmly to the belief that if the right atmosphere is established for coaching, growth will occur. Listening to advice from their peers can also benefit the student teller.

A storytelling coach never resorts to yelling or any adverse "motivation" techniques such as making the student feel less accomplished as a teller because of lack of practice or less of a person because of a character flaw. A coach simply reinforces the positive experiences of good storytelling that occur when the students are motivated to succeed. The ultimate goal is for the students to feel that they "own" their stories; that something about their unique way of telling makes the story theirs. Storytelling is not a competitive art or an art to "outdo" someone else and should never be treated as such. A good coach places young people in an environment where they want to tell stories then works with them to improve.

What Coaching Is Not

Storytelling coaching is not meant to be a counseling session; it is a place for students to work on their process as a teller and to focus on story development. Never assume there is any other agenda. Of course, some students may come for coaching because you are taking the time to listen to them, and this makes them feel wanted; but stick to the storytelling and the coaching. Do not allow it to become a therapy session. Nonetheless, you may find that some stories will help students deal with problems.

Case in Point: *In a coaching session, Michelle told a story about "someone who recently broke up with her boyfriend" and explained how that person felt about it. Even though she had recently separated from her boyfriend of two years, I did not talk about the incident; instead I focused on the story. The coaching time was used to help Michelle find the best way to relate to the story, not the best way to help her deal with her own breakup. After working with the story, however, Michelle expressed that she was beginning to develop an understanding of recent events in her own life. By coaching the story, I was also helping the student. You will be amazed how much story coaching helps students realize their own needs and motivations, because when you coach something as personal as a student's story, you are also coaching the student. —Kevin*

Storytelling coaching is not a complaint session. Even though criticism may be used in a coaching session, the student must ask for it. It is not a place for members of the group to express what they believe went wrong and why it was a terrible story. Instead, it is a place where comments expressed are for the sole purpose of improving the storytelling. Criticism is never expressed without a suggestion for improvement. For example, if a student is told, "I could not hear you," it would be followed by, "I would suggest that you move your hand away from your face because your story would sound so much clearer." This type of comment encourages the student because the listener wants to hear the story. It is far different from the comment, "I couldn't hear what you were saying," which only leaves the impression that the telling was not heard and does not acknowledge that the story was worth hearing. Using careful modeling, this type of comment is what we like to call "appreciative criticism," meaning suggestions or comments that appreciate the work of the teller. Appreciative criticism demonstrates an understanding of the process the teller used to make the story become workable and helps focus the telling so that it maximizes the full potential of the story.

In a good coaching experience, there is also more praise than criticism for the telling and teller. An effective coach uses praise to motivate the teller and modulates, models, and motivates others to use appreciative criticism. Often when praise is accompanied by criticism, only the criticism is heard. In a coaching session, praise should be the first round of comments. Instead of hearing, "I loved the story's characters, especially Jack, but you mumbled too much." Only the praise should be given, "I loved the story's characters, especially Jack." This way the teller is left with an honest and good impression of the telling. Later he or she can ask for appreciative criticism.

The Rules Of Coaching

For storytelling coaching to stay true to its definition, a storytelling coach must follow a set of rules. We have narrowed them down to four; we believe that if you follow these rules, effective coaching is bound to occur.

The four rules concern student storytellers and their needs in the coaching session. These rules reinforce the idea that if students are active participants in the process, they will improve. The underlying philosophy is that the tellers, whenever possible, should direct their own coaching session.

Of course the age of the child that you are working with will determine the level of your direction. A young or inexperienced child will need more adult direction, whereas an experienced teller (someone used to your style of coaching), middle school students, or young adults will easily adapt to the idea that the storyteller directs the coaching session. As you use these techniques, children of all ages will become familiar with this style of coaching and often request it.

Rule Number One: Students determine when they are ready to be coached

One of the primary rules is never try to coach students who do not want to be coached; it is unproductive. Young storytellers usually know when a story needs improvement and will ask for assistance. This is not to say that you can't help them with suggestions along the way, but allow students to initiate coaching sessions. You can suggest sessions, but students should agree to it. Sometimes storytellers just need to experiment further with a story. "Play Time" is a time for students to experiment with telling the story. Only after students have practiced the story on their own are they ready for coaching from the group leader. Younger children might say they don't feel comfortable with their stories at various stages. Work with these youngsters to assess if they are really uncomfortable or simply want to move on to something else.

Rule Number Two: Students decide the specific areas on which they want to be coached

The first piece of business in any coaching session is a discussion about the story and the areas of student concerns. The opening question might be something like, "Tell me how you feel about your progress with the story and your performance as a teller." By asking this first, the coach can learn how the student believes he or she is doing. Often this will set the tone for the type of coaching needed as well as the areas of concern during the session.

The coach should make notes (either mentally or with pen and paper) during the session. From this initial discussion, the coach can plan. Younger students may need a little more time to become accustomed to this practice.

You may have a student who is only searching for the positive elements in the story. This is a signal that the student's needs are ones that will build him or her as a teller. You may have to consider the criticism for another time, instead boost the confidence of the teller by telling him or her what is going right. Soon the teller may ask you how to build skills

Rule Number Three: Students control the direction the coaching session takes

Students sometimes feel uncomfortable when they are being coached. A good coach will allow students to say they are uncomfortable, and together they can work to ease stress and build skills. The old philosophy of "grin and bear it" does not work in a coaching session. A storyteller who acknowledges that something does not work will only advance the coaching session. There are also times when a student is wrestling with the story, such as plot line or struggling with a character, in these situations the struggle is positive. However, when a student says he or she does not want to discuss a topic or if he or she feels uneasy about the session, then the student being coached should be given tools to change the situation.

Rule Number Four: Students determine when to end the coaching session

Students should be able to take part in ending the coaching session. As adults we sometimes become engrossed in the coaching while the young storyteller has become too tired or simply needs a break. If students know that they are part of the process and that they can request ending a session, they will feel easier about the session. One of the first jobs of a story coach is to establish the right coaching relationship, a place where the maximum amount of student coaching can occur.

The Atmosphere of Coaching

When discussing the proper storytelling-coaching environment, one must examine two concerns, the physical setting and the comfort of the teller in the environment. First, the physical setting of a coaching environment should be one in which the student being coached is heard and seen at all times. Whether the coaching is one-on-one or in small groups, it should not be in a space where the student competes to be heard. Try to find the quietest possible environment. Clear all loud noise such as speakers that bellow unwanted announcements, outside noises, or general noise. Outside disturbances can take away from the experience. The best place for coaching is a place where the teller is able to stand or sit while the coach has a place to write notes (only if it does not disturb the student teller).

Schedule the time so that the student(s) and the coach are able to remain for the duration of the coaching session. Make sure neither you nor the student has a pending engagement that may interrupt the session and that the student is given the full time scheduled. It is helpful to allow for an extra fifteen to thirty minutes in case more time is needed. Next, make sure both of you have eaten or that you provide light snacks so that hunger pangs do not interrupt the coaching session.

After you arrange your schedules, the proper element of trust needs to be established. This is best achieved by listening to the student's needs. Set expectations to work toward those needs, then arrange mutual goals and discuss a plan to achieve them. By showing the student that you want to use the coaching session to help support his or her goals, you can establish trust and a built-in relationship. This will ensure quality telling and coaching time. It is imperative that the student is given a chance to give feedback as well, especially at the end of the session.

Three Styles of Coaching

There are three effective ways of coaching youth tellers:

1. Whole-group coaching

2. Peer coaching

3. Student-to-adult coaching

Coaching Style 1: Whole-Group Coaching

This style is best used when students are telling for the first or second time within a group. The tellers of the story and the listeners only give direct praise. At this point students should be well instructed on how to give honest and direct feedback. Hearing praise builds self-esteem and is an excellent motivator. By concentrating on what was done "well" a coach can inspire students to work harder on their strong and weak areas.

There is always something that deserves praise; it is this focus that helps the teller continue to tell the story and many that follow. Before accepting suggestions, one must first learn to tell the story, and only by appreciating the effort will the progress of learning the story continue.

Coaching involves the art of active listening. This means you listen to the telling, including the sound of the voice and the physical projection of the story. The more you provide time to listen and respond to the story, the more students will respond to coaching.

This style of coaching involves allowing the listeners a chance to encourage the teller. A room full of active listeners and wonderful praise ensures an environment of continual storytelling for the student being coached. Offering nothing but positive feedback at this point helps students achieve success. Of course, there will be many times when a coach will have to bite his or her tongue because of a half-hearted attempt at telling stories, but when he or she simply allows honest appreciation for the teller, that young person can take charge of finding his or her own excellence.

Coaching Style 2: Peer Coaching

In peer coaching, two to three students coach each other. Students follow a structure that allows the teller to maintain control of the session and to feel comfortable about the experience.

The format structure is as follows:

1. The teller chooses the story or the section of the story on which he or she wants to work. Sometimes the student simply wants his or her peers to hear the entire story. This is acceptable and encouraged.

2. When the story ends, the listeners give heartfelt praise for the story. By providing honest and sincere feedback about specific elements in the story first, the student will feel comfortable with the story and his or her telling of it.

Example: Peer Coach: "Wow, what a story! I loved the way you changed your voice for Jack. It was clever to add the grunts to show that he was having trouble going down the beanstalk. I never would have thought of that."

1.   After peers offer praise, the teller can ask for specific suggestions, or the peers might ask if the teller wants suggestions. If the student declines, then no suggestions are given. If the student does want suggestions, then those suggestions should do the following:

   • Improve the telling of the story or raise the confidence of the teller

   • Be specific

2.   Suggestions are taken for what they are—suggestions. The teller can choose to accept them or not.

Example: Peer Coach: "What a story! Would you like a suggestion?"
Teller: "Yes, please."
Peer Coach: "When you have the giant coming to chase Jack, have him fall quickly like you do when you give that final grunt when Jack falls. It is just a suggestion, if you want it, go ahead."
Teller: "Thanks, I'll try it."

It is highly effective for the coach to model this process before students engage in their first peer coaching session and then walk around the room as students are coaching one another to ensure the structure is being followed. When appropriate the coach, can break into a peer session to offer suggestions or to give honest praise on the coaching experience, either for the teller or the peers. Always ask before doing so. You will find that peer coaching is very productive once students become familiar with the process.

Coaching Style 3: Student-to-Adult Coaching

This style of coaching uses personal time between one student and the storytelling coach. Student-to-adult coaching is for more serious-minded students who want to improve their storytelling skills and who actively seek suggestions for improvement. During these sessions, individual students spend time sharing their work while the coach spends a good deal of time listening to the storytellers' concerns, responding with suggestions and honest praise.

Reflective Discussion: At the end of a coaching session, it is important to take at least ten minutes to discuss what was learned during the session, for example, what was the focus, and what was discovered? Sometimes you will see that a student is able to recap the session but may need further clarification on assessment. He or she will need your guidance to help structure the next session or even to evaluate the current one. Review what the student accomplished, whether it was a new way to begin the story or a new way to use movement. During this reflective discussion time, you should also outline the objectives and intentions for the next meeting. Sometimes it helps to keep a "Student Log" so that you can refer to coach's notes on the progress of the session.

Developing Your Coaching Skills

As you experiment with these three styles, you and your students will become adjusted to your way of coaching. Adapt any of these exercises to suit your needs and comfort level, but stay true to the four rules of coaching. They will help you become grounded in your technique.

For further study on coaching contact the National Storytelling Network at www.storynet.org or Doug Lipman, the foremost authority on storytelling coaching, at www.storypower.com. His two books, *The Storytelling Coach* and *Improving Your Storytelling: Beyond the Basics for All Who Tell Stories in Work or Play* (August House, 1999), are essential references to study the art of coaching.

You can also consult a local storytelling guild or over time build adult volunteers who assist in the listening and sometimes the coaching process. Coaching can help you see noticeable improvement and may even surprise you with the results. The more you coach, the more comfortable you will become and the more your students will respond.

Chapter 6

Nurturing the Group

You're on your way. Your storytelling group has been meeting for a number of weeks. Your students are moving along well and maybe even better than you hoped they would by this time. Kids keep coming back and some of their friends want to join. Perhaps you've even had your first performance, and it was better than you had expected. You might be asking yourself, "What more could I be doing?" Perhaps you've experienced a few glitches or problems along the way; sometimes meetings become a little out of hand. Perhaps you just want to keep the enthusiasm high and are looking for ways to keep the group motivated. Perhaps you realize that you need more books or props and need to raise funds, or just need to find an extra pair of hands to help at meetings. The topics in this chapter will address some of those concerns.

Keeping Students Motivated

Generally we find that storytelling performances are the best motivators. Knowing that they will visit a day-care or senior citizen center in a week or two will cause a flurry of practice. If you insist that only students who attend meetings will be chosen to perform, attendance will increase. Motivation really runs high after a successful performance. After patting themselves on the back, young storytellers will want to know when can they tell again.

If there is a long time between performances, interest may wane. Students will not want to keep practicing the same stories over and over again, even though "practice makes perfect." Some students will want to choose new stories to learn; others will be satisfied with their initial choice. Some will learn stories on their own and feel that they don't need to practice at meetings. This is the time to look back over the chapters on activities and choose exercises that you feel your tellers will enjoy and that will challenge them.

Keeping young people motivated also means giving them something that will reward their efforts and keep them striving to work harder.

Levels of Achievement

We believe strongly that storytelling should be a noncompetitive art form, especially for young people. This does not mean that participation, hard work, and accomplishment should go unrecognized. You want your students to put forth their best efforts, to excel and be proud of their achievements.

Establishing levels of achievement provides your storytellers something to work toward in future meetings. Determine criteria needed to attain each level, such as attendance at meetings, participation in performances, assisting and mentoring new members, acquiring a repertoire of stories. Have students keep track of their own accomplishments, listing when and where they told stories, the names of the stories they know and can tell well, and whom they have helped and mentored along the way. The best time to update or add to their lists of achievements and accomplishments is following a performance or storytelling event. This will not only give you the opportunity to praise the work they have done but remind them that good storytelling is about learning and telling new stories as well as helping each other along the way. When the club's activities are about to end, sit down with each student and together decide what level he or she has achieved. At the end of the year, recognize individual accomplishments with certificates, ribbons, or prizes. Everyone who meets the requirements receives an award. The levels of achievement are cumulative, building upon the success of the previous year. This will keep your students motivated, striving to improve without having to compete to be the best or number one storyteller in the club.

We have included a reproducible "Circle of Excellence" poster (Figure 6.1) as an example for encouraging students to achieve their best and help others along the way. It can be adapted to fit your specific needs. There is also a fill-in form (Figure 6.2) that helps students record their accomplishments.

Circle of Excellence

 Storyteller: Has attended 50 percent of meetings
Has performed at 50 percent of field trips in one year
Is able to tell one story well
Has told stories at one non-club-sponsored event

 **Yarnspinner:** has attended 50 percent of meetings
Has performed at 50 percent of field trips in one year
Is able to tell two stories well
Has told stories at two non-club-sponsored events

 **Griot:** has attended 50 percent of meetings
Perform at 50 percent of field trips
Is able to tell three stories well
Has mentored one new teller
Has told stories at three non-club-sponsored events

 **Master Student Storyteller:** Two-year club membership
Has attended 50 percent of meetings
Has perform at 50 percent of field trips in two years
Is able to tell four stories well
Has mentored two new tellers
Has told stories at four non-club-sponsored events

 **Ambassador:** Three-year club membership
Has achieved Master Storyteller level
Has completed a special project to enrich or improve the club
or has arranged for one club event or field trip.

Criteria:
Attendance, participation, accomplishment, assistance

Figure 6.1. Circle of Excellence Poster.

Circle of Excellence Fill-In Form

Directions: Fill in the blanks and update this form after each field trip or performance:

Name:_____ **Year:** _____

Grade: _____ **Years of membership:**_____

Club-sponsored performances where I have told:

Date	Place	Story Told

Stories I can tell well:

Title	Author or Country of Origin

Non-club-sponsored occasions where I have told stories:

Date	Place

My mentor's name: _____

Names of storytellers I have mentored: _____

- -

Adult leader: _____

Attendance: _____

Circle of Excellence level awarded: _____

Figure 6.2. Circle of Excellence fill-in form.

Finding Role Models and Coaches

An extra pair of hands (as well as eyes and ears) is always helpful when working with young storytellers. An adult volunteer or mature older student is invaluable. You will find this especially true as your group grows in membership. Having kids work in pairs or small groups may not be enough to keep everyone involved. Every young person wants his or her story heard and appreciated. Nonetheless, you may find that they are reluctant to listen to each other over and over again. While you work with one group or direct the group as a whole, an extra adult can listen and make suggestions to a group of two or three tellers. Your volunteer does not have to be a storyteller. Using the coaching suggestions given in Chapter 5 and a solid sense of what works, they can nurture and guide your young tellers while you work with the rest of the members strengthening and enriching skills.

Contact local storytelling guilds and leagues to find willing coaches and assistants. If that is not a possibility, consider forming your own adult storytelling group from the parents of your students or retirees living in your community. By meeting with them weekly or even monthly, you can teach them the coaching process. You can also guide them through their own storytelling journey, which will not only make them more aware and appreciative of what your young people are doing, but will enrich their own lives as well.

If you are unable to find an adult willing to devote time to your group, using mature high school students or young adults as coaches may be the answer. Of course, it is helpful if the young person has told stories themselves or at least knows something about storytelling. Choose carefully. You want someone who will be supportive and encouraging to the younger tellers, as well as someone who will take direction from you.

Things to Consider When Looking for Coaches

- Is my group large enough to warrant an extra pair of hands?

- Where can I find a suitable adult or young adult assistant coach?

- Will the person be available on a regular basis or as needed?

- What do I expect the assistant coach to do?

- Does the assistant coach need additional training from me?

- Where will the coaching take place?

- How will we determine which students will work with the assistant coach?

Tip for the Adult Leader: *Shortly after I started working with the Talespinners, in my enthusiasm to spread the word of storytelling, I created the Fitzgerald Parent-Tellers. My first idea was to involve parents in our school district, but I quickly found that most of them worked outside the home or had small children, so I began to look beyond the boundaries of our small district. I invited anyone who seemed remotely interested in storytelling to participate in weekly meetings held in the media center conference room. My purpose was to teach them storytelling techniques so they could go into classrooms throughout the district whenever a teacher requested a storyteller. Storytellers would be scheduled according to the teacher's convenience and tell to one class at a time. I offered*

Parent-Teller volunteers access to books, a copy machine, free coffee, and the opportunity to be a valued volunteer. At meetings I provided workshops. Tellers practiced stories and shared ideas. I arranged their storytelling schedules so all they had to do was show up at the appointed time. In return, Parent-Tellers often received wonderful thank-you notes and pictures from the children.

Over the years I have developed a core group of talented, highly dedicated volunteer storytellers. Most of them are retired, and almost all of them live outside the school district. Two of my Parent-Tellers come every week to coach my Talespinners and help me with the meetings. Every year one of the Talespinners first performances is to the Parent-Tellers. They are the most appreciative audience because they understand what it takes to get up in front of group of strangers to tell a story. —Judy

Dealing with Problem Situations

In our experience, we have found that a caring, supportive, and nurturing environment has kept problems to a minimum. Nonetheless, problems occasionally crop up, and you must to be prepared to take care of them. The best way to approach problems is through prevention. If you anticipate what might go wrong and how to deal with it, you will be in better shape than when you are caught unaware. Refer back to Chapter 2, "Establishing Rules" and "Structuring the Meetings." If meetings seem to be getting out of hand, take the time to reiterate the rules you set when your meetings began, or establish new rules to better fit your current situation.

Disruptive Students: Keeping your students under control is always a concern and consideration. If the group is disorderly and disruptive, it will be difficult to get them to do the tasks you want. If they are difficult to manage at meetings, you cannot be sure how they will act and react when traveling to other places to perform or when you have guests. Always discuss "performance" or company behavior. The students should be reminded that they represent your school, club, church, and the art of storytelling itself.

There will be times when you will want the group to work with partners or in small groups. Don't be surprised at the level of noise in the room or if you sometimes find students off task. This is to be expected. However, when you call the class back to order or someone is in the performance space, everyone must listen, without interruption. If necessary, remind your group of the rules each time you are preparing to have a large group activity in which everyone must listen. This is a club; don't expect the same attention and focus as you would find in a math class. Instead, be flexible but respectful of the process of storytelling and soon you will find there is a special kind of attention that arises. In some ways, this attention is more focused than a math class because of the need for students to be heard.

After reviewing the rules, you may find there is still a student who continues to disrupt, making it difficult or impossible to manage the group effectively. Some kids have a need to be at the center of attention. Sometimes they do this by making comments on everything that happens. Still others may try to put everyone else down so that he or she seems more important. If you don't resolve the problem, what may happen is that you make so many allowances and bend over backward to "work" with the child that other students drop out. On the other hand, if you raise your voice or criticize the group too many times, kids will drop out, and it will cease being fun for them or you.

Use the "lecture" method sparingly, and don't make threats unless you can and will carry them out. Tell the whole group what you expect, using "I" statements. Do not berate students in front of the entire class. Take the problem student aside and state exactly what kind of behavior you expect from him or her. Be specific, for example:

- "I need you to not call out or talk when someone else is speaking,"

- "I expect you to stay in your seat when someone is telling a story to the group."

- "I want you to keep your hands to yourself."

Try giving the student who needs attention a special job to help him or her feel useful and important. Passing out supplies, taking attendance, straightening the storytelling books, even pushing in the chairs and straightening the room when the meeting is over can make youngsters who are anxious to please you feel important.

If you are in a school situation, talk to the student's teacher or guidance counselor. Find out if there are discipline problems at school and what is usually done about them with regard to this student. If necessary, try a behavior contract. Ask how the student will change his or her behavior, what he or she will do to improve, and what the consequences will be if the behavior continues. Develop some rewards if the behavior improves. Think of rewards that are doable and may benefit the group (e.g., choose a story or activity for the meeting, pass out materials, collect permission slips, select new books for the story collection). When the contract is developed, both of you sign it, along with the student's parents. Unfortunately, if all else fails, you may have to ask the student not to participate in the meetings any more.

Behavior Contract

Date: _____

Student's name: _____

    ☐ I will not make negative comments about other members of the group.

    ☐ I will not call out or make comments while someone is telling a story.

    ☐ I will keep my hands to myself.

Consequences:

- First infraction: Warning
- Second infraction: Sit away from the rest of the group
- Third infraction: Contact parents and one meeting suspension
- Fourth infraction: Contact parents and exclusion from field trip or performance
- Fifth infraction: Dropped from membership

Rewards:

- Verbal praise
- Extra coaching session
- Tell story to the group first
- MC storytelling performance
- Choose group activity or exercise

Group leader to initial squares or comment on behavior each week:

Week 1	Week 2	Week 3	Week 4	Week 5
Week 6	Week 7	Week 8	Week 9	Week 10
Week 11	Week 12	Week 13	Week 14	Week 15

Student signature: _____

Group leader signature: _____

Parent signature: _____

Figure 6.3. Sample behavior contract.

Problems with Attendance and Participation

While the club is in its first few weeks and enthusiasm is running high, problems with attendance or participation tend to be nonexistent. But as the year wears on and practicing the same story gets a little tedious, you will find a few of your students missing meetings. Perhaps sports, band, yearbook, student government, or other activities begin to encroach on your students' time and interest. You will also find members who are always ready to participate in field trips and performances but seem to have "good" excuses for missing practice. These problems are bound to crop up, and you will have to decide just how much leeway you are willing to give your tellers.

Before you make any hard-and-fast rules about attendance and participation in storytelling events, you need to look closely at your program as well as the needs of your students. If meetings are getting a little "boring," spruce them up with activities that are lively and fun to do. All of the exercises contained in Chapters 3 and 4 are designed to get all your students involved, participating, and having fun while increasing and improving their skills. If kids are tired of listening to the same stories rehearsed over and over again, try "Exaggeration Station" in Chapter 4, in which tellers are required to tell their stories with greatly exaggerated gestures and facial expressions. Or take a break from rehearsing and practicing and create some group stories just for fun. Activities such as "Bare Bones Fables" and "Five Times Three" (Chapter 4) are fun to do and could develop into tellable tales.

Today's youngsters are provided with many activities and options for spending their free time. Middle school students in particular want to try every sport and every extra curricular activity. You will have to decide if attendance at meetings is mandatory prior to a performance or if you will allow students to miss meetings as long as they are prepared to perform. If students promise to perform but do not show up, you will have to decide if you will let them participate in the next performance or field trip.

We believe that you need to be forgiving and flexible. You want students to *want* to participate, but you also want them to understand that you expect their best efforts. Take students aside and ask them why their attendance is waning. Perhaps their grades are slipping and their parents have restricted their extracurricular activities. Maybe their parents are working and they have to be home to watch younger siblings. Ask your students if they think your speaking to their parents would make a difference. Check ahead of time with the volleyball or track coach to see if your storytellers could be allowed to miss practice before a storytelling performance. Ask other club sponsors if your members could split their time between their meetings and yours.

Whatever your rules, you must make students aware of them as soon as you see attendance slipping and then apply the rules fairly and consistently to all members. Students just may have to make a choice between storytelling and some other activity. Whatever the choice, allow the student to leave gracefully. Let students know you understand that making choices can be difficult, and no matter what they decide, you still like them. Always keep the door open. If circumstances change, let students know that they are welcome to come back.

Things to Consider When Setting Attendance Rules

- Students who choose storytelling over other activities and show up on a regular basis should be given the first option to perform.

- Tellers must know their stories before performing in front of an audience. You owe it to the audience as well as the other tellers.

- Require that stories be rehearsed in front of the group, adult leader, or coach.

- Never allow a student to choose a story and perform it on the spur of the moment.

Special Note: *When asked to talk about dealing with problem students, Judy and I had the same response: What problems? In the many years that we have been coaching kids, we simply don't have a large number of problems because we establish an environment of respect and understanding for one another. I cannot think of a single time when we had such a disruption that it caused a bad meeting. Of course, we have had minor annoyances, such as idle talking and fidgeting, but these are almost always short-term difficulties. The students want to hear the stories; they volunteer to hear and tell. This simple fact will alleviate most problem situations.* —Kevin

Section III

Performing and Beyond

Before you move on to performance, it is a good idea to review the goals you set for yourself and your youth storytellers. Was your goal to increase the reading and understanding of folk literature? Was it to develop a group of young people who could tell stories to younger children in the school? Was your goal to have your class learn a variety of stories to tell one another? Was your purpose to build a sense of community and increase poise and self-expression? Had you wanted to form a club that would use storytelling as a form of community service? Have your goals remained the same or have they changed along the way? Are you satisfied with the way the work is going? After meeting with your group five or six times, you have a good idea if things are going the way you had anticipated.

This is a learning experience for both you and your storytellers. Rework and revise your goals as needed with the understanding that your club members will be adjusting, too. Do not become discouraged when some students drop out, while others are just catching on to the idea of storytelling and want to jump in. If the momentum has begun to taper off, don't worry—you'll find that much of the initial excitement and fervor will be rekindled after that first performance. In this section, we discuss ways to ensure a good first performance. And once you have experienced the heady feeling of success, you'll want to provide more and more storytelling opportunities for your group. Chapter 7 lists some performance venues that work well, and other suggestions can be found in Chapter 9, "Raising Funds While Telling Stories."

Chapter 7

Telling the Tales

Are We Ready?

After weeks of learning, strengthening, coaching, and practicing you may wonder if your group will ever really be ready. Don't worry, they will be! You will find that most of your young storytellers are anxious and ready to test their skills on a "real" audience. If you have that first performance date set well in advance, your students will know what they are working toward. Although some may be reticent and almost all will be nervous, it is time to begin planning that first performance.

During the first few meetings, plan your first performance or field trip so your students will have a goal in mind as they choose stories and get ready to tell. Knowing where they will perform and who the audience will be helps students—and you—decide if a story they want to tell will be appropriate. Choosing a story to tell to a preschool group will be quite different from one they would tell to an upper-elementary group or even to family members. If you hope to do several field trips or storytelling events, make the first excursion an easy one. Pick an audience that will be accepting, appreciative, patient, and nonjudgmental. Young children usually fit these criteria, and so do other storytellers. Make arrangements to visit the neighborhood preschool or invite them to come to your classroom or library. Talk to the kindergarten or first-grade teacher in your local elementary school and send small groups of your tellers to visit their classrooms. Ask the media specialist if a storytelling performance can be held in the school library. Perhaps arrangements can be made with the coordinator of the Latchkey or after-school program to have your tellers perform for their program. Contact the local public librarian and ask whether your club can participate in the public library story hour.

Invite a group of storytellers from the local guild or league to attend one of your meetings. Family members may also attend, but keep the performance low-keyed. Although you want everyone to be impressed, you also want the stories to shine, not the decorations and hoopla. The more informal that first performance is, the more comfortable your tellers will be performing and the more confidence they will gain for the next engagement.

From Our Experience: *Often I have my Talespinners perform during a Parent-Tellers' meeting (see Chapter 6, Finding Role Models and Coaches). As storytellers themselves, the Parent-Tellers appreciate the effort that goes into learning and performing a story. In addition, they give feedback, especially positive feedback, to the young tellers. Hearing what they did well gives my students a sense of pride and an eagerness to do it again. It also points out to the rest of the group what good storytelling looks like. —Judy*

Using a Microphone

Your first performance provides your tellers with a good opportunity to gain experience using a microphone. It will also provide a professional environment for telling and for improving performance. Often students are not familiar with microphone management. If you can find a stage performer or audio-visual technician, ask them to help your kids rehearse. If this is not possible, use the microphone in the school's multipurpose room or auditorium or purchase a portable amplification system that you can take along to performances and field trips. There are many good and relatively inexpensive portable amplification systems. If you cannot borrow a sound system, consider fundraising as a means to purchase one so you can have it available at all times.

A microphone with a stand works the best and usually gives the best sound. Remote microphones that attach to the teller's shirt require a pocket to keep the battery pack. They are somewhat delicate and require time to put on and take off. For a seamless program, assign one student to raise and lower the microphone stand for each storyteller as needed.

Having your tellers rehearse their stories in front of a microphone not only gives them extra practice, but they can experiment with holding the microphone in their hands and with standing in front of it. The microphone should be held at chin level. This will eliminate "popping" sounds caused by words beginning with P, B, T, and D. With the mic stand, have the students remember where they stood during rehearsal to get the best sound. Some may need to stand closer to be heard clearly; others will be heard better if they stand farther away from the mic.

Rely on your storytelling group to help you adjust the sound level. Although the sound may seem right to the teller, it may not be acceptable to the audience. If you get feedback or a loud screeching sound, the mic is either too close to the amplifier or the volume has been turned up too high.

Reminders for Using the Microphone

- Speak in a natural voice.

- Hold the mic at chin level.

- Keep the mic at least the width of your hand away from your mouth.

Field Trip/Performance Checklist

There are so many things to remember the day of the field trip or performance and you do not want to forget anything. There are many people to contact and materials to get ready. The Field Trip Checklist in Figure 7.1 can help you remember all of the details. And remember, the more thorough the arrangements you make ahead of time, the less stress you'll have and the less likely you'll forget something on the day of the event.

Arrive at the appointed performance location at least a half hour to an hour ahead of the show. You want plenty of time to make sure everything is the way you had planned and to take care of any last-minute details or unforeseen problems. The greater the distance you'll be from your own home base, the more extra time you should allow.

Field Trip and Performance Checklist

Initial Preparation

☐ Reserve date of field trip/performance: _____

☐ Check school, district, and office calendar to avoid scheduling conflict

☐ Arrange transportation (school bus, private cars)

☐ Schedule performance space (library, auditorium, multipurpose room):

Field Trip/Performance Information

☐ Place:_____

☐ Contact person: _____

    Address: _____

    Telephone: _____

    E-mail: _____

☐ Map and directions

☐ Entry fees: *Amount required*_____

Publicity

☐ Flyers, invitations

☐ Posters, signs, directions to performance space

☐ Local newspaper

    Contact person: _____

    Telephone: _____

☐ TV or cable station

    Contact person: _____

    Telephone: _____

☐ School newspaper or yearbook

Permission slips
Include:

☐ Place of performance: _____

☐ Date, time: _____

☐ Times to be absent from school: _____

☐ Mode of transportation: _____

☐ What to bring along: lunch, snack, spending money, costume (group T-shirt, vest, hat)

☐ Parent signature

Field Trip and Performance Checklist (continued)

☐ Date _____

☐ Emergency phone _____

☐ List of chaperones _____

☐ Notify teachers of date and time to be absent from school

Responsibilities

☐ Welcoming committee/ushers: _____

☐ Master of ceremony (introduces program, tellers): _____

☐ Keeper of the props:_____

☐ Keeper of the sound system: _____

☐ Videotaping and photographer: _____

☐ Program designer/producer: _____

☐ Refreshment committee: _____

   ☐ Purchase   ☐ Bake

☐ Setup/cleanup committee: _____

Order of performance

☐ Welcome or opening: _____

☐ Sequence of tellers: _____

☐ Stories to be told: _____

☐ Group stories and/or chants: _____

☐ Closing: _____

Emergency Kit
Don't forget to bring

☐ Bandages, sewing kit, hand wipes, hair spray, safety pins

☐ Clipboard   ☐ paperwork   ☐ props   ☐ extension cord   ☐ duct tape

☐ 35mm or digital camera   ☐ video camera   ☐ sound system

☐ extra film, batteries   ☐ videotape   ☐ cell phone

Figure 7.1. Field trip and performance checklist.

Initial preparation: Arrange for the date, time, and place of your field trip or performance. Check the school, library, district, or any other calendar that might list a conflicting event. Don't schedule your event a day or two before or after a holiday. Families might extend their vacations. You will need time after a vacation for an extra rehearsal or for last-minute publicity. In schools you want to make sure your dates do not conflict with other field trips, school assemblies, scheduled standardized tests, rehearsals for band or music concerts, or sporting events. If there is a school concert or family night that week, consider whether families would attend two events in one week. Find out if something is occurring in another school in your area that might compete for your audience.

When your performance is in another location, arrange for transportation. Fill out proper forms to order a school bus or arrange for carpools. Find out the school or organization policy for transporting students in private cars.

If you are using a room other than your own for the performance, check with the person in charge to secure the date. Make arrangements, in writing, with the custodial staff to arrange chairs, to put up refreshment tables, and to set up the sound equipment.

Two to three weeks before the performance date, verify your arrangements. Is the contact person expecting you on the scheduled day? Has the bus been secured? Has a member of the custodial staff been assigned for that time?

Field trip/performance information: Keep a notebook or folder with the name, address, telephone, and email of your contact person. Include directions and maps. Keep the signed permission slips in the same place as well as the names of the students performing, order of performance, title of the stories they are telling, and list of responsibilities.

Publicity: Arrange for publicity at least a month before the event. Assign one of your students the task of making posters and flyers to advertise the event. Perhaps the art teacher can find a student who is especially talented at designing posters. Get permission to distribute flyers and hang posters throughout the school. Having your students write invitations adds a special personal touch. Even if you don't expect certain people to attend, invite them anyway. Don't forget to invite the principal, superintendent, school board members, and parents. It lets them know about your group and what you are doing.

Prepare a press release for the local newspaper and television news station; describe your group and how you have been preparing. Invite reporters to attend a meeting as well as the final performance. Small local papers are especially interested in writing about positive events involving youth. Don't forget to notify the school newspaper or yearbook, and invite them to send along a reporter or photographer.

Permission slips: Send notices home to parents (Figure 7.2) two weeks before the field trip or performance. Include date, location, time, and mode of transportation. Invite mom and dad along. An extra pair of hands is always helpful. Let them know if they need to send items such as a lunch or snack, spending money, and attire for the day. Be sure to ask for a phone number where parents can be reached during the performance in case of emergency. It is also helpful if you give a deadline for the return of permission slips. Make it several days before the field trip so you won't have to make last-minute calls to parents.

Use your permission slips request chaperones or parent help, or, better yet, call parents directly and ask for their assistance. Ask your parents to take care of the refreshments or to help monitor your storytellers while you are doing something else.

Don't forget to notify teachers of the date and time your storytellers will miss class. In some schools, you will need to have the teacher's signature as well as the parent's. Be sure students will be allowed to make up work they have missed. You can win points with teachers if you insist that your tellers have their assignments turned in before they are allowed to participate in a field trip or performance. Remind your tellers several weeks ahead of time and follow through if they haven't fulfilled their obligations.

Sample Performance Permission Form

March 7, 2002

Dear Parents of Talespinners,

On Tuesday, March 20, 2002, the Talespinners will be going to Neigebaur Early Childhood Center to perform for Mrs. Mayer's, Ms. Stager's, and Ms. Baker's preschoolers. Because there is no school bus available for us that day, we will be walking to Neigebaur. We will leave Chatterton at 9:00 A.M. and return around 2:15 P.M. We will tell our stories to the preschoolers and give each one a book to take home as a "Gift of Reading."

Talespinners will need to pack a bag lunch, including a drink (no glass bottles). Please remind your student to wear black slacks or skirt and a white shirt or blouse for the field trip.

In addition, the Talespinners have been asked to perform for the After-School Program at Westview and Schofield on Friday, April 6. The field trip will take place from 3:00 to 6:00 P.M. Our performance at Westview will take place from 3:30 to 4:30 and at Schofield from 4:40 to 5:45. A school bus will take us from Chatterton to Westview and Schofield and back to Chatterton.

As always, parents are invited to join us on any of our field trips. We would love to have you. Please sign below to give your Talespinner permission to attend either or both field trips.

Have students return the form to Mrs. Sima by Friday, March 16, 2002.

If you have any questions, please feel free to call me.

Judy Sima

Chatterton Talespinners Advisor

– –

My Talespinner _____ has my permission to attend the following field trips.

☐ My Talespinner may walk to Neigebaur Early Childhood Center on Tuesday, March 20, 2002.

☐ My Talespinner will participate in the Friday, April 6, 2002, After-School Program.

☐ On Friday April 6, my son or daughter has my permission to walk home at 6:00 P.M.

☐ I will pick up my son or daughter after the field trip on Friday April 6 at 6:00 P.M.

☐ I plan to attend the following field trip(s):   ☐ March 20   ☐ April 6

Parent Name _____

Parent Signature _____

Date _____

Daytime phone number _____

Figure 7.2. Sample performance permission form.

Responsibilities: It is always a good idea to keep a visual record of your performances. Keep a photo album to remind your kids what a great time they had. Traditional and digital photos are also helpful when you are looking to gain support for your program. Assign someone ahead of time to take pictures or run the video camera during the performance. Who is going to keep track of the props and sound system and ensure that everything arrives on time and in good working order?

Having program notes to introduce your tellers and their stories makes the performance more professional. Find someone in your group who is a good artist or who is willing to create the program on the computer. Design the program ahead of time but wait until the last minute to duplicate it in case there are changes to the line-up of tellers and the stories they are telling.

Order of performance: To avoid confusion, determine ahead of time the order in which the stories will be told. Make sure all tellers know who precedes them. Some kids will always want to be first and get it over with; others will want to be last. Use a stopwatch to time the stories during the last rehearsal. If you know the program will run longer than the allotted time or than the audience's attention span, divide your tellers, having some wait until the next event. It may also be possible to stagger the performance times or separate the audience into two rooms so half of your storytellers can tell to one group and the other half to the second group. Place your stronger tellers at the beginning and at the end of the program to keep audience interest high until the end.

Unless your audience members are experienced listeners, it is best to keep the program under an hour. If you have a large number of storytellers, plan a break or intermission in the middle so that people can stretch, use the restroom, or get something to drink. The program itself should be no more that an hour or an hour and a half. It is difficult for even the most eager audience to stay focused through a long performance, especially if this is your first time performing.

Decide ahead of time who is going to welcome the audience and introduce the storytellers. Assign group chant or group story parts ahead of time so the transition from group to individual teller and back to group can be as seamless as possible.

Emergency kit and last-minute reminders: Have a box or bag on hand with emergency and extra supplies such as bandages, a sewing kit, hairspray, hand wipes, safety pins, tape, extra batteries for the camera, film, videotape, and an extension cord. Have the props and cameras checked and ready to go the day before the performance. If possible, bring along a cell phone for emergencies, but make sure it is turned off during the performance. Keep your folder or clipboard with your field trip checklist, important information, and the order of the stories close at hand.

Rules of the Road

Students need to understand that their behavior reflects not only on the storytelling group but also on their sponsoring organization—whether it is a school, church, scouting organization, or library—as well as on the art of storytelling. This is especially true if you are taking your group to another school or to a library, senior residence, bookstore, or festival. Let your storytellers know their responsibilities and your expectations ahead of time. Stressing appropriate behavior and decorum sets the mood for a professional environment and can enhance the storytelling experience. Good behavior also includes being helpful and supportive of one another. There is no place for teasing or joking around in a storytelling performance. If the stories go well and tellers are proud of their behavior, it only serves to enhance their good feelings.

Things to Consider When Setting Rules for Field Trips

- Stay together as a group; no wandering off without permission.
- Ask permission to leave the performance to go to the restroom.
- Give your undivided attention to the storyteller.

- No loud talking, running, or goofing off.
- Respect others' privacy and property.
- Be on time.
- Listen to the coach at all times.
- Be flexible.
- Be helpful.
- Be polite.

Silent Signals

Young storytellers will often speed up or lower their voices as they tell their stories especially when they are nervous. The leader can provide simple hand signals to remind tellers to alter their presentation without stopping the performance (Figure 7.3). Determine ahead of time what signals you will use. Instruct your group to glance your way as they are telling to see if they need to make an adjustment. The adult coach should be the only one making the signals, otherwise the teller might become confused or flustered. Practice the signals ahead of time so your tellers will become familiar with them and become accustom to looking in your direction for guidance.

Silent Hand Signals

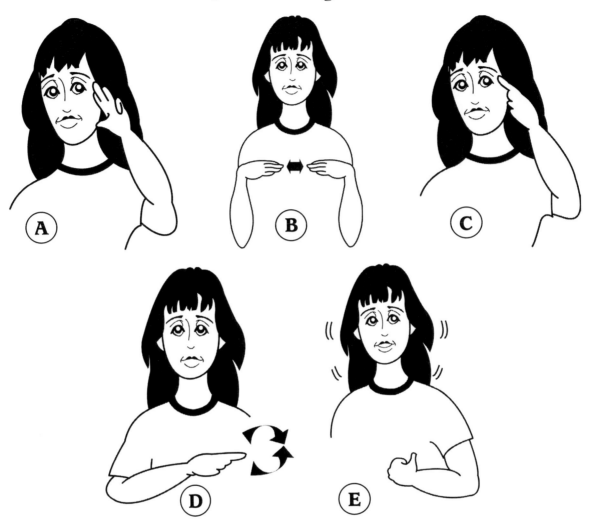

Suggested hand signals

A. Not loud enough: place your hand behind your ear, indicating that you cannot hear.

B. Talking too fast: put the fingers of both hands together and slowly pull them apart as if you were stretching a rubber band.

C. Not enough eye contact: touch the corners of your eyes, indicating they should take a look at the audience.

D. Talking too slow: make small circles with the index finger of one hand to indicate the need for increased speed.

E. Doing a great job: smile, nod your head, or give them a thumbs up to give encouragement.

Figure 7.3. Silent hand signals.

Then Let's Get Set

Dressing the Part

Whenever your group goes out to perform, you want to make a good impression. Dressing alike or wearing T-shirts, vests, or even hats with the club's logo builds a sense of unity and pride. Designing a group logo will give your group an extra sense of belonging, plus it gives your group a recognizable identity.

If you don't have a club uniform, be sure to discuss appropriate dress. You may even want to hand out "dress code" or uniform standards. Dressing up not only makes everyone feel better but also gives an air of professionalism to your performances. Skirts, dresses, or slack outfits for the girls and dress shirts and slacks for the boys make a good impression. Clothing should be modest and subdued. Bright, wild clothing or eye-catching T-shirts tend to draw the audience's attention away from the story. Discuss appropriate footwear as well. If your performance attire is black pants or skirts and white shirts, you don't want anyone wearing vibrant color tennis shoes!

Suggested Nonuniform Types of Attire

- Khaki pants or skirts and denim button-down shirts, brown shoes

- Black pants or skirts and white shirts or blouses, black shoes

- Black or navy pants or skirts and school T-shirt or sweatshirt

- Navy pants or skirts and pastel dress shirts, blouses, or polo-type shirts with collars

- Dress pants, shirt and tie for boys; dress or skirts and blouses for girls

---

From Our Experience: *The Voices of Illusion use black derby hats for their performances. The school's Life Skills classes designed and sewed black and teal corduroy vests with "Chatterton Talespinners" embroidered on the front for their performances. In Mendon, Michigan, members of a group that calls itself the Coat Tales wear blazers with extra-wide lapels sewn on them.*

Choosing Stories

If you know where your group is going to perform before the members begin choosing stories to learn, you can point them in the right direction. With your more experienced tellers, help them to choose which stories would work best with each audience. Folktales are appropriate for any audience. Short, lively stories using audience participation, music, and props work well for preschool and early-elementary audiences. Middle and high school as well as adult audiences enjoy stories with more complicated plots. Kids love ghost stories, but they are not appropriate for some schools. If there are scary tales or stories of witches, devils, or the supernatural in your group's repertoire, it is wise to check ahead of time whether there would be any objections from the hosting school or the audience.

Group Chant

Teaching a group story, chant, or song is another way to liven up meetings and get everyone to participate. This goes a long way in creating community. A group chant helps make your group unique and fosters a sense of identity. A signature song to open a performance or a finale piece that involves everyone not only binds your students together, but connects them to future and past groups. Have students create one for the group or use a published story.

The Judge (Farrar, Straus, & Giroux, 1979) by Harve Zemach makes a wonderful group story with parts for the judge, bailiff, five prisoners, and the "horrible thing," with everyone chanting the refrain. The Talespinners' favorites are a string figure story "The Mosquito," which comes from Anne Pellowski's *The Story Vine* (Macmillan, 1984), and "The Jazzy Three Bears" chant included in this chapter (Figure 7.4). The Folktellers have a version on their cassette tape, *Stories for the Road* (Mythic Stream Productions, 1992). See also "Little Rap Riding Hood" from Naomi Baltuck's *Crazy Gibberish* (Linnet Books, 1993.)

Jazzy Three Bears

Once upon a time in a wee little cottage there were Three Bears.

(I said, "Three Bears.")

One was the Papa Bear, and one was the Mama Bear, and one was the Wee Bear.

(I said, "Wee Bear.")

One day they went walking in the deep woods a-talking

When along, along, along came a little girl with blonde hair.

(I said, "Blonde hair.")

Her name was Goldilocks, upon the door she did knock

But no one was there,

(I said, "No one was there.")

So she walked right in and had herself a ball.

No, she didn't care. No, she didn't care.

Home, home, home came the Three Bears …

"Someone's been eatin' my porridge," said the Papa Bear

"Someone's been eatin' my porridge," said the Mama Bear.

"Hey baa baa wee baa baa," said the little Wee Bear,

"Someone has broken my chair!" CRASH (*clap*)

Just then Goldilocks woke up and broke up the story and beat it out of there.

"Bye, bye, bye – bye," said the Papa Bear.

"Bye, bye, bye – bye," said the Mama Bear.

"Hey baa baa wee baa baa," said the little Wee Bear.

And so ends the story of the Three Little Bears…

Na na-na-na na-na na-na-na na…… CHA!

(*Wave right hand to the audience. Bow with left hand extended.*)

Figure 7.4. Jazzy Three Bears—Chant (origin unknown).

From Our Experience: *Every year at our annual Fitzgerald Family Storytelling Festival, graduated Talespinners, current members, and all their younger siblings end the program with* "The Jazzy Three Bears." *It's something they never forget and binds them forever to their middle school experience. One of the Talespinners' signature stories is* "The Mosquito" *from Anne Pellowski's* The Story Vine *(Macmillan, 1984.) We not only tell it at every performance, but also teach it to other youth groups we meet along the way. See listings in the bibliography. —Judy*

Puppets, Props, and Instruments

Youth storytellers love to use puppets, props, and instruments in their stories. A strategic or well-placed prop can also enhance the meaning or presentation of a story. In some cases, a prop may give an extra shy student something to hang on to.

Props are especially useful and effective when telling to preschool audiences. Puppets fascinate young children. A storyteller ensures participation when a preschooler is given a prop to hold. Drums, percussion instruments, and other musical instruments can enhance a story by providing musical accompaniment, sound effects, or background music. A rattle or maracas could be used to signify the rattlesnake's rattle or the rattling of the skeleton's bones.

A nonspecific prop may also be useful in telling a story. A scarf or bandana can become a hat, tablecloth, billowing cloud, or a wall to hide behind. A stick can become a cane, violin, conductor's baton, or shovel. Give your group practice using yarn, stick, scarves and other items as props in their stories.

A Word of Caution about Props

The story should be the focus of the performance. If your storytellers want to use props, be sure that they do not get in the way of the story and that the story is able to stand on its own. Anything that detracts from the story takes away its special meaning and value. Once you allow kids to use props, the prop often becomes the central motivation for choosing a story rather than the love of the story itself. Always have your tellers practice their stories without props in case they forget these items on the day of the performance.

Several companies that carry unique props, instruments, and puppets are listed in the bibliography at the end of the book. Some of our favorites are the Upper Sarahsville Clog Dancers made by Bill Saling in Caldwell, Ohio (see listing in the bibliography). These are artistic renditions of Appalachian limberjacks—wooden puppets with hinged arms and legs that dance on a paddle.

Stories That Work Well with Props (see Storytelling Resources for brief description of each book)

- *Caps for Sale* (Harper, 1968) by Esphyr Slobodkina. A checkered cap to throw on the ground represents the monkeys throwing the peddler's gray, brown, blue, and red caps.

- *Very Hungry Caterpillar* (Collins, 1972) by Eric Carle. A caterpillar puppet and food made out of construction paper to show how much he eats before turning into a butterfly.

- *The Gingerbread Man* (Holiday House, 1993) by Eric Kimmel. A plain wooden limberjack dancing on a paddle while the audience joins in to say, "Run, Run, as fast as you can. You can't catch me, I'm the Gingerbread man."

- *Abiyoyo* (Macmillan, 1986) by Pete Seeger. An out-of-tune ukulele to accompany the little boy as he tricks the monster into dancing to exhaustion.

- "Wide-Mouth Frog" from *Stories to Play With* (August House, 1999) by Hiroko Fujita. Directions are given for making a handmade frog puppet or use a store bought puppet.

- "The Rain-Hat" from *Stories to Play With* (August House, 1999) by Hiroko Fujita. A piece of newspaper is used to take a little girl through her rainy day.

- *Millions of Cats* (Penguin Putnam, 1956) by Wanda Gag. Handmade cat finger puppets on each finger are used to show the hundreds, thousands, millions of cats.

Tip for the Adult Leader: *The Story Stagers of White Bluff Elementary School in Savannah, Georgia, use hats, masks, ears, tails, and simple costumes to perform group stories such as* Hattie and the Fox *(Bradbury, 1987) by Mem Fox or* The Judge *(Farrar, Straus & Giroux, 1979) by Harve Zemach. The costumes and props can be interchanged depending on which child is doing the telling.*

Warm-Up Exercises

Be sure to arrive at your storytelling performance space a half-hour to an hour ahead of time. You want to make sure everything is set the way you had planned and that your storytellers are ready to greet the audience in a calm, confident manner. Your students will experience excitement, anxiety, and nervousness, especially if this is their first performance. Alleviate pre-performance jitters and channel excess energy by spending ten to fifteen minutes warming up and creating a ready attitude. These exercises may be set to music to keep the practice fun and relaxed. Have your tellers stand or walk in a circle as they perform the exercises that follow.

Physical Exercises

- Body rag doll: With feet placed apart, stand up straight. Then collapse like a rag doll with your arms relaxed and your head dangling to the ground. Relax. Then slowly rise to a standing position. Repeat several times until the body is relaxed.

- Numbers and letters: Using the entire body, bend, stretch, and twist to make letters of the alphabet and numbers from 0 to 9.

- Deep breathing: Sit or stand with body relaxed. Breathe in slowly from the nose until the chest is fully expanded. Hold breath for a few seconds, then release slowly through the mouth. Repeat several times until body feels relaxed.

Vocal Warm-Ups

- Vowel stretch: Using exaggerated facial expressions, repeat the vowel sounds slowly several times. Now say "ahhh-ooooo" and "booo-hooo."

- Tongue stretch: Roll up tongue and touch the soft palate at the back of the throat. Then, push your right cheek as far as you can with your tongue. Repeat with the left cheek. Repeat until tongue feels relaxed.

- Tongue twisters: Repeat the following tongue twisters several times. Use exaggerated tongue, lip, and jaw movements.

  1. Two teamsters tried to steal twenty-two keys.

  2. The thirty-three thieves that they thrilled to the throne throughout.

  3. Would Wheeler woo Wanda if Woody snoozed woozily?

  4. Much whirling water makes the mill wheel work well.

  5. Odd birds always gobble green almonds in the autumn.

  6. Can you can a can as a canner can can a can?

  7. She makes a proper cup of coffee in a copper coffee pot.

  8. Around the ragged rock the ragged rascal ran.

  9. Send toast to ten tense stout saints' ten tall tents.

  10. A big black bug bit a big black bear.

  11. Six slim sleek samplings.

- Count down: Count from one to ten or ten to one in the following ways:

  1. Count pennies on a table.

  2. Counting out a man in a boxing ring.

  3. Counting like you won the lottery.

  4. Counting people in a crowded room.

  5. Counting like the Count on Sesame Street.

  6. Counting like the space shuttle lifting off.

Master of Ceremonies (or Maestro)

Being a good master of ceremonies, or MC, is a valuable skill all its own. MCs move the program along and set the tone for the entire concert. The MC has to be poised and must be able speak extemporaneously. Often it is the adult leader who introduces the youth storytellers, but you can provide students with valuable experience by choosing one of them.

The MC or maestro welcomes the audience and introduces the tellers. He or she can begin the program with the group's ritual opening and tell a little of the group's history. The maestro usually introduces the storyteller and the name of the story, but he or she may also relate information about the teller such as school, grade, years of experience, and something personal about the teller. With a younger group, choose two members to share the job. This relieves some of the stress and provides variety.

Case in Point: *As the MC, Cheryl let the audience know that Barbara first heard her story from her grandmother, that Jacob and Ryan were brothers who put aside their sibling rivalry to work on their tandem story, that Nicole had just won a role in a community theater play, and that Chris was the club comedian and had to work especially hard to tell his story without making people laugh.* —Judy

And Off We Go!

Public Performances

Most of the places for your group or troupe to perform suggested here are nonpublic performances (e.g., your own or other schools, senior residences, day-care centers) and can be considered to be an extension of classroom lessons. Once your group begins performing in public venues (e.g., bookstores, festivals, paid performances), however, students will need to get permission from the copyright holder to tell their stories. If the story they are planning to tell comes from a book or published work, or if the story comes from a professional storyteller's video or audiotape, students need to write for permission to tell the tale. Chances are that no one will sue your storytelling group for copyright violations, but students must be made aware of the rights of the person who created the work that they are performing. The tellers need to be told of their responsibility to respect that right.

In any storytelling performance, student storytellers must credit the author of the story they are telling. When performing a folktale, legend, or myth, tellers should also acknowledge the country or culture of origin. Having students research a story's origin or background of a culture, adds an extra dimension to the story they are telling and can be used as an introduction to the tale. It demonstrates the storyteller's respect and appreciation of the work he or she is about to perform.

In the classroom, students are taught the dangers of plagiarism, especially in this day and age of the computer, when it is so easy to copy, paste, and use someone else's work. In storytelling, we hope to teach students a higher level of respect. We emphasize respect for the story, the storyteller, and one another. Therefore, it is the responsibility of the adult leader to teach their students respect for an author's book or tape. In a public performance and especially in a paid performance, giving credit to the author is not enough. Storytellers must write for permission. Most authors are more than happy to have their work performed and gladly give permission. Many storytellers, however, are protective of their work and may suggest that your students create their own version from several folktale collections. Some authors do not own the copyright to their book and will refer you to their publisher. Students should write to the publisher for permission. If the book is in print, the publisher usually processes the permission or forwards it to the author. Students must be prepared for an answer of "no." Occasionally, publishers ask for a fee for the privilege of telling one of their copyrighted stories.

If you know ahead of time that your group will be using storytelling to raise funds for the group, school, or a charitable cause, have members write for permission as soon as they select a published story to tell. Perhaps your group started out telling in your school, church, or scout meetings, but after a while you begin receiving calls from schools, bookstores, public libraries, and other venues requesting a performance by your tellers noting that they are willing to pay. Begin immediately to write for permission. It may take weeks and even months to receive a response from the author or copyright holder. Do not write, "If I do not hear back from you, I will assume it's OK." Not receiving a response cannot be considered permission. If your group plans to produce a video or audiotape for sale, it is absolutely essential that you get permission from the copyright holder.

From Our Experience: *When asking for permission, the responses will vary. A friend of mine wrote to a book company in Africa that said the book was out of print, but the only way to keep the story alive is to tell it—the company's response actually stated the need to tell it. Some authors will simply say no, but it never hurts to ask. Be prepared to tell another story. More often than not, the Voices of Illusion members and I have found that tellers and authors are more than willing to allow you to tell their story. They often encourage young people, even providing tips for telling.* —Kevin

---

There are a number of resources that list authors and publishers' addresses (e.g., *Biography Today*, published annually by Omnigraphics; *Books in Print,* published annually by H.W. Wilson). Most publishers and many authors have Web sites where you can get their address. Storytellers usually have their contact information printed on the J-card, the paper insert that covers the audiotape or compact disk. Many storytellers are listed on the National Storytelling Network Web site (www.storynet.org). We have included a "Sample Request for Permission" in this chapter (Figure 7.5). When writing for permission, include the following:

- Student's name

- Name of your group

- Sponsoring organization

- Places the story will be told

- Estimated number of times the story will be told

- Include a form the author or copyright holder can sign giving permission

- Include a self-addressed stamped envelope

- Optional: include newspaper clipping, brochure, or other information about your group

One way to avoid asking permission is to encourage students to create their own version of folktales. Folktales, legends, myths, and some stories written before the twentieth century are considered "public domain" and therefore do not require permission to tell or perform. Direct tellers to consult several sources containing the folktale and develop their own unique version of it.

Sample Letter—Request for Permission to Tell

Date:

Return address:

Author/Copyright holder/Storyteller's name: _____

Address: _____

City: _____ State: _____ Zip Code: _____

Dear Mr./Mrs./Ms. _____ :

I am a member of the [*Name of storytelling club*]. We are a student storytelling club from [*Sponsoring organization*] in [*City, State*]. We read many stories and books to choose those we tell in our storytelling performances. Most often, we tell our stories to younger children in our school district or other schools. People who have heard us have begun to ask us to perform at local book stores and storytelling festivals.

When I read your story [*Title of the story /book*], I loved it right away and knew I wanted to tell it. My club leader, [*Adult leader's name*], said it would be a perfect story for me.

I would like permission to tell your story. When we tell stories for others, we usually receive $50 to $100 for the performance. My story is one of eight to ten stories performed by our group. I always credit you as the author of the story and, in the future, I will acknowledge that I have your permission to tell the story.

I have enclosed a permission form and stamped self-addressed envelope for your response. I look forward to hearing from you,

Yours truly,

- -

COPYRIGHT HOLDER'S PERMISSION FORM

As the copyright holder of [*Title of the book or story*], I hereby give my permission to [*Student's name*] of the [*Storytelling Club*] to tell my story in paid, public performances. I understand that the storyteller will credit me as the author/copyright holder of the book before or after the telling of the story. In addition, I ask that the storyteller meet the following stipulations and/or conditions:

_____

_____

Author/copyright holder's signature: _____

Please print name: _____ Date: _____

Figure 7.5. Request for permission to tell (sample letter).

For a more detailed discussion of copyright and the rights and responsibility of performers, refer to The Storyteller's Guide (August House, 1996) by Bill Mooney and David Holt; Susan Klein's article "Ethics, Apprenticeship, Courtesy, and Copyright," in *Storytelling World Magazine* (Winter/Spring 1999, pp. 4–24); William Wilder's article "Public Domain and Copyright: Information for Storytellers," *Storytelling World Magazine* (November/December 2000, pp. 4–6).

Places to Tell

There are a multitude of places that make for good storytelling venues to display your group's talents and skills. If you think of youth storytelling as a special talent or gift, remember that it is only valuable when it is shared with others. Encourage your students to think of storytelling as a way they can give back to the community. In planning field trips and events, consider who will benefit from your students' performance and how the experience will enrich your tellers.

Suggestions for Places in Your Community Where You Might Perform

- Local elementary schools
- Preschools and day-care centers
- Latchkey or school-age child-care programs
- Senior citizen residences, senior centers, nursing homes
- Family reading nights
- "Turn off the TV" celebrations
- "Festival of the Arts" nights
- Talent shows
- Book stores, public library story hours
- Children's hospitals, youth homes, scouting troops
- Shelters for battered women or homeless families
- Civic and church holiday celebrations
- Local storytelling festivals and meetings

A Word of Caution

Outdoor carnivals and fairs are not good places to celebrate your art. Storytelling needs a quiet place with an attentive audience. At outdoor picnics, carnivals, and the like, families are in a constant flux of activity. This can be difficult even for the most experienced storyteller and certainly for a youth teller. If you are asked to be part of the school fundraising fair then insist on a quiet location or room set apart from the band, magicians, face painters, and clowns. Have set times when storytelling is to take place. Limit the length of the program to twenty minutes or a half-hour with a break between each session. Station someone at the door so that no one enters or leaves while a story is being told.

From Our Experience: *When I created the Talespinners, one of my first goals was to increase my students' self-confidence and self-esteem, but I also had two other goals in mind. First, I wanted to use storytelling as a vehicle for community service. Next, I wanted to use storytelling to teach lessons of tolerance and acceptance by bringing them in contact with people different from themselves. So I began to look for places they could perform that would meet these goals.*

Over the years Talespinners have visited day-care and Head Start programs, nursing homes, and elementary schools in the inner city to tell their stories. We have performed at national and local storytelling festivals that have taken place in Detroit and at meetings of reading teachers and media specialists. Our favorite audience is the Change of Pace Stroke Club, *which pays a visit to our school once a year just to hear our stories. The members of this club are all seniors who have suffered a stroke and meet weekly through the local parks and recreation. Many of the seniors have been coming for years.* —Judy

Gift of Reading

Make arrangements to tell stories at a local preschool or Head Start program in your area around the holiday season. Collect or purchase new or gently used picture books and have your storytellers tell stories based on the books they've collected. After telling the stories, give the picture books to the young children in your audience. Allow time for your students to be paired with a preschooler so they can read each child's gift book to them. Your students can raise money to purchase the books or collect them from friends and family. Don't forget the camera. This field trip makes for wonderful photos.

From Our Experience: *During the holiday season each winter, the* Detroit Free Press *sponsors a community-wide program called the "Gift of Reading" in which residents are asked to donate new picture books. Collection points are set up in public libraries and bookstores throughout the metropolitan area. The books are then distributed to young children in Head Start, preschool, and day-care centers in disadvantaged areas of the city and suburbs. One of the Talespinners' annual outings is to the Head Start in our school district. We collect inexpensive, paperback picture books, wrap them in the Sunday comics section of the newspaper, and give the books to the preschoolers after our storytelling performance. Then the Talespinners sit on the floor with their adoring young audience members and read their gift books to them. We also have milk and cookies, and if there is time, we play with the puppets, blocks, sandbox, dress-up clothes, and play kitchen. It is difficult to tell who has more fun—the Talespinners or the preschoolers watching the Talespinners play!* —Judy

Youth Storytelling Exchange

Find another youth storytelling group in your area and bring the two groups together for a morning or day of stories and shared activities. This valuable and enriching experience is especially beneficial when the groups come from different ethnic and racial backgrounds. It encourages tolerance and gives youngsters an opportunity to meet in a noncompetitive atmosphere. Plan activities that foster interaction and encourage the students to get to know each other. Form teams or pairs from each group. A number of activities described in Chapters 3 and 4 engage the students, teach storytelling, and encourage sharing.

Before the visit, have the students develop a list of questions that they would like to ask about each other. Create an information sheet that can be filled out by members of both groups, along with a place to write their address or e-mail address. Paste a recent photo or school picture on the form as well. The information sheets can be exchanged with their partner from the other group to encourage continued contact. Use the Storytelling Pen Pal form (Figure 7.6) or create one of your own.

Sample Questions

- What is your favorite color?

- Where were you born?

- How old are you?

- What are your favorite music groups?

Youngsters usually find it difficult to interact and talk to new people. Storytelling games can break the ice and bring strangers together. Plan one or more introductory activities to encourage the two groups to interact. "Hello Bingo" and "Storytelling Scavenger Hunt" (Chapter 3) are effective group mixers. Have the kids team up with a partner from the other group by matching similar birthdays, favorite TV shows or musical groups, same family birth orders, or playing the same sports or musical instruments. Once partners have been established, a number of entertaining activities can be done in small or large groups. Many of these activities are described in Chapter 3. The "Me" Story Bag is always a favorite. Have partners interview one another using the "I am, I can, I like, I hope" or "Meet My Friend" activities, then introduce their partner to the rest of the group. Other activities that work well are "Toy Stories," "Point of View," and "Bare Bones Fables" (Chapter 4).

Allow time for several members of each group to tell stories. It is also fun to have the groups teach or demonstrate something to each other or teach their favorite group chant or story. If possible, plan a meal together, or at least refreshments. Eating always encourages camaraderie and conversation. Partners can exchange their information sheets over pizza or lemonade and cookies.

If another youth storytelling club is not available, you can still provide your group with this valuable experience. Contact a public or parochial school, Boys and Girls Club, Scout troop, or public library in another part of the city. Encourage the teacher, media specialist, youth director, or librarian to gather a group of young people together for the purpose of meeting with your storytellers. The ages of the students are not important. Invite the group to your school, church, or library or visit theirs, whichever is more convenient. In addition to the activities and meal, have your group tell stories and talk about storytelling. Encourage the other group to ask questions about how your students go about finding stories to tell, how they learn and remember their stories, how they overcome the fear of standing up in front of a group of strangers, and what they like best about being a storyteller.

Storytelling Pen Pal

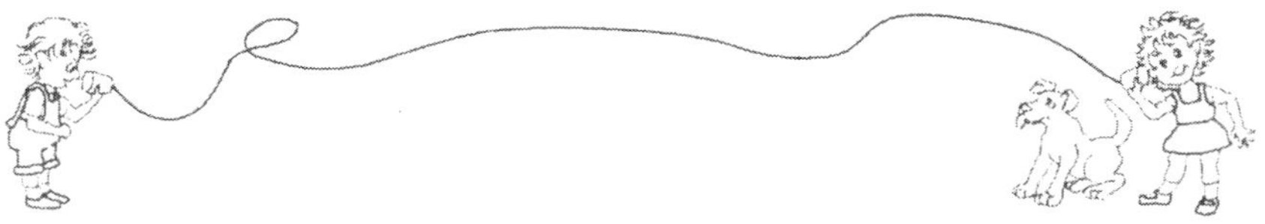

STORY TELLING PEN PAL

NAME ____________________

ADDRESS ____________________

GRADE ____________________

BIRTHDAY ____________________

HOW LONG HAVE YOU BEEN
TELLING STORIES? ____________

FAVORITE STORY ____________

FAVORITE COLOR ____________

FAVORITE TV SHOW ____________

HOBBIES AND
INTERESTS ____________________

____

____

PETS ____________________

I'M REALLY GOOD AT ____________

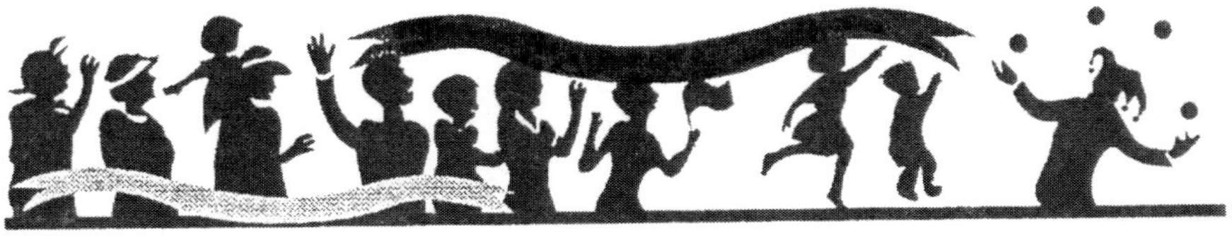

Figure 7.6. Storytelling Pen Pal.

From Our Experience: *In 1992, friend and storyteller, Karen White, and I realized a dream of using storytelling to build understanding and friendship between inner-city and suburban kids. Karen's students were fourth- and fifth-grade African Americans. Their school was located in Detroit near where the 1967 riots took place. My students were mostly white, sixth-, seventh-, and eighth-graders from blue-collar families in a suburb north of Detroit. We met twice, first at my school, then at Karen's. When the two groups met for the first time our objective was to increase the comfort level. We also wanted each club to share something meaningful with the other. Each student had to find a partner from the other group whose birthday was close to his or hers, who liked the same TV show, who had the same family birth order, or who had more than one of these things in common. When the students were matched, they interviewed each other, asking such questions as what is your favorite school subject, what is your favorite color, what do you like to do in your free time? We formed circles and each student introduced his or her partner to the group. Before sharing a pizza lunch, Karen's students taught us about Kwanzaa, and the Talespinners taught the younger students the story of "The Mosquito" from Anne Pellowski's* The Story Vine. *It was a great way to get kids interacting and made for fabulous photographs in the* Detroit Free Press. *Both groups also performed their version of the "Jazzy Three Bears."*

When we met several months later, Karen's students presented a description and demonstration of the Kalimba or African thumb piano. The Talespinners taught Karen's group two sign-language songs. Each group told a few stories, and the local Kentucky Fried Chicken donated box lunches for each of the tellers. Just before we caught the bus for our ride back to Chatterton, the kids exchanged addresses and promised to keep in touch. We met once more the following year before Karen took a job in the district office. Since then, we've met with other inner-city groups and a school in a southern suburb of Detroit where most of the students are Muslim Arabs. Each time, we pair students, tell stories, share activities, and teach or demonstrate something to the other group. Our favorite activity is sharing the contents of our "Me" Story Bags, described in Chapter 3. Our Storytelling Exchanges made the local newspapers and were even featured in NEA Today *(a publication of the National Education Association).* —Judy

Family Storytelling Festival

Plan a festive storytelling event featuring local talent from your school or community. Everyone loves to perform for an appreciative audience, and who could be more appreciative than members of your own family? Hold the festival in the evening so that working parents can attend. Encourage younger siblings or children from the elementary schools to perform as well as older students and even staff members and grandparents. Include your group's favorite chant or story and encourage everyone to participate.

If there is time, include a group activity in which everyone gets involved (e.g., "The Storytelling Scavenger Hunt" or "Hello Bingo" found in Chapter 3). Display the photos you have taken of your field trips during the year. Set up a TV and VCR to display the videos you have taken or create a PowerPoint presentation of your digital photos so folks can enjoy past performances as they come in or during refreshments. Don't forget to invite the local newspaper and yearbook staff, as well as the administration and school board.

From Our Experience: *We've held a festival for ten years. Every year I invite former Talespinners to come back and tell a story. Many of them come back from high school and even after they have graduated. Some tell a new story, others tell one they learned in middle school. Jason and Mary came back to perform their high school drama club mono-logues. Kim recited several poems she had written. Theresa returned several times with a new folktale. Each time brothers Jonathon and Jason returned, they retold* Boo Baby Girl and the Ghost of Mable's Gable *(Brotherstone, 1992) by Jim May, which became longer and longer with each retelling. At the end of the concert, everyone joined in for a rousing chorus of the "Jazzy Three Bears," from alumni to current Talespinners to younger brothers and sisters.* —Judy

---

Tellabration

Consider having your storytellers participate in Tellabration in your area or create one of your own. Tellabration was originated in 1988 by J. G. Pinkerton, who envisioned this event as a means of building community support for storytelling. Sponsored by the National Storytelling Network the third weekend of November each year, its purpose is to create a network of storytelling enthusiasts bonded together in spirit at the same time and on the same weekend throughout the world. From its humble beginnings in six locations across Pinkerton's home state of Connecticut, Tellabration has spread to more than four hundred sites in almost every state and more than fourteen foreign countries. It is still growing.

A new Youth Tellabration program was started in 2001. Originated by the Youth Telling Special Interest Group of the National Storytelling Network, its goals are to

- Introduce children as young as preschool to the art of storytelling

- Enhance understanding of cooperation and community spirit through story

- Bridge the gap between generations by sharing tales with elders

You can register your event and receive ideas for activities and publicity by checking www.storycraft.com/youthtellabration or www.youthstorytelling.com or call 1-800-525-4514. Anyone can produce a Tellabration event. Many groups include youth storytellers. The National Storytelling Network publicizes the events worldwide and offers a *Manual and Guidebook* that can be ordered through its Web site (www.tellabration.org). Find a Tellabration event in your area and ask how to take part. Besides telling stories, your club can provide invaluable assistance to the organizers by selling tickets, setting up chairs, serving refreshments, and assisting with cleanup.

National Storytelling Youth Olympics

For young storytellers and sponsors who are willing to work with them, consider entering your tellers in the National Storytelling Youth Olympics, an event that takes place in spring. Originally it was held on the campus of East Tennessee State University (ETSU); it has now relocated to Hanford High School and California State University in Fresno. Established in 1996 by Dr. Flora Joy, its purpose is to encourage young storytellers to develop and fine-tune their storytelling skills and to encourage every classroom in America to discover, or rediscover, the beauty and value of storytelling and story performance. "Special Youth Storytelling Torch-bearers" are chosen from three or more age groups, not only for their storytelling talents but also for their ambassadorship abilities in the world of storytelling. Details and an application form are at www.youthstorytelling.com. Some of the finalists have performed in the Youthful Voices Tent at the National Storytelling Festival, held annually in Jonesborough, Tennessee, the first weekend in October.

> **From Our Experience:** *I have had the privilege of being the new di-rector of the National Youth Storytelling Olympics. It is amazing to know that thousands of students are involved in the event. What better way to help youth celebrate their excellence in storytelling? I hope everyone can become involved. Be sure to contact us at www.youthstorytelling.com.*
> —Kevin

Home Again

Evaluating the Performance

Once the group completes a performance or returns from a field trip adventure, it is impor-tant to reflect on the experience. During this time, evaluate and examine the strengths and weak-nesses of the performance. Always begin on a positive note by acknowledging the efforts of your storytellers. Keep notes during the performance so you can say exactly what you liked about their individual efforts (e.g., "When you roared and showed your claws, I could really see the lion trying to scare the mouse." "I laughed out loud when you used that squeaky voice of the mouse talking back to the lion."). When giving criticism, it should always be given in the form of a suggestion (e.g., "Next time, why don't you try using your hands to show how big the giant was." "If you take a breath and look around at your audience when changing from one character to another, it might help you to talk more slowly."). Even if the performance was less than per-fect, find something to praise (e.g., "Good job! You did it! I know you were nervous, but it didn't show and you got through the whole story without forgetting anything.").

Reflection gives the troupe time to learn from and build upon each experience. If you make time for comments after each performance, students will anticipate it and will learn that with each show, a discussion follows. This tradition helps establish better communication with your troupe or student tellers.

This is also a good time to remind your tellers that there are no "stars" or "super stars" in storytelling. Some storytellers may have done better because they were less nervous, had prac-ticed more, or simply have had more experience in front of an audience. Maybe the audience laughed more at one story, or perhaps one story was more appropriate for the audience than an-other, but you need to emphasize that your storytelling group is not competitive. Instead, ev-eryone works together for the common good. While the performance is fresh in everyone's mind, encourage some of the stronger, more experienced storytellers to mentor weaker or less experienced tellers. Let the more successful tellers share the techniques that worked well for that audience.

Things to Consider When Evaluating the Storytelling Performance

- What went well?
- What do you think the audience enjoyed most?
- What improvements were seen?
- What areas need more work?
- Were some of the problems due to nervousness, lack of experience, or circumstances beyond your control?
- What did you like about your own storytelling?
- What did you like best about your own performance?
- What improvements could you see in your own performance?
- What changes would you consider making the next time out?

Case in Point: *After each performance, we have what I call "Cordi (my last name) Notes." This is a time when I can say thanks for a job well done or mention how we might strengthen the performance next time. It is also a time when my students can respond to the performance. They often say, "That African story was more for older students" or "The microphones are having trouble, can we get them checked?" or simply, "A little girl came up and hugged me, and it felt good." This is valuable time, time that is meant to help build cohesion for the next show.* —Kevin

Use the first meeting after the field trip or performance to review and record your tellers' accomplishments. In Chapter 6 (Figure 6.2), we introduced the Circle of Excellence, which recognizes and rewards storytellers' efforts and achievements. Each level takes into account attendance at meetings, participation in performances, assisting and mentoring new members, and acquiring a repertoire of stories. Have your students keep track of where they told stories and what stories they told. The form also provides a place to list the name of the person whom they are mentoring.

Thank-You Letters

Writing a thank-you note to your host immediately upon returning from your storytelling field trip is not only a good idea, it also teaches your students the rules of proper etiquette. It may also ensure an invitation for a return visit. Use letterhead with the name or logo of the group. Compose a letter as a group and have all of the students sign it. Make the letter personal by mentioning the name of the place you visited as well as specific occurrences that your group appreciated or enjoyed.

Wrapping Things Up

After all is said and done and you are looking at the end of your time with your youth story-tellers, take time to reflect on the past year. This is a good time to have a party. Order pizza and soda or let the kids bring cookies and chips. Play back the videos you've taken of performances and let the tellers see how well they have done and how much they have improved. Give participation certificates or Circle of Excellence Awards (see Chapter 6) to each student. Allow time to have your storytellers evaluate their experiences (see the evaluation form in Figure 7.7). Ask them to think about what events they enjoyed the most and what they learned. Ask, too, what could be done to make the experience even better next year. Discuss their opinions, but also require students to write down their evaluation so you can refer to them in planning for the next year.

Things for Students to Consider When Evaluating the Storytelling Club

- What did they like best about being a member of the storytelling club?
- What was their fondest memory?
- What suggestions do they have for new storytellers coming up?
- What suggestions do they have to improve the club next year?

Storytelling Club Evaluation

Name: _____ Today's Date: _____

Grade: _____ Years of membership: _____

1. What did you like best about being a member of the storytelling club this year?

2. What was your favorite memory from the meetings, performances, or field trips?

3. What was the most important thing you learned as a storyteller?

4. What skills or knowledge did you learn in storytelling club that you would use in your daily life?

5. What advice would you give to new storytellers?

6. If you were a storyteller last year, how was your experience better or worse this year?

7. What suggestion(s) would you give to the adult leader to make the storytelling club even better next year?

8. How would you rate your overall experience in storytelling club this year?

   1 (not very good)   2 3 4 5 (just ok)   6 7 8 9 10 (Fantastic)

Figure 7.7. Storytelling club evaluation.

Planning for the Future

While the experience is still fresh, the adult leader should also evaluate the year and think about ways to make next year even better. There is always room for improvement. First, think about all the things that went well and pat yourself on the back. Perhaps you were new to storytelling as well as to coaching youth tellers. List the stories you learned to tell, and write a sentence or two about how it was received. If your experience was less than optimal, give yourself credit for trying and honestly evaluate ways to make improvements. Perhaps you had hoped to attract more young tellers, or maybe some members dropped out during the year. Begin planning new ways of recruiting students. Think about which activities went well and which ones you would like to add to the schedule. Look for new places to perform or ways of raising funds so that you can offer club T-shirts or vests next year. Perhaps you were spread too thin and felt you were not able to address the needs of all your tellers. Begin looking for another adult who would be would be willing to help coach tellers in small groups.

Be sure to sit down with the principal of the school, the head of the youth center, the director of the library, or the administrator of the program that sponsored your storytelling group. We hope you invited your administrator to attend some of your performances and that he or she is just as pleased with the kids' accomplishments as you are. Brag about the students' accomplishments, and be frank about what did not go well and what improvements you plan to make next year. Ask for suggestions and let your administrator know ways that he or she can help. If money has been a problem, perhaps your administrator can suggest sources of funding.

In planning for next year it is also wise to secure the day and room ahead of time. Make arrangements with storytellers or guests that you wish to bring into your meetings. Many professional storytellers book performances six months to a year or more in advance. If you have a favorite storyteller, early planning will ensure that you secure the teller you want.

Things for the Adult Leader to Consider When Evaluating the Storytelling Club

- Did you meet your goals and objectives?

- Are there new objectives you wish to add next year?

- Which experiences went better than expected?

- List two or three things you would like to change, improve, or add next year (e.g., limit number of members, add a Family Storytelling Festival, find an adult coach or assistant to help with meetings, increase publicity efforts, hold students more accountable for learning stories on their own, etc.).

- List the activities, field trips, performances that you plan to repeat next year and others that you hope to add.

As the storytelling year ends, you look back with a smile and perhaps a lump in your throat. Your young tellers have accomplished more than you had expected. There are fond memories and thoughts of bigger and better things to come. Keep a notebook handy to jot down ideas. And be sure to put all of those wonderful photos you've taken throughout the year in an album to remind returning members of past glories and get those new ones all revved up.

National Youth Storytelling Pegasus Awards

As you wrap up the year, consider submitting nominations for the National Youth Storytelling Pegasus Awards. Plaques and recognition are given to young storytellers who exemplify distinction in the art of storytelling. Each year a "Coach Extraordinaire" is recognized and honored for his or her work and for making a difference in the lives of young people through storytelling.

More than seventy storytellers and educators take part in the annual review. Winners of the award are broadcast online and featured in national magazines. For nomination forms and a list of past winners, visit www.youthstorytelling.com.

Chapter

Creating a Traveling Troupe

Once young people catch the "storytelling bug," you will find an endless supply of tellers who never can do enough storytelling. These are the members of your group who are content to have their monthly or even weekly calendars filled with opportunities to perform their stories. You may even find that some of them want to seriously study storytelling as an art form or profession.

As people become aware of your storytelling troupe, calls will come in for bookings. You will find there are schools, libraries, and other community organizations such as Optimist and Rotary Clubs calling to ask your group to perform for programs and events. Soon your group will become featured at art festivals, community events, storytelling festivals, and more. The number of requests you are able to fill as well as the distance your group can travel depends largely on your time and resources. Often requesting organizations are willing to provide "traveling funds." For other performances, you will have to raise funds to pay for travel expenses. See Chapter 9 for suggestions for "Raising Funds While Telling Stories."

At this point you may wish to form a special performing troupe in addition to your regular storytelling club. A traveling troupe is a dedicated group of storytellers to which all members can aspire and work toward joining. A troupe differs from storytelling club in that the main function of its members is to take their show on tour. Troupe members are not necessarily the best and most talented tellers but rather those who show the most commitment to storytelling and the storytelling group as a whole. Excellence in telling should only be one criterion. Other aspects to consider are dedication to storytelling, length of membership, willingness to help less experienced tellers, ability to take on some of the responsibilities of running meetings and organizing field trips and performance venues, and a commitment to learning new stories and improving performance.

Troupe members should come from the established storytelling club. It could be regarded as reward for service to storytelling. You will need to establish a separate set of standards and criteria for inclusion. Create a special application for students who are interested in participating in the traveling troupe. Because there should be a greater sense of commitment and higher expectations of these tellers, tryouts, letters of recommendation, an inventory of skills and interests, interview with the adult leader, as well as a pledge to service should be included as part of the selection process.

From Our Experience: *In addition to commitment and attitude toward storytelling and the group, students who wish to be in the Voices of Illusion Troupe must learn and tell four separate stories, complete an interview with me, and successfully answer a riddle in the form of a story. The four types of stories they must tell are an experimental story, a funny story, a serious story, and a tandem story. They are expected to work with other club members and act as ambassador of storytelling. I never use "storytelling excellence" as a prerequisite for troupe membership. I find it more effective to allow group cohesion to help foster dedication, and talent will follow. My philosophy is this: Talent comes with time. Some of my more reluctant tellers have even had the opportunity to tell at the National Storytelling Festival and the National Youth Storytelling Olympics.*
—Kevin

Creating a Troupe Identity

It is important that your regular storytelling club and others begin to see your traveling troupe as a unique performing arts group. Providing your troupe members with wallet sized membership cards is one way to give them a sense of pride and identity. You also need to create a visual identity for your traveling troupe. If you have not already done so, decide on a specific name for your troupe. It can be the same as your storytelling group, or you can create a catchy name that reflects what you are doing. There are many troupes across the country that take on names indicating their town or school (e.g., The Lemoore Tellers or The Seashore Storytellers), while others take on a name that conveys the idea of storytelling (e.g., Off the Page Storytellers, The Freedom Train Storytellers, and Imagine Nation Tellers). Troupe members should vote on the name and discuss why it is an effective name for your troupe. As the adult coach and group leader, the name must be acceptable to you as well.

Once you have decided on a name, consider logo T-shirts, posters, or even uniforms to help spread the word. Students should be noticeably identified as a traveling troupe teller. Performing in a standard shirt and jeans sends the wrong message about your troupe. It tells others that the kids are casual about their work and does not speak to the numerous hours of rehearsal. When they "dress the part," troupe members will begin to act differently about the group.

To help pay for uniforms and publicity, students can raise funds by traditional means such as candy bar or candle sales and walk-a-thons; however, the next chapter offers some effective storytelling fundraisers that have worked for both of us.

Initiation into the Troupe

Once the students have fulfilled the requirements to become part of the troupe, plan an initiation ceremony. This can be done as a formal induction or an informal gathering. Encourage troupe members to help plan the ceremony. Students can sign a "Storytellers Hall of Fame" declaring that they have earned the honor of troupe membership. During this time, a ceremonial ritual can be established for all troupe members. For example, troupe members can light a candle and dedicate themselves to the art of storytelling. It is important that the troupe members see themselves as the ambassadors of the art. If students know they have an honored role, they must take the role seriously.

Scheduling Separate Meetings

In addition to regularly scheduled meetings of the storytelling club, schedule an additional weekly or monthly get-together with your troupe where you can rehearse and discuss upcoming shows. Each meeting should be engineered to help build skills. Your expectations of troupe participants should be higher than those for the general membership. Encourage members to take risks in telling stories and to build their storytelling repertoires. Students should also know that they are seen as "Ambassadors of the Arts." Whenever someone asks about the storytelling group, they are responsible for representing storytelling in a way that encourages involvement.

It is also advisable that the troupe members elect their own officers and establish their own set of rules, with the supervision and veto power of the adult leader. Having a constitution or printed guidelines helps to ensure that meetings go well and that all troupe members understand their responsibilities.

Assigning Leadership Roles

Because troupes often have a busy schedule, assign roles to your troupe members to assist with running meetings and preparing for shows. Depending on the age and maturity of your group, these roles can be assigned by you or elected by the members of the troupe.

Suggested Leadership Roles

- Chairperson or co-chairs to act as the troupe leaders and to run the meetings

- Secretary for taking minutes of the meetings

- Treasurer to assist with the group's finances and its fundraising efforts

- Historian to maintain a scrapbook of newspaper clippings, letters, and other memorabilia

- Videographer or photographer to record events and performances

- Publicity chair to contact newspapers and make flyers and posters

- Performance chair to set up sound equipment and to make sure the show runs smoothly

From Our Experience: *Voices of Illusion actually has a student who serves as "story manager." This is similar to the position of stage manager in drama troupes in which the student helps organize of the performance, for example, by providing water, checking on the space, ensuring the troupe arrives on time, and so on. The story manager takes care of any of the coach or the students' needs before, during, and after each performance. This helps the group function smoothly and become more cohesive.* —Kevin

Provide Storytelling Opportunities

Provide as many opportunities as possible to have your troupe share its stories. To ensure that your troupe is telling and your members are hearing stories, ask the troupe members to rotate times that they share a story.

Your troupe members should be the first to go on field trips to see other storytellers or storytelling events in your area. Find out if there is an adult storytelling guild with meetings in your area that your students could attend; perhaps they could tell their stories at some of the meetings. Some adult guilds may even have youth members. Because the students have chosen to invest their time in storytelling as an art form, they need to see as many events and storytellers as possible. They also need to explore other arts, including dance and drama, where they can build their storytelling style by watching others.

Your entire storytelling club will benefit from an end-of-the-year award ceremony where awards are given and stories are told. This can be formal or informal. Troupe members make excellent tellers at these events. If the troupe members also speak to the year's accomplishments and the goals for next year, you will be "priming the pump" for next year's troupe of tellers.

From Our Experience: *We have both a formal and an informal award ceremony. During the formal part, we actually give out a student storytelling scholarship and formal certificates. During the informal ceremony, we design it like a comedy variety show and poke fun at the foibles of the year. Both of these are events that are well attended, and they give us a chance to say thank you to our group.* —Kevin

Troupe and Leadership

For the adult leader, having members of the traveling troupe assist with meetings and performances is a comfort and help. Troupe members are the leaders of your group. As long as you treat them with this honor, people will vie to be in the troupe. Never let it go to their heads; always remind them of the honor of being in the troupe. We are proud to have such active troupes, and we know that you will enjoy hours and hours of fun with yours. It is definitely an investment in time, but to see the growth of the students is well worth the effort.

From Our Experience: *In Voices of Illusion, my students hear me tell a "troupe only" story, which contains a message or most often a universal riddle that explains the value of working together. Then my students are given an explanation of what it means to be in the troupe, then they share what they think they will do as a troupe member. We have separate troupe meetings that reinforce the principles of their commitment. Often students aspire to be in the troupe because they, too, want to be the first considered for trips or extra storytelling assignments. Having a storytelling troupe is a wonderful recruitment for further years of storytelling. —Kevin*

Having a storytelling troupe is another way to help students connect to stories. It is rewarding to watch community members light up when they see students telling stories. Coordinating a storytelling troupe takes time, but it is time well spent. Just ask the students who are honored to be the tellers.

Chapter  9

Raising Funds While Telling Stories

When starting a storytelling group or troupe, you might naturally wonder, "Where am I going to get the funds to support this group?" We are here to tell you that you can have a very successful storytelling group or troupe with no budget. Many storytelling youth groups have started and continue to function with little or no budget. All that is really required are the following:

- A place to meet

- An adult story coach or guide

- Kids to tell and listen to stories

Unlike football or band, there are no expensive uniforms or instruments to purchase. You don't have to go on a field trip to listen to stories. If you simply provide a safe, encouraging, and inviting place for kids to tell stories, you have all the necessary ingredients for each meeting. With additional funding or support, you can do more, such as organize a student storytelling festival, acquire a storytelling library, or even produce your own youth storytelling tapes, but none of these extras are required for a storytelling group or troupe to be successful.

From Our Experience: *Voices of Illusion began simply because students wanted to hear and tell stories. We ran for about a year with no budget, having the time of our lives. We sat hour after hour listening to each other tell ghost stories. We invited adults or senior citizens to share community stories, and we played game after game to keep motivated. No amount of funding would be able to replace the wonderful laughter, tears, and sharing that were created in our storytelling circle. It cost us nothing, but we gained a great deal from simply listening to each other. We were never bored, but soon word spread and people from the community hired us to perform for them. I am quite certain if we simply stayed at a school meeting place and did not expand to giving fifty-five performances a year, we would still be having fun and enjoying the storytelling environment. I think storytelling is one of the last free joys in this world.* —Kevin

From Our Experience: *Like Kevin, I, too, started my storytelling group without any additional funds. After fifteen years, I find that very little money is needed to run the troupe. I fund the Talespinners' limited expenses through the media center's petty cash account, which is created by selling school supplies. Also, in past years, we have received gift certificates from the local bookstores where we performed. The money is used to purchase picture books and books of story collections, refreshments for our end of the year party and on-site performances, and paperback picture books for our Gift of Reading program (see Chapter 7). Recently, I purchased bolts of corduroy to make vests for our performances, which were sewn by eighth-grade students in our Life Skills program. The local trophy shop embroidered the vests at a very reasonable price.* —Judy

Even though telling stories to obtain funding is not necessarily your goal, it beats selling candy bars door to door or having students run car washes every weekend. These activities can be fun, but the primary purpose of a storytelling group is to learn more about storytelling. And if in the process of telling stories, you secure funding by accepting donations or charging admission for future events or activities, does this not serve a twofold purpose: providing additional learning for your kids and raising funds that will help to sustain the group? By charging a small price or asking for voluntary donations you can ensure the longevity of your group. After performing in your area, public awareness of your group will grow. You may find that businesses will call and offer donations.

There may be troupes or clubs that will look to expand beyond a place for telling. There is nothing wrong with this; in fact, we encourage growth within the youth storytelling community. As student interest grows you may require additional funds. For example, after hearing King Arthur tales, your students may take a particular interest in finding out about medieval myths and legends, and they may want to acquire a collection for the group. Perhaps they may want to put on a medieval festival to showcase the stories.

From Our Experience: *I was surprised when I received that first phone call from our Rotary Club asking if I had students who could tell stories at a luncheon. I told him that I would have to rent a van and thanked him for the opportunity to perform. The man stated, "We can provide a $100 donation for their work." I graciously accepted the donation. I was shocked, and continue to be shocked, by the outpouring of support from our small town of Hanford over the years. These funds help us reach more than fifty-five audiences a year, including senior citizens homes and children from poorer school districts. One year we raised $11,000 by telling stories and appealing to our community for funds. After I realized that storytelling is something people enjoy and don't have problems supporting, I sold fewer candy bars and instead raised my expectations with my students to become a professional student storytelling troupe.* —Kevin

Establishing Rates

One of the questions that every storytelling group leader will eventually ask is, "How much do we charge for a show?" First, keep in mind that you need to charge for more than just the show itself. You also need to request money to help with travel, room accommodations, hours of practice and rehearsals, students' time and yours, along with your professional expertise. Although the objective is not to make so much profit that it becomes a business, quality requires an investment.

You need to determine what is a fair and reasonable fee to charge for your services and what amount will help you continue your storytelling group. You should also consider the audience and their resources. A group of business people can usually pay more than a day-care center or seniors group. Be flexible but realize that your kids work hard and should be compensated for their work. If you are uncertain about the rates charged by professional storytellers in your area, you can find out by contacting the following:

National Storytelling Network (www.storynet.org)

Voices Across America Youth Storytelling Project's list of youth groups (www.youthstorytelling. com)

Calling local guilds and asking about "local" rates

Tip for the Adult Leader: *Voices of Illusion charges about $100 an hour for a local show, which brings about nine student tellers and an adult coach. This rate is usually under the rate of professional storytellers. We also have an out-of-local-area rate, which varies according to the distance traveled. We have performed at numerous charity shows as well. These are performances for which we do not receive monetary payment but "earn" a sense of having a new and appreciative audience. Often we perform shows for people who have never heard a storyteller. The real reward is seeing their faces light up when they hear stories for the first time.* —Kevin

Taking the Show on the Road

There are many ways to raise money while telling stories. In this chapter we suggest a number of projects that you and your group can organize to provide a means for both storytelling and financing your group. There are many others. Begin by brainstorming the organizations, events, and places that might use storytellers (e.g., country fairs, schools, churches, and civic service groups such as Optimist or Rotary Clubs; consider programs to which you can add storytelling such as "A Reading Marathon" or a book fair). Your group members can help by naming some of their own connections (e.g., Does a member have a parent who works in a day-care center or is a member of the Rotary Club?).

With a younger storytelling club, it is best if the adult leader secures the storytelling gigs. High school students are capable of making phone calls and writing letters to prospective venues. Have your members write letters or design a flyer advertising the talents of your group and send them to places that might have a need or interest in hiring your group. As the adult leader, always keep control over what is sent out and insist on retaining the final approval of where your young tellers perform. Start small. Send out a few flyers at a time and wait to see the results. Word of mouth is usually the best advertisement. Once you have held a successful performance, ask the contact person to pass along information about your group to others in the field.

Telling for Civic Service Groups

Local civic service groups like the Masons, Optimists, and the Lion's Club have guest speakers every month. They often invite representatives of community groups to discuss their programs or give a presentation. These groups are not offended when the speaker also asks for support for their group in the way of time, funding, or joint sponsorship. Ask to be part of that support. Even venture as far as suggesting the amount of the donation. To arrange a presentation, the first thing you should do is contact a member of this group and ask for the name of the person in charge of programs. Explain the specific needs of your group (e.g., to raise funds for books, to travel to a storytelling festival, to help with expenses of the National Youth Storytelling Olympics, etc.). After making that initial contact, arrange a time to actually present a storytelling show or meet to discuss a future storytelling presentation.

Schools and Day-Care Centers

Schools and day-care centers often have a "budget for speakers or artists." Contact these event educational organizers early in the school year to determine the best time to present. The earlier you determine the dates for performing, the sooner you can suggest prices for the performance. Schools and day-care centers are always looking for educational programs that teach the principles of learning. Having students perform their stories is a powerful reminder to educators that storytelling helps promote literacy and collaboration.

Country Fairs or Special Community Events

When towns celebrate a certain holiday or plan their annual fair, they often look for people to entertain children and adults. Contact the local fair advisor or the nearest youth fair board and inquire how your group can become involved in the event. Don't be afraid to request a donation for the time spent working or performing.

Word of Caution: *Avoid arranging storytelling in high-traffic and noisy areas. Many storytelling programs are conducted at a location away from the main activities of the fair. Insist that the storytelling take place in a small makeshift theater or tent. Arrangements should be made so that your storytellers can be heard and people can take some time out to listen to a show.*

Conferences and Conventions

Many library and educational organizations such as the International Reading Association, National Council of Teachers of English, American Association of School Librarians, and the American Library Association have state and local chapters that are looking for educational presentations and will donate funds to support literacy programs such as your youth storytelling group. Other community organizations such as the YMCA, Boy and Girl Scouts, and Boys and Girls Clubs might appreciate storytelling programs that teach the kids nature skills or folklore. Be certain to pay particular attention to deadlines. Most organizations have dates for accepting proposals after which they cannot accept speakers or presenters for the annual events calendar.

The Public Library

Some youth storytelling groups establish a yearly or quarterly contract with their local library. The storytellers come and perform up to forty-five minutes of shows for various ages. This also serves as an excellent way to recruit for other programs, because kids come to the libraries to hear stories and usually bring their parents. Word of mouth is always the best form of advertising. Your students may be asked to perform at birthday parties, schools, latchkey, or other student organizations.

Retirement Homes and Senior Centers

Many youth groups have arranged to receive a donation for telling stories in retirement homes or special care facilities. Even though the students are there to perform, there is a greater reward after the program, when students take time to interview and listen to the stories of the elders living in the retirement homes. This experience is unforgettable when you see the students serve as tellers and then learn from the wisdom that comes with age.

Camps and Outdoor Programs

Church camps, community camps, and nature centers, along with organizers of family reunions, often look for that extra entertainment to help them make their event special. Consider exploring the outside programs in your local region and making an initial contact to ensure a booking.

These are only suggestions of places that have worked for us. Your town or city is unique. It holds its own events and programs. For example, sometimes a local store or coffeehouse will hold a special event in the town. Be aware of the community calendar. A call to the chamber of commerce can often keep you updated on future events. One thing we have learned is that every performance and every new place provides another opportunity to hand out a business card or invite someone to see our show.

Bringing the Audience to You

Another way to raise funds is to bring people to see your group. If you are lucky enough to already have a performance space outside of your practice area, the only thing required is promoting the program. If you don't have a performance space, you can always call your local YMCA, library, college, or school and ask if they will donate a room or theater with seating capacity of one hundred to three hundred. You may be surprised at the generosity of others for the program. By charging admission, you will be able to secure funding and at the same time provide quality shows for the audience. Some libraries, schools and other organizations have policies that prohibit charging for events, so check with the administration before making your plans.

Tellabration and Youth Tellabration

Every year during the month of November, the National Storytelling Network (NSN) holds National Storytelling Week. One effective means of fundraising is to become part of the event known as Tellabration. (Tellabration is a night of storytelling when tellers in nearly every state and a number of foreign countries simultaneously tell stories throughout the week.) You can create your own Tellabration or start a Youth Tellabration that specifically showcases young people telling stories. Once you print tickets and contact the media about the program, you will be surprised at the number of people who attend the event. Charge a small admission price or even hold a bake sale or book fair in combination with the event. Design flyers about your storytelling troupe and make them available at all events. Provide a donation box where people can further contribute to your program. The NSN has a full promotion kit you can use by calling 1-800-525-4514.

Thematic Programs

Students can study and learn stories based on a specific theme or event. For example, to celebrate Mother's Day, a church can help sponsor a "Salute to Mothers" and your students can tell stories. This type of program can be done for stories about holidays, civil rights, family stories, veteran stories, and so on.

Special Programs to Promote Literacy

Storytelling programs promote literacy. Libraries and schools regularly celebrate reading themes during the year. This is especially true in schools because of the national thrust to increase literary achievement. Encourage people to donate a "story book" to your storytelling library. Aligning your program with literacy awareness programs such as National Book Week can help you market a show that promotes literacy.

Storytelling Festival

Festivals are exciting, but they require a group of volunteers to assist with the planning. This includes finding a location, arranging ticket sales, handling hospitality, catering to the tellers, and more. You will also need to ask professional storytellers to tell with your students. Start your planning well in advance and you can raise a hefty sum for your youth storytelling group. Contact the National Storytelling Network (1-800-525-4514) and ask for their handbook on developing storytelling festivals.

Renaissance Dinner

Students and adults love to take part in this entertaining event. Find local establishments to donate food prepared during the time of the European Renaissance. Cornish hens, chicken, turkey legs, or stew and some touching up with simple food items like potatoes, vegetables, and desserts can easily be made to resemble a Renaissance meal. The flavor of the "old days" is the most important consideration. Speak with a local Renaissance guild or festival organizer. You will find they are generous with their help. After consulting books on the Renaissance, have your students dress up in authentic attire and serve the food and stories. Some possible stories could include King Arthur tales, such as "The Holy Grail" or "Sir Gawain and the Green Knight," the adventures of Robin Hood, or even some tales of Geoffrey Chaucer. This is a sure-fire fundraising event that requires some work but pays off in the end.

Ghost Story Program in a Haunted House

Every town has their haunted places, and ghost stories are extremely popular with audiences. Call the city officials and ask if an alleged haunted place could be used for an evening to share ghost stories. Charge an admission and tell the haunted stories of the house.

Ethnic or Cultural Festival

Pick a country or ethnic group and share stories of that culture. Work to make the experience a cultural event including dances, stories, and music. Have your students provide a day of custom and culture or create a multicultural extravaganza. For a small charge, this will bring great educational benefit to all.

Additional Programs to Provide Funding

Mime-a-Thon

This enjoyable program is similar to a bowl-a-thon or walk-a-thon in which participants receive pledges per hour or per day that someone bowls or runs. In this case, pledges are made to have storytellers keep quiet for a day. Adults and other students sponsor the storytellers for each day they act as a mime and do not talk. Prior to the Mime-a-Thon, participants dress up like mimes and practice doing mime for their communication. Students wear badges, which state that they are in a Mime-a-Thon for the day. The badge lists the time they started. If they are found talking, except during break times, they turn in their badge and pledge sheet. This is done during a school day, with the cooperation of teachers and administration, or on full-day outings. It is great fun and a good way to raise money for the club at the same time.

Book and Story Drive

Invite children to a gathering and ask them to bring a donation for the group (i.e., money, books). Every time someone gives the group a donation, you share a story. This is an entertaining way to have others listen to stories and collect for the group.

Story Delivery Service or "Story-a-Gram"

People will pay to have a story delivered with a personal message. Hearing a beautiful folk-tale or a personal tale attached with a message from someone who cares about them is a wonderful gift. This type of fundraiser works especially well for birthdays, Valentine's Day, and Mother's or Father's Day. It is a special way to connect with loved ones using storytelling. For safety reasons, if you offer this service, be sure that you have safe drivers and that students never travel alone. Groups of three and four are recommended.

Personal Story Program

People can also pay you to tell their favorite story or collection of stories. Most individuals really want to hear stories, especially stories that have personal significance to their lives. Create a form using a publishing computer program such as Print Shop or Print Master announcing that you will cater stories to the wishes of the listener. You may be surprised at the variety and number of requests you receive.

Case in Point: *A local doctor offered a donation if we would come to his home to tell "Casey at the Bat." He said he had loved the story poem as a child and longed to hear it again. I found the original poem, as well a story in which Casey returns and another about Casey teaching a young boy about baseball in his old age. To perform the stories, we all dressed up in baseball outfits. His smile was a great reward! We knew our "Story Delivery Service" had brought that smile.* —Kevin

---

Surefire small-amount fundraising efforts such as car washes, bake sales, and book fairs generate cash for single events. However, if you can develop an annual or biannual event that becomes tradition for your town, you can secure a steady base of support. For more fundraising ideas, explore the Fundraising Web site (www.fundraising.com). It features a variety of traditional fundraising efforts (e.g., T-shirts, candy bars, wrapping paper) that have worked in the past.

Section IV

Storytelling Resources

Building a Storytelling Collection

Having an assortment of books and stories available for club members to read, appreciate, and use for selecting tales to tell is vital to any storytelling group or troupe. Although every group leader should encourage his or her students to look for books at the public and school library, it is also helpful to have a special collection of books to use at meetings, so that students will have immediate access while interest is high. Middle and high school students may not have ready access to picture and folktale collections, which makes it all the more important to have your own set of books. Begin with *your* favorite books and add to the collection in response to student preferences and requests.

As you and your students develop favorites, you will need to devise ways to finance a collection that is to be used exclusively by your youth storytellers. Books are expensive, and often funds are limited. Ask your school principal, school board, or parent group for money or a one-time gift to begin your storytelling collection. Check with your local arts or humanities councils, civic and church groups, educational organizations, or even local merchants to see if grants are available. Storytelling can fit into grants aimed at at-risk or gifted and talented students, career education, or arts instruction. For other ideas see Chapter 9 on fundraising.

Once your group is established, offer a storytelling program at the local bookstore. In return, ask for a gift certificate so you can shop for relevant books. Take a list of titles with you. Try offering the club's services at birthday and holiday parties for younger children. Start a "Birthday Book" program. Parents can donate money in honor of their child's birthday. In return, place a special bookplate with the child's name in the front of the book.

If all sources of "free," gift, or grant money prove insufficient or unavailable you can always resort to bake sales, candy sales, or other fundraisers. Pass the hat at your concerts advising members of the audience that their donations will go to the purchase of storytelling books for the group.

Work with your local public librarian or school media specialist. Ask if for an extended loan period for some of their picture books or folktale collections. Ask to have first pick of picture books and folktales that are being discarded. Make friends with your local used bookseller. Many picture books and collections of fairy tales are beautifully illustrated but may be difficult to adapt to an oral retelling or simply are not suited to storytelling. If you are going to invest, look for books that contain interesting and uncomplicated plots. In the meantime take your group to the public or school library and introduce them to the folklore section (398.2) and the mythology section (291 and 292). Make arrangements ahead of time for the librarian to book talk some favorites for you. Try downloading stories off the Internet and keeping the master copy. Check the bibliography at the end of this chapter to find a list of Web sites.

Purchase books in quality paperback whenever possible. They usually cost less, and with a little love and extra care, they can often last as long as hardcover books. Invest in a rubber stamp with the name of your storytelling club and stamp all of your books. Devise a sign-out system with a limited loan period to ensure maximum use and return of the books.

While you are searching for books, be sure not to neglect the hundreds of storytelling compact disks and audiotapes that are available. Build a listening library as well as a reading one. Listening to nationally renowned storytellers such as Jackie Torrance, Donald Davis, or The Folktellers can be an inspiring experience, even on a recording. Hearing master storytellers' words come alive with characterization and expression often tempts students to check out the book or learn the story on their own. A tape library is especially helpful to your bilingual students and those with reading difficulty or special needs.

Bibliography

This bibliography includes titles of suggested books that we have used and found helpful. Most of these resources are in our own personal collections. We have found that the world of storytelling is addictive and expensive. There is always one more "must have" book to purchase and one more fantastic story to tell. Our recommendations should not to be considered as an all-inclusive compilation of books to be used for and by youth storytellers, but rather a selective sampling. More and more wonderful books published each year are also worthy of your consideration. We have included a list of publishers that specialize in storytelling materials. You may wish to check their Web sites or request a catalog.

The audio and videocassettes identified at the end of the bibliography are only a tiny sampling. Storytellers all over the country have produced excellent works. As you attend festivals and listen to other storytellers, you will want to build up your own collection of tapes, compact disks, and videos. The ones listed here are currently available and easy to find.

We have grouped the selections by a number of categories. Each entry includes the name of the author, title of the book, publisher, copyright date, and level of difficulty. In addition, every entry is annotated to help you make the best choice for your particular needs. When appropriate, we have highlighted in bold-faced print the culture or country of origin (e.g., Hispanic, African American, Denmark) and unique or special theme or focus (e.g., ghost stories, activities, puppetry). We have designated books that are especially designed for young people as "Youth."

> E: Elementary-aged tellers, aged 10 and under; easier to learn
>
> M: Middle school–aged tellers, aged 11 to 13; intermediate level of difficulty
>
> H: High school and young adult, aged 14 and up; for the advanced teller
>
> A: Teachers and coaches to be used with youth tellers

Categories

Storytelling Theory, Practice, and How-To Guides: Professional reading, these books may be used with your storytelling group or to the build confidence and ability of the group leader. Some of the books focus on using storytelling in the classroom, giving the rationale and educational benefits of storytelling as well as stories and activities, whereas several others focus specifically on youth storytellers.

Storytelling Collections: Collection of world tales, short stories, and stories based around a central theme. Some collections are suited to beginning tellers with stories that are one or two pages in length and can be embellished for the more advanced teller. Other collections are suited to intermediate and advanced storytellers with stories that are longer, more complex, and may contain more sophisticated subject matter.

Single Stories: Picture books that make good tellable stories. We have indicated in bold-faced print stories that are suited for two or more tellers.

Video, Compact Disks, and Audiotapes: Nationally known storytellers tell some of their favorite stories.

Storytelling Web Sites: Well-established sites of storytelling organizations, storytellers, and others, which provide stories, activities, information about storytellers and festivals, and links to other storytelling sites

Storytelling Organizations: State, regional, and national guilds and organizations nurturing the storyteller and promoting the art of storytelling.

Publishers and Distributors Specializing in Storytelling Books: All of these publishers are committed to publishing quality books about stories and storytelling.

Storytelling Theory, Practice, and How-To Guides

Barton, Bob. *Tell Me Another: Storytelling and Reading Aloud at Home and in the Community.* Des Plaines, Ill.: Heinemann. 1986. A

Another excellent book on using stories in the classroom with games, Story Theater, dance, call and response, multipart narration. Also how to select a story and make it your own. Barton is a Canadian storyteller and educator.

Barton, Bob, and David Booth. *Stories in the Classroom: Storytelling, Reading Aloud and Role-playing with Children.* Des Plaines, Ill.: Heinemann. 1990. A ACTIVITIES

Drawn from the authors' thirty-plus years of classroom experience, the book shows teachers how to find, choose, and use stories and includes lots of follow-up activities, such as retellings, reading of similar stories, writing new versions, dramatizing, thematic art projects, and more.

Bauer, Caroline Feller. *New Handbook for Storytellers: With Stories, Poems, Magic, and More.* Chicago: American Library Association, 1993. H A PUPPETRY, MAGIC, PROPS

More than 500 pages of ideas, activities, themes, kinds of stories, multimedia, props, and developing programs for preschool children to young adult. Practical resource for anyone who tells stories to children and wants to find new ways to present stories. Includes ideas for decorating and promoting programs; using objects, magic, puppets, poetry, and music; book talks; and lists of books to go along with every storytelling idea and theme.

Brand, Susan Trostle, and Jeanne M. Donato. *Storytelling in Emergent Literacy: Fostering Multiple Intelligences.* Albany, N.Y.: Delmar Publishers. 2001. A

This book creatively integrates multiple intelligences and related activities with methods of effective storytelling. Based on recent brain research and multiple intelligence theory, the text combines the art of storytelling with popular selections from children's literature; it is organized by themes around the calendar and is useful for anyone interested in developing effective storytelling skills.

Brody, Ed., and others. *Spinning Tales Weaving Hope: Stories of Peace, Justice, & the Environment.* Philadelphia: New Society Publishers. 1992. M H A ACTIVITIES

Stories from many cultures are accompanied by a variety of follow-up activities involving discussion, writing, music, drama, and crafts. The book focuses on using story to promote self-esteem, conflict resolution, and problem solving. Activities are for classroom use. Many well-known tellers contributed to the stories.

Champlin, Connie, and Nancy Renfro. *Storytelling with Puppets.* Chicago: American Library Association. 1997. H A PUPPETRY

A comprehensive guide to creating and using puppets in storytelling. Puppets are correlated to specific stories, books, and themes.

Collins, Rives, and Pamela J. Cooper. *The Power of Story: Teaching Through Storytelling.* Boston: Prentice-Hall. 1996. A ACTIVITIES

Excellent resource. The eight chapters cover the "why" and "how to" of storytelling with activities, lists of resources, and an interview with the storyteller who wrote each chapter. Includes the value of telling stories, choosing and preparing stories, finding your own voice, dramatization, personal narratives, and storytelling activities along with a bibliography and listing of Internet sites.

Dailey, Sheila. *Putting the World in a Nutshell: The Art of the Formula Tale.* Bronx, N.Y.: Wilson. 1994. A

Easy-to-learn stories that follow set patterns for such tale types as the chain story, cumulative tale, circle story, endless tale, good-bad, question, air castles, and the catch story are accompanied by an explanation of each type of formula tale and mention of additional stories. Useful for creating your own stories or helping students create formula stories.

Davis, Donald. *Telling Your Own Stories: For Family and Classroom Storytelling, Public Speaking, and Personal Journaling.* Little Rock, Ark.: August House. 1993. E M H A

A small book packed full of "story starters" and memory joggers written by America's foremost teller of personal stories. Gives ideas on how to build plot, structure stories, developing crisis, expanding descriptive skills, recovering memory, and telling personal stories.

De Vos, Gail, and Anna E. Altman. *New Tales for Old: Folktales as Literary Fictions for Young Adults.* Englewood, Colo.: Libraries Unlimited. 1999. A

Discusses the nature of folktales, their cultural context, and characteristics that make them attractive to young adults. Describes the reworkings of many familiar tales and offers suggestions for use with young people. Other titles by the same authors: *Tales, Then and Now: More Folktales as Literary Fiction for Young Adults; Tales, Rumors, and Gossip: Exploring Contemporary Folk Literature with Young Adults; Storytelling for Young Adults: Technique and Treasury.*

Garrity, Linda K. *The Tale Spinner: Folktales, Themes, and Activities.* Golden, Colo.: Fulcrum. 1999. A ACTIVITIES

The eight chapters are centered around various themes; this book includes folktales from various countries and provides discussion questions, a bibliography, and activities to go along with the tales. Themes include the origin of fire, don't believe everything you hear, never give up (the Cinderella theme), beware of strangers. The activities focus on geography, games, science, arts and crafts.

Gillard, Marni. *Storyteller Storyteacher: Discovering the Power of Storytelling for Teaching and Living.* York, Maine: Stenhouse. 1996. A

The author relates her journey of discovering how storytelling can affect learning and the lives of both children and the people who teach them. Includes choosing and performing stories, personal tales, reviving early memories, encouraging reluctant readers and writers through storytelling, using storytelling to build community, and using storytelling for personal growth and understanding.

Greene, Ellin. *Storytelling: Art & Technique,* 3rd ed. R. R. New Providence, N.J.: Bowker. 1996. A

Often used as a text for storytelling classes, this guide presents the history of the storytelling movement, discusses the purpose and value of storytelling in libraries, and provides guidelines for selecting stories, preparing to tell, and presenting stories. Lists of resources are included.

Griffin, Barbara Budge. *Storyteller's Guidebook Series: I—Students As Storytellers. II—Student Story Fest.* Medford, Ore.: Griffin McKay. Order direct: P.O. Box 626; Medford, OR 97501; telephone: 541-773-3006. A YOUTH

Book I: contains lesson plans, reproducible handouts, curriculum calendars, and educational skills for a complete classroom program in traditional tales. Book II: contains full instructions, including reproducible handouts, for organizing and coordinating an intramural or multischool festival. Also from the same author: *Storyteller's Handbook* and *Storyteller's Workbook.*

Hamilton, Martha, and Mitch Weiss. *Children Tell Stories; A Teaching Guide.* Katonah, N.Y.: Richard C Owen. 1990. E M A YOUTH

The most well-known book on teaching storytelling to children. Includes how to prepare a storytelling teaching unit, helping children choose and learn stories, coaching tellers, developing family stories, and integrating storytelling into the curriculum. Also gives twenty-five stories that range from beginners to advanced.

Haven, Kendall. *Super Simple Storytelling: A Can-Do Guide for Every Classroom, Every day.* Englewood, Colo.: Libraries Unlimited. 2000. A ACTIVITIES

Gives directions for learning how to tell stories and how to use them across the curriculum. Includes forty storytelling exercises and guidelines for teaching students to tell. Also by this author: *Stepping Stones to Science: True Tales and Awesome Activities.*

Lipman, Doug. *The Storytelling Coach: How to Listen, Praise, and Bring Out People's Best.* Little Rock, Ark.: August House. 1995. A

Lipman is considered the foremost authority on storytelling coaching, and this book presents principles for giving and receiving good coaching help for classroom, stage, and other venues. Also by Lipman: *Improving Your Storytelling: Beyond the Basics for All Who Tell Stories in Work or Play.*

Lipman, Doug. *Storytelling Games: Creative Activities for Language, Communication, and Composition Across the Curriculum.* Phoenix, Ariz.: Oryx Press. 1995. A ACTIVITIES

Step-by-step methods on how to find a storytelling game, learn it, present it, adapt it, and use it to teach a variety of subjects. The games can be used to encourage flexible thinking, imagination, cooperation, acceptance of diversity, self-confidence, and freedom of expression, as well to reinforce learning.

Livo, Norma J., and Sandra A. Rietz. *Storytelling Activities*. Englewood, Colo.: Libraries Unlimited. 1987. A ACTIVITIES

A collection of activities designed to expand storytelling experiences. Combines stories, songs, ballads, games, and other play forms with art and research projects. Includes activities for finding, learning, and presenting stories. Provides some stories to tell from folklore, mythology, and family stories.

MacDonald, Margaret Read. *The Parent's Guide to Storytelling: How to Make Up New Stories and Retell Old Favorites*. Little Rock, Ark.: August House. 2001. H A

Contains ideas for making storytelling easy, spontaneous, and affirming. Includes traditional stories in easy-to-follow formats, helpful hints, and techniques. Focuses on storytelling for the youngest listeners, bedtime stories, expandable tales, scary stories, improvisational ideas, and family folklore.

MacDonald, Margaret Read. *The Skit Book: 101 Skits from Kids*. Hamden, Conn.: Linnet Books. 1990. E M H YOUTH

Improvisational skits passed along by word of mouth by scouts, at camps, and so on. Each skit gives title, characters, story, and punch line. Dialogue, costumes, and props can be added. Good for creating dialogue and creating stories with more than one teller. While designed for use with theater and creative dramatics, the activities are lots of fun and can be used to strengthen storytelling skills.

MacDonald, Margaret Read. *Storyteller's Start-Up Book; Finding, Learning, Performing, and Using Folktales*. Little Rock, Ark.: August House. 1993. M H A

Basic startup information on finding stories, learning to tell the story in one hour, playing and teaching with story, teaching others to tell, and the role of the storyteller. Twenty unusual world folktales are given in short tellable paragraphs.

Maguire, Jack. *Creative Storytelling: Choosing, Inventing, and Sharing Tales for Children*. New York: McGraw Hill. 1985. A

Comprehensive book describing types of stories, how to find the right story for children of different ages and interests and how to adapt stories, create your own stories, improve your storytelling technique, and extend the story experience through music, poetry, puppetry, and so on. Includes several stories to illustrate story types.

Mooney, Bill, and David Holt. *The Storyteller's Guide: Storytellers Share Advice for the Classroom, Boardroom, Showroom, Podium, Pulpit, and Center Stage*. Little Rock, Ark.: August House. 1996. A

The authors interviewed more than fifty well-known storytellers who are also teachers, librarians, clergymen, actors, and musicians, as well as full-time professional storytellers. The book gives their opinions and advice on many topics, such as shaping stories from printed text, controlling stage fright, marketing, worst performance experiences, learning and rehearsing a story, creating original stories, making a program flow, copyright, using storytelling in the library, and recommendations for the "storyteller's bookshelf." Excellent source for anyone who is serious about telling stories.

Rubinstein, Robert. *Curtains Up! Theater Games and Storytelling.* Goldern, Colo.: Fulcrum. 2000. M H A ACTIVITIES, YOUTH
> Former middle school teacher and storytelling coach provides more than eighty easy-to-follow games and activities for creating and performing stories. Includes tips for learning and performing stories as well as warm-up exercises and tips for telling stories

Rubright, Lynn. *Beyond the Beanstalk: Interdisciplinary Learning Through Storytelling.* Des Plaines, Ill.: Heinemann. A
> Educator and storyteller Rubright demonstrates how teachers can use storytelling and expressive arts to motivate students and develop their skills. Lots of tried-and-true methods that teachers can put to immediate use are provided, including specific activities, stories to tell, drama games, movement, family folklore, creative writing, oral history, poetry, storytelling and music, and more.

Schimmel, Nancy. *Just Enough to Make a Story: A Sourcebook for Storytelling.* 3rd edition, 1998. Order from Sister Choice Press, 1450 6th St., Berkeley, CA 94710. A
> Ideas for choosing and using stories in various settings. Includes several stories including "The Tailor," as well as two paper-folding stories. Annotated bibliography.

Sierra, Judy, and Robert Kakminski. *Twice Upon A Time; Stories to Tell, Retell, Act Out, and Write About.* Bronx, N.Y.: H. W. Wilson. 1989. M H A ACTIVITIES
> A collection of twenty-four world folktales accompanied by instructions for dramatics, creative writing, and illustrating. Tips are given on how to learn, introduce, and tell stories effectively. Besides storytelling, there is a chapter on creative dramatics. The stories are written simply and can be used by student tellers.

Spolin, Viola. *Theater Games for the Classroom: A Teacher's Handbook.* Evanston, Ill.: Northwestern University Press. 1986. M H A ACTIVITIES,
> Theater and improvisational games and activities that may be used to develop creativity and strengthen performance skills.

Tales as Tools: the Power of Story in the Classroom. Jonesborough, Tenn.: National Storytelling Press. 1994. A
> This book highlights the major areas in which storytelling makes a difference—in the teaching of reading, writing, history, science and math, language development, multicultural education, creations of classroom communities, and social and environmental education. Each article is written by an educator in the field and reproduced from another source. Includes teaching children to tell stories, making history come alive, telling stories to write, collecting oral histories, telling and writing family stories, therapeutic storytelling, using stories to teach science and math, a bibliography of books about storytelling, and recommended stories for various age groups. Also contains an article by Judy Sima, "Turning Parents into Tellers," reprinted from the *Yarnspinner* (December 1993).

Storytelling Collections

Babbitt, Natalie. *The Devil's Storybook.* New York: Farrar Straus, & Giroux. 1974. E M H
> Ten wonderful tales of a scheming practical joking devil that comes to earth to play tricks on clergymen, goodwives, poets, and pretty girls but is almost always bested. Also by this author: *The Devil's Other Storybook.*

Baltuck, Naomi. *Crazy Gibberish and Other Story Hour Stretches (from a* Storyteller's Bag of Tricks). North Haven, Conn.: Linnet Books. 1993. Includes book and audiocassette. E M H A AUDIENCE PARTICIPATION

>   Wonderful collection of chants, short audience participation stories, action songs, musical games, jokes, tongue twisters, plus section on how to use the story stretchers and creating and adapting your own. It is a good idea to have a few of these in your own bag of tricks for those times when you have a few extra minutes or need to get the audience with you. Student storytellers can use these as group stories and chants. Also by same author: *Apples from Heaven: Multicultural Folk Tales about Stories and Storytellers.*

Bang, Molly. *The Goblins Giggle and Other Stories.* Magnolia, Mass.: Peter Smith. 1973. H GHOST STORIES

>   Five great tellable stories, spooky and unusual, including "Mary Culhane and the Dead Man."

Best-Loved Stories Told at the National Storytelling Festival and *More Best-Loved Stories Told at the National Storytelling Festival.* Twentieth Anniversary Edition. Jonesborough, Tenn.: National Storytelling Press. 1991. M H

>   Respectively containing thirty-seven and thirty-nine stories from some of the most well-known and best storytellers in the country, told at the twentieth anniversary festival in Jonesborough, Tennessee.

Bruchac, Joseph. *Iroquois Stories: Heroes and Heroines, Monsters and Magic.* Trumansburg, N.Y.: Crossing Press. 1985. E M H NATIVE AMERICAN

>   This book contains some of our favorite Native American tales. Thirty-two stories with an introduction on the Iroquois people. Our favorites: "Turtle Makes War on Human Beings," "Turtle's Race with Bear," and the "Vampire Skeleton." Another collection by Bruchac, beautifully illustrated by Murv Jacob, is *The Boy Who Lived with the Bears and Other Iroquois Stories.*

Cabral, Len, and Mia Manduca. *Len Cabal's Storytelling Book.* New York: Neal-Schuman. 1997. M H AFRICA

>   Popular Rhode Island storyteller Cabral shares twenty-three familiar and not-so-familiar stories from Africa and other traditions with directions for telling and activities for integrating the stories into the curriculum.

Caduto, Michael J. *Earth Tales from Around the World.* Golden, Colo.: Fulcrum. 1997. M H NATURE

>   Organized into ten themes such as earth, water, sky, plants, fire, and wisdom, the stories come from every continent. Includes suggestions for lessons inspired by the stories and additional extensions for further exploration.

Caduto, Michael J., and Joseph Bruchac. *Keepers of the Earth: Native American Stories and Environmental Activities for Children.* Golden, Colo.: Fulcrum. 1988. M H NATIVE AMERICAN, NATURE

>   Twenty-three Native American stories about creation, fire, earth, water, seasons, plants, and animals are presented along with discussion questions and activities. Tribe of origin is given. The authors have written several other books along the same lines: *Keepers of the Animals: Native American Stories and Wildlife Activities for Children; Keepers of the Night: Native American Stories and Nocturnal Activities for Children.*

Carle, Eric. *Treasury of Classic Stories for Children.* New York: Orchard Books. 1996. E M H

>   Twenty-two familiar and not-so-familiar tales by Aesop, the Grimm Brothers, and Hans Christian Anderson.

Climo, Shirley. *A Treasury of Princesses: Princess Tales from Around the World.* New York: HarperCollins. 1996. M H
> This book presents retellings of seldom-heard princess tales, featuring such heroines as White Jade from China, Gulnara of Arabia, and Vasilisa the Frog Princess from Russia. A discussion of princess lore precedes each selection. Also from the same author; *A Treasury of Mermaids: Mermaid Tales from Around the World* and *Magic and Mischief: Tales from Cornwall.*

Climo, Shirley. *Someone Saw a Spider: Spider Facts and Folktales.* New York: Harper Collins. 1985. E M H NATURE
> Myths, folklore, and superstitions about spiders accompany facts about how they live. Stories from Japan, American Indian cultures, Africa, Russia, Islamic cultures, and Scotland.

Cohn, Amy L. *From Sea to Shining Sea: A Treasury of American folklore and Songs.* New York: Scholastic. 1993. M H UNITED STATES
> The book is a wonderful collection of stories, poems, and songs from the American folk tradition, including creation stories, scary stories, immigrant stories and stories from the Revolutionary War, slavery, pioneers, tall tale heroes, and baseball. Each section is illustrated by one of fourteen Caldecott Medal and Honor Book artists. Many of the stories are written by well-know authors, songwriters, storytellers, and poets

Cole, Joanna. *Best-Loved Folktales of the World.* New York: Doubleday. 1982. M H
> This collection of two hundred tales is arranged by regions of the world—Eastern and Western Europe, the British Isles, Middle East, Asia, Africa, North and South American, the Caribbean, and the Pacific. An index in the back lists stories by categories. Includes humorous tales, legends, tales with a moral, witches, ogresses, and female monsters, trickster-heroes, married couples, and others. One of the best collections of world tales.

Courlander, Harold, and George Herzog. *The Cow-tail Switch and Other West African Stories.* New York: Henry Holt.1986. M H AFRICA
> Newbery Honor Book contains seventeen tales about animals, kings, warriors and hunters, clever and foolish people, good and bad people, and how things came to be. Courlander is one of the foremost collectors of African folklore. Other books by the authors for children: *The Fire on the Mountain and Other Stories from Ethiopia and Eritrea; People of the Short Blue Corn: Tales and Legends of the Hopi Indians; The Tiger's Whisker and Other Tales form Asia and the Pacific.*

Creden, Sharon. *Fair Is Fair: World Folktales of Justice.* Little Rock, Ark.: August House. 1994. M H
> Thirty folktales from countries such as Israel, Jamaica, Ancient Greece, India, Turkey, Ireland, Burma, Japan, and Mexico and well as from the Apache and Navajo tribes. Each tale is followed by comments on the moral issue at hand and legal precedents. Included are "Mr. Fox" (Ted Bundy: Serial Killer), "General Moulton and the Devil" (Salem Witch Trials), and "Bell of Atri" (Animal Rights). Written by a former deputy prosecuting attorney. Also from the author: *In Full Bloom: Tales of Women in Their Prime.* In this book, she pairs a folktale with a vignette about a notable American woman.

Czarnota, Lorna Macdonald. *Medieval Tales That Kids Can Read and Tell.* Little Rock, Ark.: August House. 2000. M H YOUTH
> King Arthur, William Tell, Robin Hood, Roland, and other tales are written in a simplified way that allows kids to add their own details. Also includes historical background to each story, tips for telling, and a section on characteristics of medieval tellers and the ways children might adopt a medieval persona.

Davis, Donald. *Southern Jack Tales*. Little Rock, Ark.: August House. 1992. (Also published as *Jack Always Seeks His Fortune: Authentic Appalachian Jack Tales)*. M H APPALACHIA
  Thirteen stories of Jack who is sometimes foolish, sometimes wise, but always ends up on top as he goes off to seek his fortune, wins a wife, and fools giants and ogres.

DeSpain, Pleasant. *The Emerald Lizard: Fifteen Latin American Tales to Tell*. Little Rock, Ark.: August House. 1999. E M H LATIN AMERICA
  These traditional folktales, myths, and legends from fifteen Latin American countries are written in English and Spanish. Also by the same author: *The Dancing Turtle: A Folktale from Brazil*.

DeSpain, Pleasant. *Sweet Land of Story: Thirty-Six American Tales to Tell*. Little Rock, Ark.: August House. 2000. M H UNITED STATES
  Stories from every region of the country; silly, scary, and wise; stories from the Native American tradition, Civil War heroes, tall tale heroes.

DeSpain, Pleasant. *Thirty-Three Multicultural Tales to Tell*. Little Rock, Ark.: August House. 1993. E M H
  Brief stories from around the world. Easy enough for students to tell but should probably be embellished by adult tellers. Includes stories from Mexico, Korea, Tibet, India, Russia, China, Fiji, Africa, and Japan. Also by DeSpain: *Eleven Turtle Tales: Adventure Tales from Around the World*; *Eleven Nature Tales: A Multicultural Journey*; *Twenty-Two Splendid Tales to Tell: Volumes I and II*; *The Emerald Lizard: Fifteen Latin American Tales to Tell*.

DeSpain, Pleasant. *Twenty-Two Splendid Tales to Tell from Around the World*. Volumes I and II. Little Rock, Ark.: August House. 1990. E M YOUTH
  Simplified folktales from sixteen countries are easy to read and tell and may be embellished. Other books include *The Books of Nine Lives* series: vol. 1, *Tales of Tricksters;* vol. 2, *Tales of Nonsense & Tomfoolery;* vol. 3, *Tales of Wisdom & Justice;* vol. 4, *Tales of Heroes;* vol. 5, *Tales of Holidays;* vol. 6, *Tales of Insects*.

De Van Etten, Teresa Pijoan. *Spanish-American Folktales*. Little Rock, Ark.: August House. 1990. E M H SPANISH-AMERICAN
  "The practical wisdom of Spanish Americans in twenty-eight eloquent and simple stories." The stories are sprinkled with Spanish words, collected by the author from her relatives and neighbors in New Mexico.

Dubrovin, Vivian. *Storytelling for the Fun of It: A Handbook for Children*. Order from Storycraft Publishing. P.O. Box 205, Masonville, CO 80541-0205. Phone: 970-669-3755. E M YOUTH, ACTIVITIES
  Written especially for children, telling them how to find, learn, and tell stories for campouts, slumber parties, and classroom projects and how to plan storytelling parties and start storytelling clubs. Suggestions for using costumes, puppets, and props. Author has several other works directed at young people including a quarterly newsletter, *Junior Storyteller,* which presents ideas for storytelling activities. Other books include *Create Your Own Storytelling Stories* and *Storytelling Adventures: Stories Kids Can Tell*.

Erlich, Amy. *The Random House Book of Fairy Tales*. New York: Random House. 1985. M H
  Retellings of nineteen well-known fairy tales from Hans Christian Andersen, Charles Perrault, and the Brothers Grimm, including Beauty and the Beast, Rumpelstiltskin, Red Riding Hood, Steadfast Tin Soldier, Hansel and Gretel, and Cinderella.

Forest, Heather. *Wonder Tales from Around the World.* Little Rock, Ark.: August House. 1995. E M H
    Twenty-seven folktales that ask the listener to "suspend the logic of ordinary reality and leap into and imaginative world where impossible events can occur." Forest adds a touch of poetry in each tale. Simply written and good for intermediate tellers. Cultures included are Australia, Babylonia, China, Ecuador, Finland, France, Iceland, Siberian Arctic, Middle East, and Indonesia among others. Also by same author: *Wisdom Tales from Around the World.*

Friedman, Amy. *Tell Me A Story.* Kansas City, Mo.: Andrew and McMeel. 1993. M H
    Nineteen stories from around the world adapted by Friedman first appeared as featured newspaper articles. Folktales, myths, and fairy tales including stories of ghosts, dragons, talking animals, and flying ships. Also by this author: *The Spectacular Gift and other Tales from Tell Me a Story.*

Fujita, Hiroko. Adapted and edited by Fran Stalling. *Stories to Play With: Kids' Tales Told with Puppets, Paper, Toys, and Imagination.* Little Rock, Ark.: August House. 1999. E M H PUPPETS, PROPS, JAPAN YOUTH
    Written for beginning storytellers who work with young children, these short, easy-to-tell tales use drawing, participation, and easy-to-find materials to enhance the telling. Some may be well known, such as "Wide-Mouth Frog," "The Tailor," "Rain Hat," and "Mr. Brown and Mr. Black"; others come from Japan where Fujita-san is an author and educator. These stories are easy enough for even young children to do and tell. Contains diagrams and instructions on how to make the simple props. Most of the necessary materials can be found around the house.

Gellman, Marc. *Does God Have a Big Toe? Stories about Stories in the Bible.* New York: Harper & Row. 1989. E M H BIBLICAL
    There are sixteen modern *midrashim* (a *midrash* is the Jewish term for a story that explains a story in the Bible) written for children about stories in the Old Testament. Includes stories about the first rainbow, the Tower of Babel, Moses, and others.

Greaves, Nick. *When Hippo Was Hairy and Other Tales from Africa.* Hauppauge, N.Y.: Barron's. 1988. E M H AFRICA, NATURE
    Thirty-six animal stories from Africa. Each story contains a color illustration as well as "Facts about" the animals; map of Africa locating the animal's habitat and information about height, weight, life span, identification, diet, habitat, breeding, and diet. Some of the animals are very unusual. Each chapter states the tribe where the story originates. Also by the same author and in the same format: *When Lion Could Fly and Other Tales from Africa.*

Hamilton, Martha, and Mitch Weiss. *Stories in My Pocket; Tales Kids Can Tell.* Golden, Colo.: Fulcrum. 1996. E M H YOUTH
    Presents how to choose, learn, and tell stories as well as a guide for adults to help kids tell stories. Thirty stories are offered, from starter stories to the most challenging. Stories are written in two columns, one with the story, the other with directions for telling, including gestures, facial expressions, and what words to emphasize. Also by the same authors: *How and Why Stories: World Tales Kids Can Read and Tell, Through the Grapevine,* and *Noodlehead Stories.*

Hamilton, Virginia. *The People Could Fly: American Black Folktales.* New York: Alfred A. Knopf. 1985. H AFRICAN AMERICAN
    Twenty-four tales from the African American tradition including Brer Rabbit, slave tales of freedom, tales of the supernatural. Written with a hint of dialect. Includes notes on the origin of each story. Also by this author: *Her Stories: African American Folktales, Fair Tales, and True Tales.*

Harrison, Annette. *Easy-to-Tell Stories for Young Children.* Jonesborough, Tenn.: National Storytelling Press. 1992. E M AUDIENCE PARTICIPATION
> A collection of twelve stories aimed at young children with suggestions on how to incorporate the tale into the curriculum. Each story contains sidebars to encourage participation and how to tell the story.

Haven, Kendall. *Amazing American Women: 40 Fascinating 5-Minute Reads.* Englewood, Colo.: Libraries Unlimited. 1995. M H UNITED STATES
> Stories of well-known and not-so-well-known American Women in the fields of women's and civil rights, politics, sports, science and exploration, medicine, education, military service, business and the arts. Good resource for historical stories without having to do the research yourself. Includes questions to explore and a bibliography for each story. Also by the author: *Marvels of Math: Fascinating Reads and Awesome Activities; Marvels of Science: 50 Fascinating 5-Minute Reads; Close Encounters with Deadly Dangers: Riveting Reads and Classroom Ideas.*

Haven, Kendall. *Voices of the American Revolution: Stories of Men, Women, and Children who Forged our Nation.* Englewood, Colo.: Libraries Unlimited. 2001. H UNITED STATES
> Diverse stories of real people of the American Revolution: Patriots, Tories, pacifists, African American slaves, Native Americans, Hessian mercenaries, as well as women and children. Includes extension activities and suggestions for research projects. Also by this author: *Voices from the American Civil War: Stories of the Men, Women, and Children who Lived Through the Raging Fire.*

Haviland, Virginia. *Favorite Fairy Tales Told in Norway.* New York: William Morrow. 1961. E M H NORWAY
> Seven stories retold in an easy-to-read format. Good for young readers and tellers. This is one of sixteen in the Favorite Fairy Tales Told in … series. All of the books have been reprinted in paperback format. Other countries include Czechoslovakia, Denmark, England, France, Germany, Greece, India, Ireland, Italy, Japan, Poland, Russia, Scotland, Spain, and Sweden.

Holbrook, Belinda. *String Stories: A Creative, Hands-On Approach for Engaging Children in Literature.* Worthington, Ohio: Linworth Publishing. 2002. E M H PROPS
> Contains nineteen string stories with step-by-step directions from the easiest to the most complex. A sure hit with kids.

Holt, David, and Bill Mooney, editors. *Ready-To-Tell Tales: Sure-fire stories from America's Favorite Storytellers.* Little Rock, Ark.: August House. 1994. M H
> Forty of the country's most popular professional storytellers—all of whom have been featured at the National Storytelling Festival—contribute stories they believe a beginning storyteller can be successful with. Multicultural collection includes stories from Africa, India, Ancient Greece, Egypt, Japan, Mexico, Thailand, as well as stories from African American, Cajun, Appalachian, Jewish, and Native American oral traditions. Includes "a word about fair use" for storytellers who wish to tell the tales. Telling tips and story sources are given. Also by these authors: *More Ready-to-Tell Tales from Around the World.*

Holt, David, and Bill Mooney. *Spiders in the Hairdo: Modern Urban Legends.* Little Rock, Ark.: August House. 1999. E M H URBAN LEGENDS
> Urban legends are stories told as true but "always having happened to a friend of a friend." (You know the ones; they often show up in your e-mail inbox!) These fifty-five tales include some well-know and not-so-well-known urban legends that can be told as is or changed a little to fit a student's own setting and circumstances.

Jacobs, Jacob. *English Fairy Tales.* New York: Dover Dell. 1967. M H ENGLAND
  Reprinted from the 1898 edition by one of England's most well-known folklorists. Many of the forty-three tales are among our most familiar fairy tales: "The Three Sillies," "Jack and the Beanstalk," "Teeny-Tiny," "Henny-Penny," "Three Bears," "Mr. Fox," "Tom Thumb," "Lazy Jack," "Three Pigs," and "Golden Arm." Other Jacob's books in this series: *Celtic Fairy Tales, More Celtic Fairy Tales,* and *Indian Fairy Tales.*

Jaffe, Nina, and Steve Zeitlin. *The Cow of No Color: Riddle Stories and Justice Tales from Around the World.* New York: Henry Holt. 1998. M H
  Stories from Asia, Africa, Europe, and North America give readers the opportunity to play judge and jury by answering the question at the end of the tale.

Jaffe, Nina, and Steve Zeitlin. *While Standing on One Foot: Puzzle Stories and Wisdom Tales from the Jewish Tradition.* New York: Henry Holt. 1993. M H JEWISH
  These short clever folktales come from many eras of Jewish history in many parts of the world. The reader is invited to guess how the hero or heroine solved the problem or escaped the predicament and then read the solution.

Justice, Jennifer, editor. *The Ghost and I: Scary Stories for Participatory Telling.* Cambridge, Mass.: Yellow Moon Press. 1992. M H GHOST STORIES
  Eighteen well-known storytellers share their favorite scary stories with notes on how to tell them and where to add participation. Includes a page on the ten "basics of participation." Great, fun collection of ready-to-tell tales.

Kennedy, Richard. *Richard Kennedy: Collected Stories.* New York: Harper & Row. 1987. H
  Contains sixteen original, beautifully written stories—a favorite of many professional tellers.

Kipling, Rudyard. *Just So Stories.* New York: William Morrow. 1996. H
  This beautifully illustrated (by Barry Moser) version contains twelve of Kippling's original stories, including "Elephant's Child" and "How the Leopard Got His Spots."

Leach, Maria. *How the People Sang the Mountains Up: How and Why Stories.* New York: Viking. 1967. E M H
  This out-of-print book gives brief stories from cultures all over the world that explain the "how and why" of man, animals, earth, sea, sky, plants, and constellations. The stories need a little embellishing to become good tellable tales.

Leach, Maria. *Whistle in the Graveyard: Folktales to Chill Your Bones.* New York: Puffin. 1974. E M H GHOST STORIES
  Forty short, easy-to-tell stories about ghosts, bogeys, witches, and other haunters. Some are true, others come from folktales in England, the United States, and other countries.

Lester, Julius. *How Many Spots Does a Leopard Have? And Other Tales.* New York: Scholastic. 1989. M H AFRICA, JEWISH
  A collection of twelve African and two Jewish folktales. Very readable and tellable. Also by same author: *Black Folktales, Tales of Uncle Remus, The Adventures of Brer Rabbit,* and *Further Tales of Uncle Remus: The Misadventures of Brer Rabbit, Brer Fox, Brer Wolf, the Doodang and Other Creatures.* These books use a slight dialect but are easy to read and understand.

Lewis, Shari. *One-Minute Bedtime Stories.* New York: Dell Yearling. 1982. E M
  Twenty compact, easy-to-tell versions of familiar and not so familiar tales, including "Rumpelstiltskin," "Paul Bunyan," "The Golden Goose," The Lion and the Mouse," and "The Sorcerer's Apprentice." Other books by Lewis in the same series: *One-Minute Favorite Fairy*

Tales, One-Minute Animal Stories, One-Minute Bible Stories, One-Minute Greek Myths, One-Minute Christmas Stories, and *One-Minute Stories of Brothers and Sisters.*

Livo, Norma J. *Story Medicine: Multicultural Tales of Healing and Transformation.* Englewood, Colo.: Libraries Unlimited. 2001. M H
> Contains sensitive, inspiring stories about healing the self, relationships, the community, and the earth. Includes old-time medicinal cures. Other books by the author: *Celebrating the Earth: Stories, Experiences, and Activities; Enchanted Wood and Other Tales from Finland; Folk Stories of the Hmong;* and *Teaching with Folk Stories of the Hmong; Story Medicine: Multicultural Tales of Healing and Transformation; Bringing Out the Best: Values Education and Character Development Through Traditional Tales.*

Lobel, Arnold. *Fables.* New York: Harper Trophy. 1983. E H M
> Twenty original fables about an array of animal characters from crocodile to ostrich.

Loya, Olga. *Momentos Magicos, Magic Moments: Tales from Latin America Told in English and Spanish.* Little Rock, Ark.: August House. 1997. M H LATIN AMERICA
> Fifteen stories grouped into scary stories, tricksters, strong women, and myths. The stories come from Mexico, Guatemala, Nicaragua, Puerto Rico, Cuba, Colombia, and the Maya, Chol, and Aztec peoples.

MacDonald, Margaret Read. *Twenty Tellable Tales: Audience Participation Folktales for the Beginning Storyteller.* Bronx, NY: H. W. Wilson. 1986. M H AUDIENCE PARTICIPATION
> Written in short paragraphs with repetitious lines and phrases, these stories are broken down in an easy-to-tell format. The stories are mostly "can't miss" and fun to tell. MacDonald has written other wonderful books of tellable stories, including *Look Back and See: Lively Tales for Gentle Tellers; Peace Tales: World Folktales to Talk About; When the Lights Go Out: Twenty Scary Stories to Tell; Celebrate the World: Twenty Tellable Folktales for Multicultural Festivals;* and *Shake-It-Up Tales!: Stories to Sing, Drum, and Act Out.*

Many Voices: True Tales from America's Past. Jonesborough, Tenn.: National Storytelling Press. 1995. M H UNITED STATES
> Thirty-six stories arranged chronologically from 1643 to 1989, meant to breathe life into history. The stories are essentially true; they describe actual events and people or are based on fictional characters in true-to-life situations. Written by storytellers. Stories include Abraham Lincoln, Sacagawea, Scott Joplin, Sitting Bull, Rosie the Riveter, and many ordinary citizens who lived during extraordinary times. Stories can be read aloud or adapted for telling. The companion volume, *Many Voices Teacher's Guide,* offers helpful teaching tips, learning objectives, questions for discussion, worksheets, and variety of classroom activities.

Marsh, Valerie. *Storyteller's Sampler.* Fort Atkinson, Wisc.: Alleyside Press (available through Highsmith Press). 1996. E M H ACTIVITIES, PROPS, PUPPETS
> A sampler of five types of stories: paper cutting, mystery fold, sign language, story puzzles, and storyknifing. Marsh describes each method and how to use them and offers four stories of each type. The directions come with patterns and are easy to follow. Great for young audiences and for the "artistically challenged." Other titles by the author include *Beyond Words: Great Stories for Hand and Voice: A Treasury of Trickster Tales, Puppet Tales, Story Puzzles: Tales in the Tanagram Tradition, Terrific Tales to Tell: From the Storyknifing Tradition, True Tales of Heroes and Heroines, Paper-Cutting Stories for Holidays and Special Events, Mystery-Fold: Stories to Tell, Draw, and Fold, Paper-Cutting Stories from A to Z,* and *Storytelling with Shapes and Numbers.*

Marshall, Bonnie C. *Tales from the Heart of the Balkans.* Englewood, Colo.: Libraries Unlimited. 2001. M H BALKANS

   This book includes thirty-three stories representing major population groups of the former Yugoslavia. Includes historical overview, background information, maps, and color photos of the people and land. This book is part of an excellent and growing series from Libraries Unlimited, the World Folklore series (see World Folklore Series).

Martin, Rafe. *Mysterious Tales of Japan.* New York: Putnam. 1996. H JAPAN

   Ten wonderful stories retold by one of America's best-know author/storytellers. Great for older readers and tellers. Illustrated and contains notes on each story.

Miller, Theresa. *Joining In: An Anthology of Audience Participation Stories and How to Tell Them.* Cambridge, Mass.: Yellow Moon Press. 1988. M H AUDIENCE PARTICIPATION

   Eighteen storytellers share their favorite participation stories with notes on how to tell them and where to add participation.

Norfolk, Bobby, and Sherry Norfolk. *The Moral of the Story: Folktales for Character Development.* Little Rock, Ark.: August House. M H

   Contains twelve stories presented by two nationally known storytellers, including suggestions for incorporating character development into the classroom.

Orgel, Doris. *The Lion and the Mouse and Other Aesop Fables.* New York: DK Publishers. 2001. E M H

   Twelve familiar Aesop fables plus information on the life and times of Aesop.

Osborn, Mary Pope. *Favorite Greek Myths.* New York: Scholastic. 1989. H MYTHOLOGY

   Twelve simplified myths, some familiar and some not so familiar, including the stories of Cupid and Psyche, Atalanta and Hippomenes, Orpheus and Eurydice, and Minerva and Arachne. Also by the same author: *Favorite Norse Myths.*

Osborne, Mary Pope, and Troy Howell. *Favorite Medieval Tales.* New York: Scholastic. 1998. H

   This beautifully illustrated book contains nine retellings of well-known tales from the European Middle Ages including Beowulf, Robin Hood, and Finn MacCoul. Also by the author: *American Tall Tales* and *Mermaid Tales from Around the World.*

Pantheon Fairy Tale and Folklore Library. New York: Random House. H A

   All of the collections are written by scholars and folklorists from the culture they write about. While many of the stories are not in tellable form, the myths and legends can be reworked and adapted for telling. Titles include *African Folktales: Traditional Stories of the Black World, Afro-American Folktales: Stories from the Black Traditions of the New World, Russian Fairy Tales, Norwegian Folk Tales, Swedish Folktales and Legends, An Encyclopedia of Fairies: Arab Folktales, Italian Folktales, The Old Wives' Fairy Tale Book, Folktales of the British Isles, The Norse Myths, America in Legend: Folklore from the Colonial Period to the Present: Irish Folktales, The Complete Grimm's Fairy Tales, The Victorian Fairy Tale Book, Northern Tales, American Indian Myths and Legends, Tales from the American Frontier, Folktales of India, French Folktales, Chinese Fairy Tales and Fantasies, Gods and Heroes, Japanese Tales, Yiddish Folktales, Favorite Folktales from Around the World.*

Parent, Michael, and Julien Olivier. *Of Fools and Kings: Stories of the French Tradition in North America.* Little Rock, Ark.: August House. 1996. M H FRENCH AMERICAN

   Includes a glossary. Some of the stories are based on the authors' family experiences; others were originally collected by folklorists. The stories come from French Canada, the Great Lakes region, and Louisiana.

Pellowski, Anne. *The Story Vine; A Source Book of Unusual and Easy-to-Tell Stories from Around the World.* New York: Collier/Aladdin. 1984. E M H PROPS
   Contains stories and directions for using string, nesting dolls, riddles, drawing, African thumb piano, finger games, sand paintings. Includes string stories "The Mosquito" and "The Yam Farmer." Other titles: *The Family Storytelling Handbook: How To Use Stories, Anecdotes, Rhymes, Handkerchiefs, Paper; and Other Objects to Enrich Family Traditions; Hidden Stories in Plants: Unusual and Easy-To-Tell Stories from Around the World, Together with Creative Things to Do While Telling Them.*

Pellowski, Anne. *The Storytelling Handbook, A Young People's Collection of Unusual Tales and Helpful Hints on How to Tell Them.* New York: Simon & Schuster. 1995. E M H YOUTH
   Introductory chapters on how young people can get into storytelling and how to select and learn stories. Twenty-three stories from different parts of the world grouped into categories, such as cumulative tales, stories that use objects, stories for holidays, and stories written by young people. Stories range from easy to learn to more difficult. *Pellowski* has two other books of unusual world tales, using objects and unusual ways of presenting the stories: *The Family Storytelling Handbook* and *The Hidden Stories in Plants.*

Phelps, Ethel Johnston. *Tatterhood and Other Tales.* New York: The Feminist Press. 1978. M H
   Contains folktales and legends from around the world in which the protagonists are clever, strong, resourceful, and successful women. Also by the same author *The Maid of the North: Feminist Folk Tales from Around the World.*

Pinkney, Jerry. *Aesop Fables.* New York: Seastar Books. 2000. E M H
   Contains more than sixty bare-bones versions of Aesop's fables. Also by the same author: *The Tales of Uncle Remus: The Adventures of Brer Rabbit; Same and the Tigers; The Talking Eggs: A Folktale from the American South;* and *John Henry.*

Reneaux, J. J. *Cajun Folktales.* Little Rock, Ark.: August House. 1992. M H LOUISIANA
   Contains twenty-seven animal tales, fairy tales, funny folktales, and ghost stories from the Cajun people of French Louisiana. Also by the same author: *The Haunted Bayou and Other Cajun Ghost Stories* and *Cajun Fairy Tales.*

Ross, Gayle. *How Rabbit Tricked Otter and Other Cherokee Trickster Stories.* New York: Harper Collins. 1984. M H NATIVE AMERICAN
   Fifteen "how and why" stories and tales of how Rabbit tricks friends and enemies alike. Beautiful illustrations. Also by the same author: *The Legend of Windigo.*

Ryan, Patrick. *Shakespeare's Storybook: Folk Tales That Inspired the Bard.* New York: Barefoot Books. 2001. M H
   Seven folktales that Shakespeare may have heard growing up that later became the foundation for some of his most famous plays, including *Romeo and Juliet, Hamlet, King Lear, Taming of the Shrew,* and others.

San Souci, Robert D. *Cut from the Same Cloth: American Women of Myth, Legend, and Tall Tale.* New York: Philomel Books. 1993. M H UNITED STATES
   Divided into regions of the country, these are fifteen tales of strong-hearted, strong-willed women from Anglo American, African American, Spanish American, and Native American traditions.

San Souci, Robert D. *Short and Shivery: Thirty Chilling Tales.* New York: Doubleday. 1987. M H GHOST STORIES
   "The stories have been carefully selected from international ghost lore and retold with ghastly details and strong, shuddery endings." Good scary stories for older children for reading

and retelling. Stories from Russia, Japan, the United States, England, Costa Rica, the Jewish culture, Iceland, France, and other cultures. There are also stories by well-known authors such as Nathaniel Hawthorne and Washington Irving. Sequels by the same author: *More Short and Shivery: Thirty Terrifying Tales, Still More Short and Shivery,* and *Even More Short and Shivery.*

Schram, Peninnah. *Jewish Stories One Generation Tells Another.* Northvale, N.J.: Jason Aaronson. 1987. M H JEWISH

Sixty-four Jewish folktales collected and retold by America's best-know Jewish storyteller, written in tellable form. Also edited by Schram: *Chosen Tales: Jewish Stories by Jewish Storyteller* and *Stories within Stories from the Jewish Oral Tradition.*

Schwartz, Alvin. *Scary Stories to Tell in the Dark.* New York: Harper. 1981. E M H GHOST STORIES

Perennial favorite of all kids for reading and retelling. Stories are short and easy to learn for beginning storytellers, and kids love them. Scary illustrations by Stephen Gammell add to the popularity. Additional books by the author: *More Scary Stories to Tell in the Dark, Scary Stories Dark 3: More Tales to Chill Your Bones.*

Schwartz, Howard, and Barbara Rush. *The Diamond Tree: Jewish Tales from Around the World.* New York: Harper Collins. 1991. M H JEWISH

Fifteen folktales and fairy tales dating back as far as the third century from such countries as Turkey, Yemen, Iraq, and Morocco, including stories of rabbis and prophets, angels and goblins, wise kings and fools. By the same authors: *A Coat for the Moon and Other Jewish Tales; The Sabbath Lion.*

Shannon, George. *Stories to Solve: Folktales from Around the Word.* New York: Morrow/ BeechTree.1985. E M H YOUTH

Fifteen brief folktales are presented in which there is a mystery, problem, or riddle that the reader is invited to solve before the resolution is given. The stories make good "fillers." Also by the author: *More Stories to Solve; Still More Stories to Solve;* and *True Lies.*

Sherman, Josepha. *Trickster Tales: Forty Folk Stories from Around the World.* Little Rock, Ark.: August House. 1996. M H

Forty stories from every continent and many cultures, including ancient Babylonian, China, India, Eastern Europe, Morocco, and others. Notes as to origins and motifs are found at the end of the book. Also by the same author: *Once Upon a Galaxy* and *Rachel the Clever and Other Jewish Folktales*

Sierra, Judy. *Cinderella.* Phoenix, Ariz.: Oryx Press. 1992. H

Features twenty-five variations on the basic theme of the persecuted heroine who emerges victorious, regardless of the circumstances. Each version, from Asia, Africa, Eastern Europe, and North America, is accompanied by an introductory paragraph that discusses the cultural background of the story. Other similar titles in the Oryx Multicultural Folktale series by different authors: *Tom Thumb; A Knock at the Door* and *Beauties and Beasts.* Another Orxy book by Sierra is *Multicultural Folktales.*

Silverstein, Shel. *Where the Sidewalk Ends.* New York: Harper & Row. 1974. E M POETRY, YOUTH

This well-known book of poems is a perennial favorite with young and old alike. Contains poems such as "If you are a dreamer," "Sick," and "The Unicorn." Other favorites by Silverstein: *A Light in the Attic, Falling Up,* and *The Giving Tree.*

Singer, Isaac Bashevis. *Stories for Children.* New York: Farrar, Staus & Giroux. 1984. M H JEWISH
Thirty-six stories written by the Nobel Prize–winning Yiddish writer includes stories about Chelm, a city of fools; stories from the Polish *shtetl* (village); and Bible stories. The stories are drawn from life, legend, and fantasy. Also by the author: *Zlateh, the Goat and Other Stories.*

Smith, Jimmy Neil, editor. Homespun: Tales from American's Favorite Storytellers. New York: Crown. 1988. M H
Stories by twenty of the early pioneers in the storytelling revival, including Donald Davis, Jackie Torrence, Ray Hicks, the Folktellers, and Jay O'Callahan. Also includes the history of the National Storytelling Festival and suggestions for finding and telling your own stories. Also written by the author: *Why the Possum's Tail Is Bare and Other Classic Southern Stories.*

Spagnoli, Cathy. *Asian Tales and Tellers.* Little Rock, Ark.: August House. 1998. M H ASIAN
Over thirty stories from Japan, India, Korea, Vietnam, Cambodia, the Philippines, Bangladesh, Laos, Tibet, Pakistan, Sri Lanka, China, Indonesia, Taiwan, Burma, and Nepal. Stories are arranged around dominant Asian themes such as harmony and friendship, charity and simplicity, hard work and study.

Spagnoli, Cathy. *Asian Trickster Tales for Young Storytellers.* Ft. Atkinson, Wisc.: Highsmith Press. 2001. M H ASIAN
Contains twenty-six easy-to-learn, authentic tales from seventeen nations, as well as cultural background, storytelling techniques, and learning activities. Also by the author: *A Treasury of Asian Stories and Activities: A Guide for Schools and Libraries.*

Stavish, Corrine. *Seeds from Our Past: Planting for the Future: Jewish Stories and Folktales.* Washington, D.C.: B'nai B'rith Center for Jewish Identity. 1996. M H JEWISH
Brief tales that can be told by themselves or used as a springboard to discussion. The stories may need to be expanded upon and embellished by experienced tellers. The stories are broken down by topics: anti-Semitism, drinking and drugs, family, elderly, future, honesty-dishonesty, Israel, self-respect, stereotypes, and others. Following the stories is a discussion guide and bibliography of sources for Jewish stories.

Steck Vaugh Literature Library. *Folktales from Around the World.* Ten-book series. Austin, Tex.: Steck-Vaughn. 1990. E M YOUTH
Titles: *Tales of Wonder, Tales of Trickery, Humorous Tales, Tall Tales, Animal Tales, Tales of the Wise and Foolish, Tales of the Heart, Tales of Justice, Tales of Nature,* and *Tales of Challenge.* Each book contains ten simplified versions of stories from different cultures centered on each theme. Many of the stories have been written and adapted from well-known authors and storytelling collections.

Tashjian, Virginia A. *Juba This and Juba That: Story Stretches for Large or Small Groups.* Boston: Little, Brown. 1969. E AUDIENCE PARTICIPATION
Poems, chants, riddles, stories, finger plays, songs, and tongue twisters for the younger set. By the same author: *With a Deep Sea Smile.*

Torrence, Jackie. *The Importance of Pot Liquor.* Little Rock, Ark.: August House. 1994. M H AFRICAN AMERICAN
Written by one of America's best-known and best-loved storytellers, these twelve tales come from her childhood growing up with her grandmother and grandfather in North Carolina. Pot Liquor, the broth of simmered foods, fortified her slave ancestors. Now Jackie Torrence finds strength in another unexpected source, the stories her grandmother and grandfather told." Each set of stories is introduced by a glimpse into her childhood and the lives of her beloved grandparents. Collection includes the legend of Annie Christmas and Brer Rabbit stories.

Untermeyer, Louis. *The Firebringer and Other Great Stories: 55 Legends That Live Forever.* New York: M. Evens and Company. 1968. H

Readers will have some knowledge and awareness of the myths and legends contained in this book. They come from all over the world, including Greece, Scandinavia, France, Spain, and Great Britain; tales from the Bible are also included.

Walker, Barbara K. *Turkish Folk-tales.* New York: Oxford University Press. 1988. E M H TURKEY

Includes fables, riddles, and folktales; some stories are Turkish versions of familiar European folktales. Other titles in the Oxford Myths and Legends series: *African Myths and Legends; Armenian Folk-Tales and Fables; Chinese Myths and Legends; English Fables and Fairy Stories; French Legends, Tales and Fairy Stories; German Hero-Sagas and Folk-Tales; Hungarian Folk-Tales; Indian Tales and Legends; Japanese Tales and Legends; Tales of Ancient Persia; Russian Tales and Legends; Scandinavian Legends and Folk-Tales; Scottish Folk-Tales and Legends; West Indian Folk-Tales; The Iliad; The Odyssey;* and *Gods and Men.*

Wolkstein, Diane. *The Magic Orange Tree and Other Haitian Folktales.* New York: Schocken. 1978. M H HAITI

Contains twenty-seven unique, sometimes scary folktales and songs from the island of Haiti. A storytelling classic.

World Folklore Series. Englewood, Colo.: Libraries Unlimited.

These wonderful books highlight the folktales, myths, and legends from many diverse and unique cultures. It is difficult to find stories from many of these countries in any other source. New titles are published each year. The books are usually coauthored by native authors, folklorists, and storytellers. In addition to the tales, each book contains background information, historical overview, beliefs and customs, maps, color photographs of the people, land, and crafts. The books are a expensive but well worth the price. Several include audiotapes. Titles include *Tales from the Heart of the Balkans; The Eagle on the Cactus: Traditional Stories from Mexico; The Celtic Breeze: Stories of the Otherworld from Scotland, Ireland, and Wales; A Tiger by the Tail and Other Stories from the Heart of Korea; Gadi Mirrabooka: Australian Aboriginal Tales from the Dreaming; The Enchanted Wood and Other Tales from Finland; Jasmine and Coconuts: South Indian Tales; The Magic Egg and Other Tales from Ukraine; When Night Falls, Kric! Krac! Haitian Folktales; Hyena and the Moon: Stories to Tell from Kenya; From the Mango Tree and Other Folktales from Nepal; Why Ostriches Don't Fly and Other Tales from the African Bush; Images of a People: Tlingit Myths and Legends; Folk Stories of the Hmong: Peoples of Laos, Thailand, and Vietnam; The Corn Woman: Stories and Legends of the Hispanic Southwest;* and *Thai Tales: Folktales of Thailand.*

Young, Richard, and Judy Dockery. *Favorite Scary Stories of American Children.* Little Rock, Ark.: August House. 1990. E M H GHOST STORIES

Contain twenty-three tales collected from children aged five to ten. The authors rate each story by its "fearfulness" and give an appropriate age level range: five or six, seven or eight, nine or ten. Some of the stories are familiar, others not; all are written to tell easily. The Afterword contains advice for parents and teachers. Also by the authors: *Classic American Ghost Stories and Ghost Stories from the American South.*

Yep, Laurence. *The Rainbow People.* New York: Harper Trophy. 1992. M H CHINA, CHINESE-AMERICAN

A collection of twenty Chinese and Chinese American stories collected in the 1930s as part of a Works Progress Administration project. The stories all stem from Kwangtung province in China. The tales are divided into five sections: Tricksters, Fools, Virtue and Vices, In Chinese America, and Love.

Yolen, Jane. *Not One Damsel in Distress: World Folktales from Strong Girls.* New York: Harcourt. 2000. M H
Contains thirteen tales of clever, heroic, courageous, and ingenious young women from Europe, Asia, the Americas, and Africa.

Yolen, Jane. *Favorite Folktales from Around the World.* New York: Pantheon. 1988. M H
Yolen presents more than 150 stories from all parts of the world, including stories of ghosts, lovers, tricksters, noodleheads, and heroes; tales of wisdom; tall tales; fooling the devil tales; life and death tales; and stories of stories. One of the best story collections, some tales can be told as is, others need work to become tellable. There is no index. Also by the author: *Gray Heroes: Elder Tales from Around the World.*

Young, Richard, and Judy Dockery Young. *Race with Buffalo: And Other Native American Stories for Young Readers.* Little Rock, Ark.: August House. 1994. E M H NATIVE AMERICAN
A collection of thirty-one Native American stories about how and why, ancient times, young heroes, tricksters, and magical beasts and the spirit world from tribes such as Cherokee, Choctaw, Seneca, Iroquois, and Cheyenne. Stories are written simply and easily adapted for telling. Also by these authors: *Stories from the Days of Christopher Columbus, Ozark Ghost Stories, and Outlaw Tales.*

Young, Richard, and Judy Dockery Young. *The Scary Story Reader: Forty-One of the Scariest Stories for Sleepovers, Campfires, Car & Bus Tips—Even for First Dates.* Little Rock, Ark.: August House. 1990. M H GHOST STORIES
These tales include modern urban legends, stories with shocking endings that make the listener "jump," ghost stories from across the country, and scary stories with endings that make you laugh.

Single Stories

Ardema, Verna. *Why Mosquitoes Buzz in People's Ears.* New York: Penguin Group. 1993. M H AFRICA
Based on a West African legend, this cumulative tale tells how mosquito's big lie causes a series of unfortunate chain reaction events in the jungle.

Bang, Molly. *Wiley and the Hairy Man.* New York: Aladdin Paperbacks. 1987. M H AFRICAN AMERICAN
With his mother's help, Wiley outwits the hairy creature that haunts the swamp near the Tombigbee River.

Birdseye, Tom. *Soap, Soap, Don't Forget the Soap: An Appalachian Tale.* New York: Holiday House. 1993. H APPALACHIA
Plug Honeycutt, a forgetful young boy, gets into trouble as he sets out for the store to buy some soap for his mother.

Birdseye, Tom. *Airmail to the Moon.* New York: Holiday House. 1988. H
Little Ora Mae sets out to find the thief who has "stole" her tooth, and when she does, she promises to send them "airmail to the moon."

Blume, Judy. *Pain and the Great One.* New York: Dell Yearling. 1974. M H TWO OR MORE TELLERS
Sibling rivalry told in verse. A brother and sister think their parents love the other one best.

Brown, Marcia. *Stone Soup: An Old Tale.* New York: Aladdin Books, 1986. E M FRANCE
    Three soldiers teach a village about sharing and cooperation while making soup from a stone.

Brown, Marcia. *Three Billy Goats Gruff.* New York: Harcourt. 1997. E NORWAY, TWO OR MORE TELLERS
    Familiar Norwegian folktale of the billy goats who wanted to go up to the hillside to make themselves fat and the ugly troll who lived under the bridge and threatened to eat them.

Bruss, Deborah. *Book! Book! Book!* New York: Scholastic. 2001. E
    A retelling of an old joke. The farm animals go to the library to check out a book, and the bullfrog claims he's already "read it."

Carle, Eric. *The Very Hungry Caterpillar.* New York: Collins World. 1972. E PROPS
    Little caterpillar that goes through the days of the week eating everything in sight before becoming a beautiful butterfly. Good story to tell with a caterpillar puppet.

Celsi, Teresa. *The Fourth Little Pig.* Austin, Tex.: Steck-Vaughn. 1992. E M TWO OR MORE TELLERS
    Written in verse, the Three Little Pigs' sister helps them to escape from the Big Bad Wolf.

Charlip, Remy. *Fortunately.* New York: Aladdin Paperbacks. 1993. E M TWO OR MORE TELLERS
    As young Ned makes his way to a party, good fortune follows bad through a series of cliff-hanging escapades that lead to a fortunate ending.

Climo, Shirley. *The Korean Cinderella.* New York: Harper Trophy. 1993. M H KOREA
    Pear Blossom triumphs over her cruel stepmother with the help of magical creatures called "tokgabis" and wins the heart of the magistrate. Other titles in the same series: *The Irish Cinderlad, The Egyptian Cinderella, The Persian Cinderella.* Other picture books by the same author: *Stolen Thunder, A Norse Myth*, and *Atalanta's Race: A Greek Myth.*

Cole, Brock. *The Giant's Toe.* New York: Farrar, Straus & Giroux. 1988. M H
    The giant's toe comes to life after he chops it off his foot. It cooks the hen and throws away the harp before Jack comes knocking at the gate.

DeFelice, Cynthia. *Dancing Skeleton.* New York: MacMillan. 1989. M H GHOST STORY
    Lively version of an old Appalachian folktale. Ornery old Aaron Kelly comes back from the grave to keep his wife from marrying another man.

Ernst, Lisa Campbell. *Zinnia and Dot.* New York: Viking. 1992. M H TWO OR MORE TELLERS
    Two bickering chickens learn to cooperate to save one remaining egg from the crafty fox.

Forest, Heather. *The Woman Who Flummoxed the Fairies.* San Diego, Calif.: Harcourt Brace. 1990. H
    Asked to bake a cake for the fairies, a clever baker figures out a way to escape from the fairies and still keep her promise. Also by the same author: *The Baker's Dozen: A Colonial American Tale.*

Fox, Mem. *Hattie and the Fox.* New York: Bradbury Press. 1987. E M TWO OR MORE TELLERS
    Hattie, a big black hen, discovers a fox in the bushes, which creates varying reactions from the other barnyard animals.

Fox, Mem. *Wilfrid Gordon McDonald Partridge.* Brooklyn, N.Y.: Kane Miller. 1985. M H
    Heartwarming story of a young boy with four names helps Miss Nancy, his ninety-six-year-old friend who also has four names, recapture her memories.

Gag, Wanda. *Millions of Cats.* New York: Penguin Putnam. 1956. E M
    An old man sets out to find a cat for his lonely wife and returns with hundreds of cats, millions, billions, and trillions of cats because he can't make up his mind.

Galdone, Paul. *Obedient Jack.* Danbury, Conn.: Franklin Watts. 1971. M H APPALACHIA, TWO OR MORE TELLERS
    Jack wins the hand of the king's daughter in spite of taking his mother's advice literally. Also by the same author: *Puss in Boots; The Elves and the Shoemaker; Rumplestiltskin; The Three Bears;* and *The Monkey and the Crocodile: A Jatuku Tale from Indian.*

Galdone, Joanna. *Tailypo: A Ghost Story.* New York: Seabury Press. 1977. E M GHOST STORY
    An old man living all alone cooks and eats the tail of a hairy, scary creature that comes back to get it. Even his dogs can't protect him.

Gerson, Mary-Joan. *Why the Sky Is Far Away: A Nigerian Folktale.* Boston: Little, Brown. 1992. E M AFRICA
    The sky was once so close to Earth that people could cut parts of it to eat, but their greed and waste caused the sky to move far away.

Gilman, Phoebe. *Something from Nothing.* New York: Scholastic. 1992. E M
    A little boy's grandfather, a tailor, keeps cutting down the coat he made into smaller and smaller items as the little boy wears them out until nothing is left but the story.

Goss, Linda, and Clay Goss. *The Baby Leopard.* New York: Bantam Books. 1989. E M AFRICA
    Baby Leopard learns a valuable lesson about fire and acquires his spots.

Grimm, Jacob, and Wilhelm Grimm . *The Bremen Town Musicians.* New York: North-South Books. 1992. E M GERMANY
    On their way to Bremen, four aging animals find a new home and outwit a band of robbers.

Hague, Kathleen, and Michael Hague. *The Man Who Kept House.* San Diego, Calif.: Harcourt Brace Children's Books. 1981. M H
    A foolish husband trades places with his wife for a day because he thinks his work in the fields is more difficult than keeping house.

Hardendorf, Jeanne. *A Bed Just So.* New York: Four Winds. 1975. E
    A "Hudgen" prevents the tailor from getting a good night's sleep until he figures out what kind of bed it would like.

Harper, Wilhemina. *The Gunniwolf.* New York: Dutton. 1967. E M TWO OR MORE TELLERS
    A little girl disregards her mother's warning and meets the Gunniwolf when she enters the forest but manages to make it home safely by singing him to sleep.

Heine, Helme. *The Most Wonderful Egg in the World.* New York: Aladdin. 1983. E M
    Three proud hens enlist the help of the king to determine which one of them lays the most beautiful egg.

Hewitt, Kathryn. *The Three Sillies.* San Diego, Calif.: Harcourt Brace Jovanovich. 1986. M H ENGLAND

> A young man returns to marry the silly farmer's daughter after finding three bigger "sillies."

Hickox, Rebecca A. *The Golden Sandal: A Middle Eastern Cinderella.* New York: Holiday House. 1998. M H IRAQ

> An Iraqi version of the Cinderella story in which a kind and beautiful girl is mistreated by her stepmother and stepsister and finds a husband with the help of a magic fish.

Hogrogian, Nonny. *One Fine Day.* New York: Aladdin. 1971. M H

> Fox loses his tail to an old woman and has to beg something from everyone he meets to try and get it back.

Howe, John. *Jack and the Beanstalk.* Boston: Little, Brown. 1989. E M ENGLAND

> Retelling of the tradition tale of Jack who trades the family cow for a handful of magic beans.

Johnson, Tony. *The Cowboy and the Black-eyed Pea.* New York: Putnam. 1992. M H

> A young woman of "bodacious beauty," named Farethee Well, heeds her dying father's warning to find a "real" cowboy who is known for his sensitivity.

Kasza, Keiko. *Wolf's Chicken Stew.* New York: Putnam. 1987. E

> Mr. Wolf sets out to fatten up Mrs. Chicken with cakes, donuts, and cookies so that he can eat her but changes his mind when he receives one hundred kisses from her grateful chicks.

Kent, Jack. *The Fat Cat: A Danish Folktale.* New York: Scholastic. 1971. E DENMARK

> A cat goes on a walk after eating all of his mistress's gruel and devours everyone he meets along the way until a woodcutter with an axe saves the day.

Kettleman, Helen. *Bubba the Cowboy Prince: A Fractured Texas Tale.* New York: Scholastic. 1997. M H

> Bubba's wicked step daddy and stepbrothers won't let him go to the party given by lady rancher, but his Fairy God Cow saves the day.

Kimmel, Eric A. *Anansi and the Moss Covered Rock.* New York: Holiday House. 1988. E M AFRICA

> Anansi the spider tricks all of his animal friends out of their food, until Little Bush Deer tries to teach him a lesson.

Kimmel, Eric A. *Baba Yaga: A Russian Folktale.* New York: Holiday House. 1991. M H RUSSIA

> Kindness pays off as a young girl outsmarts the famous witch who lives in a house built on chicken feet and travels in a mortar and pestle.

Kimmel, Eric A. *The Gingerbread Man.* New York: Holiday House. 1993. E

> The traditional tale of the cookie that outruns many animals until he meets up with the clever fox.

Kimmel, Eric A. *The Greatest of All: A Japanese Folktale.* New York: Holiday House. 1991. E M JAPAN

> A humble field mouse proves himself the most worthy when Father Mouse goes searching for someone to marry his daughter.

Kimmel, Eric A. *The Old Woman and Her Pig.* New York: Holiday House. 1992. E

> The old woman encounters many problems trying to get her pig home.

Kimmel, Eric A. *Seven at One Blow, or the Gallant Little Tailor*. New York: Holiday House. 1998. M H GERMAN
> This well-known Grimm fairy tale tells about a tailor who kills seven flies with one blow who manages to become king.

Kimmel, Eric A. *The Three Princes: A Tale from the Middle East*. New York: Holiday House. 1994. M H MIDDLE EAST
> A princess promises to marry the prince who finds the most precious treasure.

Kimmel, Eric A. *Three Sacks of Truth: A Story from France*. New York: Holiday House. 1993. M H FRANCE
> Petit Jean outwits a dishonest king and wins the hand of a princess.

Kraus, Robert. *Leo, The Late Bloomer*. New York: Crowell. 1971. E
> Leo can't talk or write and is very messy. His parents must learn patience until at last Leo blooms and can do everything right.

Lester, Helen. *Tacky the Penguin*. Boston: Houghton Mifflin. 1983. E M
> Tacky might be an odd bird, but he's mighty nice to have around, especially when hunters come to the land of the pretty penguins.

Lester, Helen. *The Wizard, the Fairy and the Magic Chicken*. New York: Houghton Mifflin. 1983. M H TWO OR MORE TELLERS
> Three enemies learn to cooperate to overcome the monster they have created.

Liberman, Syd. "Debate in Sign Language" from *Sea to Shining Sea* by Amy Cohn. New York: Scholastic 1993. M H JEWISH, TWO OR MORE TELLERS
> An evil king who wants to rid his kingdom of Jews is outwitted by a simple chicken seller.

Littledale, Freya. *The Magic Fish*. New York: Scholastic. 1996. E M TWO OR MORE TELLERS
> In this old folktale a fisherman keeps going back to the sea to ask the magic fish for bigger and bigger things for his wife who is never satisfied with what she has.

Lobel, Arnold. *Frog and Toad Are Friends*. New York: Harper Collins. 1970. E M H TWO OR MORE TELLERS
> Contains five short stories about the unusual, caring, and often humorous friendship of these two loveable amphibians. Also by the author: *Days with Frog and Toad* and *Frog and Toad Together*.

Lobel, Arnold. *Ming Lo Moves the Mountain*. New York: William Morrow. 1982. M H CHINA
> The wise man teaches Ming Lo a strange dance that will move the mountain that overshadows his home.

London, Jonathan. *Froggy Gets Dressed*. New York: Puffin Books. 1992. E
> Froggy keeps forgetting to put on one article of clothing after another before he can go outside to play in the snow.

Lowell, Susan. *The Three Little Javelinas*. Flagstaff, Ariz.: Northland. 1992. M H
> Three wild, hairy Southwestern pigs build their houses out of tumbleweeds, saguaro catcus ribs, and adobe to outsmart a coyote.

MacDonald, Margaret Read. *The Old Woman Who Lived in a Vinegar Bottle: A British Fairy Tale*. Little Rock, Ark.: August House. 1995. M H ENGLAND, TWO OR MORE TELLERS
> A no-nonsense fairy grants wishes, up to a point, to an ungrateful old woman, who complains constantly about her house.

Martin, Rafe. *The Rough-Face Girl.* New York: Putnam. 1992. M H NATIVE AMERICAN
An Algonquin Cinderella story of a mistreated younger sister with a pure heart is the only one who can see the Invisible Being's bow and sled.

Martin, Rafe. *The Storytelling Princess.* New York: Putnam. 2001. M H
A shipwrecked princess tells a prince a story with an ending he doesn't know and wins his hand in marriage.

May, Jim. *The Boo Baby Girl Meets the Ghost of Mable's Gable.* Elgin, Ill.: Brotherstone. 1992. E M GHOST STORY
A little baby with big diapers outsmarts two eighth-grade football players and a ghost to win a bag of gold. This story is a perennial Talespinners favorite.

Mayer, Mercer. *There Is Something in My Attic.* New York: Dial Books for Young Readers. 1988. E
A little girl lassos her nightmare and tries to bring it to her skeptical parents. Also by the same Author: *There's a Nightmare in My Closet.*

McDermott, Gerald. *The Stonecutter: A Japanese Folktale.* New York: Viking Press. 1975. E M JAPAN
A foolish stonecutter longs to be something more powerful.

McGovern, Ann. *Too Much Noise.* New York: Scholastic. 1968. E AUDIENCE PARTICIPATION
An old man who complains about his noisy house brings in all the farm animals to help drown out the noises.

McKissack, Patricia C. *Flossie and the Fox.* New York: Scholastic. 1986. H AFRICAN AMERICAN, TWO OR MORE TELLERS
This little girl doesn't need a Woodsman to outwit a sly and smooth talking fox.

Mosel, Arlene. *Tikki Tikki Tembo.* New York: Henry Holt. 1968. M H CHINA
A little Chinese boy nearly drowns because of his great long name.

Munsch, Robert. *Love You Forever.* Toronto: Annick Press. 1986. E M
A mother sings a lullaby to her little boy every night as he grows older until she can no longer sing to him. A definite tearjerker.

Munsch, Robert. *Mortimer.* Toronto: Annick. 1985. E M
Everyone in Mortimer's family and even the policemen try to make him "be quiet" and go to sleep—to no avail.

Munsch, Robert. *Murmel, Murmel, Murmel.* Toronto: Annick. 1982. E M
A little girl finds a baby and has a difficult time finding someone to take him.

Munsch, Robert. *The Paper Bag Princess.* Toronto: Annick Press. 1994. M H
Elizabeth sets out to rescue Ronald when a dragon burns down her castle and kidnaps him, wearing nothing but a paper bag.

Munsch, Robert. *Stephanie's Pony Tail.* Toronto: Annick Press. 1999. E M
Stephanie threatens to shave off all of her hair if her classmates don't stop copying her latest hairdo.

Munsch, Robert. *Thomas's Snowsuit.* Toronto: Annick Press. 1985. E M
His mother, his teacher, and the principal all try to make Thomas wear his new snowsuit until he takes matters into his own hands.

Paulson, Tim. *Jack and the Beanstalk and the Beanstalk Incident.* New York: Birch Lane Press. 1990. M H ENGLAND
   After reading the traditional version of "Jack and the Beanstalk," the reader is invited to turn the book upside down and read an updated version told from the giant's point of view.

Pellowski, Anne "The Mosquito" from *The Story Vine.* New York: MacMillan. 1984. E M PROPS
   A string story with directions. A woman swats a pesky mosquito and unties a knot in the process. Also in the same book: "The Yam Farmer" and "Grandmother's Candles."

Polette, Nancy. *The Little Old Woman and the Hungry Cat.* New York: Mulberry Paperbacks. 1989. E
   A hungry cat eats everyone he sees, until he swallows his owner who takes steps to stop his eating rampage.

Reneaux, J. J. *Why Alligator Hates Dog.* Little Rock, Ark.: August House. 1995. M LOUISIANA, TWO OR MORE TELLERS
   This Cajun folktale tells of how sassy old Dog tricks Alligator, king of the swamps, and starts a feud that continues to this day in the Louisiana bayous.

Rosen, Michael. *We're Going on a Bear Hunt.* New York: MacMillan. 1989. E AUDIENCE PARTICIPATION
   A brave family sets out to hunt a bear. All goes well until they actually see one. Good participation story.

Schimmel, Nancy. "The Rainhat" from *Just Enough to Tell a Story.* Order from Sister's Choice Press, 1450 6th Street, Berkeley, CA 94704. E M PROPS
   A simple paper-fold story of a resourceful young girl on a rainy day.

Scieszka, John. *The True Story of the Three Little Pigs.* New York: Viking Press. 1989. M H
   The story of what "really" happened to the Three Little Pigs as told by Mr. Abner T. Wolf. All he wanted to do is borrow a cup of sugar for his poor old granny's birthday cake.

Seeger, Pete. *Abiyoyo.* New York: Macmillan. 1986. E M SOUTH AFRICA
   This story taken from a South African lullaby is about a boy who tricks a terrible monster by making him dance.

Sendak, Maurice. *Where the Wild Things Are.* New York: Harper. 1963. E
   Max takes a magical trip to the place where the Wild Things live but returns to some place where someone loves him best of all.

Simms, Laura. *The Squeaky Door.* New York: Crown. 1991. E M AUDIENCE PARTICIPATION, TWO OR MORE TELLERS
   A squeaky door keeps a little boy awake and drives his grandmother crazy as she puts one animal after another in his bed to keep him quiet.

Slobodkina, Esphyr. *Caps for Sale.* New York: Harper. 1968. E M PROPS, AUDIENCE PARTICIPATION
   Unable to sell his caps, a peddler finds he must trick a bunch of monkeys into giving him back the caps they have stolen from him.

Small, David. *Imogene's Antlers.* New York: Crown. 1991. M H
   Imogene wakes up one morning to find she has sprouted a pair of antlers. While they prove to be quite useful, nothing her family tries can get rid of them.

Stevens, Janet. *The Three Billy Goats Gruff.* New York: Harcourt, Brace. 1987. E NORWAY, TWO OR MORE TELLERS
> The old familiar tale of a family of goats who had to cross over the troll's bridge to get to grass on the other side.

Stevens, Janet. *Tops and Bottoms.* New York: Harcourt. 1995. M H TWO OR MORE TELLERS
> Rabbit tricks Bear and ends up with all the vegetables in the garden.

Stevens, Janet. *The Tortoise and the Hare.* New York: Holiday House. 1984. E M TWO OR MORE TELLERS
> A comical retelling of the familiar Aesop's fable of slow and steady winning the race.

Taback, Simms. *Joseph Had a Little Overcoat.* New York: Viking. 1999. E M JEWISH
> Joseph the tailor makes smaller and smaller garments from his wonderful little overcoat as he wears it out, until he has nothing but the story to tell about it.

Tashijan, Virginia. "The Snooks Family" from *Juba This and Juba That.* Boston: Little, Brown. 1969. E M
> This odd family has difficulty blowing out the candle so they can all go to bed.

Tolstoy, Alexei. *Great Big Enormous Turnip.* Danbury, Conn.: Franklin Watts, 1968. E RUSSIA
> A farmer needs all the help he can get to pull an enormous turnip out of the ground.

Tresselt, Alvin. *The Mitten.* New York: Lothrop, Lee & Shepard. 1964. E UKRAINE
> A number of animals make their home in a boy's lost mitten until it splits apart.

Trivizas, Eugene. *The Three Little Wolves and the Big Bad Pig.* New York: Margaret K. McElderry Books. 1993. H
> A mean pig tries violent means to get rid of the three little wolves until the smell of flowers gives him a change of heart.

Turkle, Brinton. *Do Not Open.* New York: Puffin. 1984. M H
> An old woman tricks the genie she finds in a bottle and fixes an old clock in the process.

Van Laan, Nancy. *Possum Come a-Knockin'.* New York: Alfred A. Knopf. 1990. E M H TWO OR MORE TELLERS
> This toe tapping verse can be divided into a number of parts. Possum comes knocking and everyone in the family stops what they are doing.

Van Lann, Nancy. *Rainbow Crow.* New York: Alfred A. Knopf. 1989. M H NATIVE AMERICAN
> A Lanape Indian tale of how Crow brings fire to the animals.

Vaughan, Marcia. K. *Wombat Stew.* New York: Silver Burdette. 1984. E M H AUSTRALIA
> The animals trick a dingo out of making a stew of their friend in this Australian tale.

Viorst, Judith, "The Southpaw" from *Free to Be, You and Me* by Marlo Thomas. New York: McGraw Hill. 1974. E M H TWO OR MORE TELLERS
> Through a series of letters, Janet convinces Richard to let her pitch for his Little League team.

Wahl, Jan. *Tailypo!* New York: Henry Holt. 1991. E M GHOST STORY
> An old man eats the tail of a hairy scary creature that comes back to get it back.

Williams, Linda. *The Little Old Lady Who Was Not Afraid of Anything.* New York: HarperCollins. 1986. E M AUDIENCE PARTICIPATION
> An old lady out for a walk encounters a pair of shoes, a pair of pants, a shirt, gloves, and hat, and a pumpkin head that she puts to good use. Good participation story.

Xiong, Blia. *Nine-in-one, Grr! Grr!* Chicago: Children's Press. 1989. E M LAOS
   A folktale of the Hmong people from the mountains of Laos. When the great god Shao promises Tiger nine cubs each year, Bird comes up with a clever trick to prevent the land from being overrun by tigers.

Yep, Laurence. *The Man Who Tricked a Ghost.* Mahwah, N.J.: Bridgewater Books. 1993. M H CHINA
   A brave young man meets a ghost on his way home and tricks it into revealing its secret weakness. This story is based on one of the first published ghost stories in China, published in the third century A.D.

Young, Ed. *Lon Po Po: A Red-Riding Hood Story from China.* New York: Scholastic. 1989. M H CHINA
   Three little girls trick the wicked wolf.

Zemach, Harve. *The Judge.* New York: Farrar, Straus & Giroux. 1979. E M TWO OR MORE TELLERS
   Refusing to believe the prisoners, the Judge learns the hard way that "a horrible thing is coming this way."

Zemach, Harve. *A Penny a Look.* New York: Farrar, Straus & Giroux. 1971. M H TWO OR MORE TELLERS
   Two brothers hope to get rich as they set out to find a one-eyed man they can put in a cage and charge people a penny a look.

Zemach, Margot. *It Could Always Be Worse.* New York: Farrar, Straus & Giroux. 1977. M H JEWISH
   A wise Rabbi tells an unfortunate man to bring his farm animals into his house when he complains that his house is too small and too noisy.

Sources for Puppets, Props, and Instruments

Big Brazos Children's Center. P.O. Box 567, Hearne, TX 77859. (626) 975-2120. www. bigbrazos.com
   Large variety of beautiful world instruments.

Book Props. 1120 McVey Avenue, Lake Oswego, OR 97034. (800) 636-5314. Online catalog: www.bookprops.com
   Made to accompany specific picture books; gorgeous but very expensive. Picture book can be ordered along with the props.

Elderly Instruments. 1100 N. Washington, Lansing, MI 48906. www.elderly.com.
   New and used instruments; instruments from around the world.

R & J Fial Enterprises. 5366 Camino Real, Riverside, CA 92509. (909) 360-0961.
   Custom-made state badges and pins; can be engraved with the name of your storytelling group and each storyteller. Very reasonably priced.

Folkmanis Puppets. 1219 Park Avenue, Emeryville, CA 94608. (415) 648-767. www.folkmanis.com
   Includes "Folktails," "Furry Folk" puppets. Puppets are very realistic and include endangered animals and insects. Purchased online and at many book and toy stores.

Kids & Things. Box 7488, Madison, WI 53707. (800) 356-1200.

>Folkmanis Puppets, dolls, stuffed animals, and accompanying picture book. For preschool and early elementary. Retail prices.

Lakeshore Learning Materials. 2695 E. Dominguez Street, P.O. Box 6261, Carson, CA 90749. (800) 421-5354. www.lakeshorelearning.com

>Puppets, world instruments, kid- and adult-sized storytelling aprons. They also have a "Storytelling Board" of brushed nylon surface that can be used with the cloth storytelling characters in their storytelling kits. Each kit has characters, a book, and directions for telling well-known children's picture books. Ideal for young storytellers for use when telling to very young audiences. Some of the titles include *Brown Bear, Brown Bear, What do You See?; The Paper Bag Princess; Corduroy; There Was an Old Lady Who Swallowed a Fly; Silly Sally; Anansi & the Moss-Covered Rock.*

Lark in the Morning. P.O. Box 799, Fort Bragg, CA 95437. (707) 964-5569. www.larkinam.com

>World musical instruments, books, recordings and videos: Lark in the Morning is a musician's service founded in 1974 that specializes in hard-to-find musical instruments, music, and instructional materials.

Nancy Renfro Studios. P.O. Box 164226, Austin, TX 78716. (800) 933-5512.

>Hand puppets from fairy tales and generic animals; Old Lady Who Swallowed a Fly. Reasonable prices.

Oriental Trading Company. P.O. Box 2308, Omaha, NE 68103-2308. (800) 875-8480. www.orientaltrading.com

>Toys, masks, nose masks, hats, puppets, seasonal items, and a myriad of novelty items.

Strings. $1 each plus shipping. Order from Bob Grimes; 4619 Curtis Lane, Clarkston, MI 48346. (248) 623-0482.

>Macramé strings without knots. Use for string figures and stories.

Upper Sarahsville Clog Dancers. Bill Saling. 48726 SR 285, Caldwell, OH 43724. (740) 732-2071.

>Wonderfully decorated wooden limberjacks of hillbillies, farmers, old women, dogs, cats, frogs, turtles, jesters, skeletons, and a whole slew other animals and characters. Comes with a paddle. $15 and up, plus shipping.

Audio and Videocassettes

DeSpain, Pleasant. *Thirty-Three Multicultural Tales to Tell.* Little Rock, Ark.: August House. Two Audiocassettes.

>Oral telling of stories from the book of the same title. Other audiobooks from the author: *Eleven Turtle Tales, Twenty-Two Splendid Tales to Tell,* Volumes I and II.

Folktellers. *Stories for the Road.* Mythic Stream Productions. P.O. Box 2829, Asheville, NC 28002. (800) 864-0299.

>America's best-known tandem storytellers. This tape has their version of "The Jazzy Three Bears." Other tapes include *Chillers* and *One to Grow On.*

Novak, David. *The Cookie Girl.* Audiocassette. Little Rock, Ark.: August House. 1993.

>Original and remakes of classic stories each with a valuable lesson to teach. Especially useful for youth tellers is "The Grasshopper and the Ants (3x)." David tells this Aesop's tale three ways with three morals. Also by same storyteller: *Itsy Bitsy Spider's Heroic Climb.*

O'Callahan, Jay. *Six Stories about Little Heroes and Herman and Marguerite.* Videocassette. 1986. Vineyard Video Productions. Elias Lane, West Tisbury, MA 02575. (617) 693-3584.
> Original stories told by one of America's foremost storytellers.

Schutzgruber, Barbara. *String Things: Stories, Games and Fun!* Videocassette. BGSG Storytelling, 2855 Kimberly, Ann Arbor, MI 48104. (734) 761-5118.
> Part one: string stories. Six stories using string figures in the telling. Part two: playing with string. Demonstrates how to make a number of string figures that can be used in telling stories.

Storytelling World. *"Choices of Voices."* Magazine and audiocassette. Dr. Flora Joy, Editor. Johnson City, Tenn.: East Tennessee State University, Box 70647. Johnson City, TN 37614-0647.
> Contains suggestions for using voices, sounds, and sound effects as well as eight storytellers each with their own version of the Aesop's fable, "The Crow and the Pitcher." Excellent for examples of how to make a story your own.

The Storytellers Collection. Videotape. Bethesda, Md.: Atlas Video. 1991.
> Four videocassettes featuring four well-known professional storytellers telling stories from their cultures based on a central theme. Animal stories, scary stories, magic tales and tall tales, yarns and whoppers. The storytellers are African American Alice McGill, Native American Joe Bruchac, Hispanic American Olga Loya, and European American Jon Spellman.

Tell Me a Story. Videotapes. Mill Valley, Calif.: Hometown Entertainment. 1995. (800) 786-7983.
> Four videocassettes featuring live performances from the Twentieth Anniversary National Storytelling Festival. The first video describes the National Storytelling Festival and the history behind it. The other three feature the performances of Carol Birch, Milbre Burch, Rex Ellis, Diane Ferlatte, Heather Forest, Jackson Gillman, Bob Jenkins, Syd Lieberman, Waddie Mitchell, Johnny Moses, David Novak, Jay O'Callahan, Michael Parent, Jon Spellman, and Ed Stivender.

Young, Richard, and Judy Dockery. *Favorite Scary Stories of American Children.* Two audiocassettes (for grades K–3 and 4–6). Little Rock, Ark.: August House.
> Easy ghost stories to learn and tell taken from the book of the same title.

Storytelling Web Sites

Chace, Karen A. *Researching Stories on the Internet.* Storybug@aol.com
> Karen has produced a CD-ROM of links to myriad story and storytelling Web sites, arranged by such topics as craft sites, oral history information and ideas, princess tales, puppets and puppetry, stories by culture, string figure sites, story links (myths, fables, folktales, fairytales, and legends), teaching tools, storytellers' Web sites, and more. This is a reasonably priced, excellent guide to storytelling on the Internet.

Children's Literature Web Guide. www.ucs.ucalgary.ca/~dkbrown/index.html
> Links to Children's Book Awards, Best Books, Stories on the Web, Resources for Storytellers. This site attempts to gather together and categorize the growing number of resources related to books for children and young adults.

Folklore and Mythology. www.pitt.edu/~dash/folktexts.html.
> One of the most comprehensive sites for world folklore and mythology; tales are indexed alphabetically by subject matter.

National Storytelling Youth Olympics. East Tennessee State University. www.youthstorytelling.com
> Annual event encouraging young storytellers to develop and fine-tune their storytelling skills. There are local and state events leading up to the national level each spring.

Story Arts. www.storyarts.org

Storyteller, Heather Forest's excellent site with stories, lesson plans, activities, and links to even more sites. She has ideas and resources for classroom curriculum applications and the use of story in teaching. You can also subscribe to "Musings," a monthly e-zine devoted to storytelling in education.

Storycraft. www.storycraft.com

This site is specially geared toward kids. Includes the Kids' Storytelling Club page with crafts, activities, ideas for parents and teachers, and how to join the online storytelling club.

Storynet. www.storynet.org

Official Web site of the National Storytelling Network, listing storytellers and storytelling events around the world. Membership is $50 per year. Includes subscription to *Storytelling Magazine* and *Storytelling World.*

Storytell. www.twu.edu//cope/slis/storytell.htm

Without a doubt, the best and most supportive storytelling discussion group on earth! Truly an international resource. This free service, provided by the Texas Woman's University School of Library and Information Studies, is an ongoing discussion of storytelling.

Storytelling Ring. www.pjtss.net/ring

This is a good starting point for storytelling. There are links to individual storyteller's Web pages, online storytelling resources, and storytelling organizations.

Tales of Wonder. www.darsie.net/talesofwonder

Contains dozens of stories in tellable forms collected and referenced from many cultures from Africa to Siberia.

Tampa Storytelling Festival. www.tampastory.org

They have been featuring youth storytellers since 1980. Includes an online Coaching Manual with forty-two reasons for teaching storytelling, how to choose a story to tell, sample lesson plans, coaching guidelines, and worksheets.

Tell Me a Story. www.uexpress.com/ups/features/ts/archive

Contains stories from around the world. This site has been adding new folktales since 1997.

Voices Across America. www.youthstorytelling.com

Voices Across America Youth Storytelling Project is a nationwide, soon to be worldwide, effort to build youth storytelling groups across the globe. The organization currently has more than sixty registered groups. It provides a startup package, contact lists, and idea exchanges.

Storytelling Organizations

International Storytelling Center. 116 West Main Street, Jonesborough, TN 37659. (800) 952-8392. www.storytellingcenter.net

Dedicated to promoting the power of storytelling to create a better world. Provides exhibits, teller-in-residence programs, and concerts. Co-produces the National Storytelling Festival, second weekend of October, in Jonesborough, Tennessee.

League for the Advancement of New England Storytelling. http://www.lanes.org/about.html

This organization is dedicated to the appreciation and promotion of the art of storytelling in all its aspects: traditional, creative, educational, cultural, personal, and therapeutic. "We believe that sharing stories creates understanding between people. Our purpose is to nurture family, community, and professional storytelling throughout New England and Upstate New York.

LANES functions as a resource for both storytellers and the general public through our publications, conferences, and events." Produces Sharing the Fire Storytelling Conference in March.

National Story League.
The oldest storytelling organization in the country, originated in 1903, it has many chapters throughout the United States and numerous Junior Story Leagues. Their motto is "Service Though Storytelling," and it provides volunteer tellers for schools, churches, libraries, and other institutions. Contact information is through current presidents of each league.

National Storytelling Network. 101 Courthouse Square, Jonesborough, TN 37659. (800) 525-4514. www.storynet.org
Based in Jonesborough, Tennessee, this is a membership-driven storytelling organization. It produces the National Storytelling Conference, which takes place in a different area of the country each July; publishes *Storytelling Magazine;* sponsors *Tellabration* and National Storytelling week each November; and co-produces the National Storytelling Festival in Jonesborough the first weekend in October.

Northlands Storytelling Network. http://www.northlands.net
A community of storytellers and story listeners in the upper Midwest, this is the largest regional storytelling organization in the country. It serves tellers and storytelling enthusiasts in Minnesota, Iowa, Wisconsin, Illinois, and Michigan. This organization produces a storytelling conference each April with workshops, concerts, story swaps, and a youth storytelling concert.

Storytelling Arts of Indiana. P.O. Box 20743. Indianapolis, IN 46220. (317) 576-9848. www.storytellingarts.org
Through its programs and services, Storytelling Arts of Indiana seeks to reinstill and promote the art and use of storytelling into the daily lives of individuals, families, organizations, neighborhoods, and communities. Programs include the Hoosier Storytelling Festival, Storyteller's Theater for Adults, and many family programs.

South Coast Storytellers Guild. www.storyguild.com
Located in Costa Mesa, California, the South Coast Storytellers Guild is a dynamic and diverse group of storytellers who celebrate the oral tradition of storytelling through entertaining performances, educational workshops, and the development of student storytellers.

Southern Order of Storytellers. http://www.accessatlanta.com/community/groups/sos
Based in Atlanta, with a commitment to promoting the timeless values and universal bond of story, members share stories, teach the art of storytelling, produce story events, and provide information, resources, and support to their membership, other storytelling organizations, and the extended community.

The Tejas Storytelling Association. www.tejasstorytelling.com
The Tejas Storytelling Association was formed in 1987 and unites lovers of storytelling throughout Texas and the Southwest. Storytelling is the art and tradition of passing folktales, family history, legends, ghost tales, and some downright lies from one generation to the next. TSA is based in Denton, Texas, and sponsors the Texas Storytelling Festival every spring and the Texas Conference on Storytelling, as well as numerous other workshops and performances throughout the year and around the state.

Publishers and Distributors Specializing in Storytelling Books and Tapes

August House. P.O. Box 3223, Little Rock, AZ 72203-3223. (800) 248-8784. www.augusthouse.com

Fulcrum Publishing. 16100 Table Mountain Pkwy. Golden, CO 80403-1672. (800) 992-2908. www.fulcrum-resources.com.

A Gentle Wind: Songs and Stories for Children. Box 3103, Albany NY 12203. (888) 386-7664. www.gentlewind.com

Highsmith Press. W5527 Highway 106, PO Box 800; Fort Atkinson, WI 53538. (800) 558-2110. www.hpress.highsmith.com

Libraries Unlimited. P.O. Box 5007, Westport, CT 06881. (800) 225-5800. www.lu.com

National Storytelling Press. 101 Courthouse Square, Jonesborough, TN 37659. (800) 525-4514. www.storynet.org

Shen's Books. 8625 Hubbard Road, Auburn, CA 95602-7815. (530) 888-6776. www.shens.com

Shoe String Press. P.O. Box 657, 2 Linsley Street, North Haven, CT 06473-2517. (203) 239-2702. SSPBooks@aol.com

Yellow Moon Press. P.O. Box 1316, Cambridge, MA 02238. (617) 776-2230. www.yellowmoon.com

Appendix: Youthful Voices

Listening to young people tell stories and empowering them by guiding them to become storytellers is the purpose of this book. We firmly value the voices of our students, and it is from their voices that we have built our programs. By listening to the needs of our members, we have learned a great deal about shaping our youth storytelling group or troupe.

With this thought in mind, it only makes sense to include an appendix that elicits our students' comments about storytelling, as well as sample stories created by our youth tellers. Over the years, students have created wonderful stories. We would love to include every comment and story, but this small sample will give you some sense of the intensity that students put into their storytelling group.

Youthful Voices Give Advice

1. How has storytelling or belonging to a storytelling group helped you?

"Storytelling has helped me learn how to voice variations in public speaking and acting. Storytelling has helped me become more confident on stage." —Tamara Roberts, freshman, Hanford High School

"Storytelling helped me to channel my emotions and my thoughts in a relaxing and helpful atmosphere. By listening to stories I came to appreciate and understand how different people all really are. There's a story out there for each and every one of us." —Michael Lovan, junior, Hanford High School

"Stories have changed the way I think about life and even my point of view." —Jose Gonzales, one of the founders of Voices of Illusion

"My experience in Talespinners taught me to take risks and embrace creativity. This has helped me in many ways, especially in theater and public speaking, but also in working on group projects and presentations in college." —Heidi Bennett, Talespinners graduate, 1995

"Talespinners helped me decide to switch from law to education. Telling and reading stories to young children was very rewarding. Also, when we helped others learn stories during exchanges and workshops, I felt very comfortable and confident with the role of trying to relate the information." —Lori Stone, Talespinners graduate, 1994

"It helped me with my public speaking abilities during presentations at school. It also helps me in my future career as a speech pathologist because I use the skills I learned in Talespinners when I read or tell stories to my clients. I also competed in forensics in high school where I made it to state finals. I find that I am very dramatic in my interactions with others. Every story that I tell, even about my own experiences, is dramatic." —Jennifer D'Uva, Talespinner graduate, 1991

221

"Storytelling has helped my life in many ways including improving my ability to control my tone of voice when speaking in different situations and environments, the ability to use words to enhance my position when involved in debates or opinionated conversations, and by giving me a good basis to communicate with others in general conversations. Storytelling is always a good icebreaker with new people." —Mary Muzzarelli, Talespinner graduate, 1995

"Storytelling helped me be able to really talk in front of big groups and it helped me be able to act on stage." —Lauren Sroka, Talespinner graduate, 2000

2. Can you remember a storytelling experience when you said, "I like storytelling?"

"It was the recording studio this month. It was really fun and I loved the way I told the story. I had to show the sign language that I use with the story in a way that would translate on the tape. I think by explaining the detail I did it very well. I think my poetic skills helped me as well." —Tamara Roberts

"This feeling occurred in my senior year when I went to the retirement home. When I arrived I realized I personally knew several people who had a hand in watching me grow up. I had gone there because I wanted to tell stories and I was practicing for the National Youth Storytelling Olympics. I told several stories. The audience listened and was very polite. After I told for a half-hour, I went around and greeted them. The residents shook my hand and even gave me a few of those famous 'old lady hugs.' Just seeing their smiles and the happiness in their eyes touched my heart." —Dawn Escobar, senior, Hanford High School

"The moment I told my first story, the other teens raised their hands to give me praise; I was unaware I would get suggestions as well. I heard lots of good advice for my first time telling, and I heard a fair share of constructive criticism to go along with it. I was thinking in my head, 'this is helpful, they're really being honest.' " —Michael Lovan

"It was a simple experience but I shall never forget it. A little shy boy approached me after a show and despite his shyness, he said to me, 'Hey I like storytelling.' I knew then what I was doing was making people see storytelling in a new and fun way." —Jose Gonzales

"My brother and I told stories together, which helped us become friends as well as brothers. We fed off of each other's creativity and had a lot of fun in the process." —Jonathan Napper, Talespinners graduate, 1991

"I remember Mrs. Sima coming to Mound Park Elementary School when I was in third or fourth grade and telling stories for Halloween. I was pretty mesmerized by her, and I think it was then when I began to love performance and wanted to do it myself. Since then my life has pretty much centered around the performing arts. I don't know what else I would be doing if I hadn't been exposed to the arts early in my life." —Heidi Bennett

"Probably when I started telling stories, my sister looked up to me. Then she wanted to tell stories. She looked up to me and I was proud to be her brother." —Brandon Yuker, Talespinner graduate, 2000

"I remember once trying to tell the story of the 'Twelve Dancing Princesses.' It was one of my favorites, and I told it more than once. All of a sudden, about halfway through, my mind went blank. I couldn't remember what happened next. I think I paused for a moment, then I began elaborating. The audience never even noticed. I figured, if I could pull that off, I must have learned something. If I had let myself be afraid and nervous, if I had given into my doubts, it would have been a disaster. Sometimes if you believe in yourself, it's enough." —Theresa Johnson, Talespinner graduate, 1992

"When I used to tell 'Obedient Jack' in sixth grade, I remember the reactions of the children at the elementary school we told stories for. They were laughing so hard at everything we said and did, and it gave me such a sense of excitement. I never wanted to sit down. I remember Mrs. Sima had to give a cue to shorten it up because we were running out of time and other people still had to tell stories. The audience definitely gives you the energy to continue telling! Storytelling is not complete without an audience to bring the story alive." —Jennifer D'Uva

"Actually telling and listening to the stories told in Talespinners was of great importance to me. Some of the people I became friends with in that group remained my friends all the way through high school." —Mary E. Muzzarelli

"When we told stories for the 'Family Storytelling Festival' in the 2000–2001 school year, my younger sister and I told a story together about how two kids think that their parents love the other one better. It put me in touch with my sister (for at least a little while!)." —Lauren Sroka

3. Why are (were) you in storytelling?

"I am in storytelling because I like it and it gives me chances to do things I otherwise would not have been able to do. Storytelling helps me develop my people skills, so when it is time for me to get a job I won't be too nervous. Overall I am in it because it is so much fun." —Tamara Roberts

"I was in storytelling not for friends. Sure I made friends but I was in storytelling because I knew if I had something to say I could send a peaceful message to people without yelling or constantly repeating what I had to say. I could say it in a way that people remember or enjoy; I could say it in a story. I also enjoyed storytelling because I knew that this would make me a better person. Storytelling is a unique art. It is a unique art that calls for you to give stories away. You don't keep stories. You give them away. I love the idea that I didn't have to buy a gift; I would share a gift of story to fit a need of someone. Put simply, stories are gifts I just love to give to others." —Dawn Escobar

"Storytelling, quite simply, made me happy. It helped keep me in check with my surroundings and helped to remind me how diverse people really are. Plus, the stories always had me grinning." —Michael Lovan

"I was in storytelling because my family told stories. I wanted to keep this tradition going. I had an obligation to be the storyteller of my family. This is a title that I am honored to have and one that does not come lightly. I take my job as storyteller seriously because I am the keeper of my family's traditions." —Jose Gonzales

4. What suggestions would you give students who want to tell stories?

"You should always consider your voice. Are you varying it to meet the needs of the story? Also never forget that the characters in your story are real, their feelings motivate their actions; let your stories complement those feelings. Lastly, you set the atmosphere of the story. Let the story take shape based on your frame for the story." —Tamara Roberts

"Don't hold back what you want to say. Sometimes the first descriptions and sudden plot twists you think of on the spot stand out the best. Be yourself when you tell stories. Keep your own style and please yourself before your audience. Don't be scared to look like a fool. If you want to characterize a bizarre character and the only way to do that is to hunch over and squint an eye, then hunch over and squint an eye. Make your own world with your story and [wrap] your audience up into it." —Michael Lovan

"1. Storytelling is the chicken soup that people rarely feed you. 2. Your story is like wildfire; once it is out, it is like gossip, and it goes on forever. 3. Storytelling is a unique, dynamic tool where you learn tons of new ideas and concepts like public speaking, proper grammar skills, listening skills, creativity, and much more. Just pick up a story, unravel it, and tell it to discover more." —Dawn Escobar

"Don't be afraid. It is a story worth telling. No one knows when you mess up. Make the story yours." —Jose Gonzales

"Try it. Don't care what your friends think and have fun." —Jamie Favreau, Talespinners graduate, 1991

"Never limit yourself to what you can do. There is no such thing as a bad story, only bad storytelling. Keep your audience enthralled by convincing them that you didn't memorize your story, but that you lived through it personally. Always listen to how you speak on a day-to-day basis so that you can hear the mistakes you make in normal speech and correct them before you perform." —Mary E. Muzzarelli

"Have fun; if you're having fun, your audience will have fun. They are there to see you in the first place; they won't criticize you nearly as much as you criticize yourself. —Theresa Johnson

"Start out telling stories to people you know— your friends and family. Don't give up if you don't perform your best the first time—practice makes perfect!" —Jennifer D'Uva

5. What suggestions would you give adults who want to help young people become storytellers?

"Let the students make their own decisions regarding what story to tell and how to do it; only act as a guide. Encourage and praise them but give them things to improve. Provide them with as many experiences to tell stories as possible."—Heidi Bennett

"Make sure there are lots of books. A wide variety of stories, especially from around the world, can make a huge difference. Take them to see professional storytellers. Invite them in. Let them see other ways of telling stories. If there are kids who are a bit scared of telling up there, all alone, in front of an audience, have them participate as part of a group or a two-person piece. The less lonely it is, the less scary it is." —Theresa Johnson

"Provide constructive criticism. Offer as many compliments as criticisms but make sure to provide ideas for improvements. Having the silent signals Mrs. Sima provided during performances was very important." —Lori Stone

"Have them practice by first reading a story using expression before they begin memorizing. Sometimes for a beginner, a story can lose its expression if the person is too caught up in remembering it and reciting it perfectly. Have the students first watch videos of professional storytellers so they can see how it is done and have a goal to reach for." Jennifer D'Uva

"Try some tongue twisters and word games to help them speak better in front of a crowd.

Always encourage them to do it their way. It might not be what the author intended; however, it should always be told as the storyteller sees it. And always let them choose the story. If you choose it for them, then the story becomes an assignment. Teaching children the value of words and giving them the ability to speak loudly and clearly is what is going to give them the confidence and intelligence they need to become the leaders of the world." —Mary Muzzarelli

"Take your time teaching them. Don't get frustrated with your students, and most important, have fun!" —Brandon Yuker

"1. Let them come to you for help first. 2. Let them know how good their story is going. 3. Have some fun with the kids." —Lauren Sroka

6. What are you doing now in your life that uses skills you learned in storytelling?

"I am now a high school band teacher, so I am interacting with students and the public every day." —Jonathan Napper

"I'm still finishing high school, but it helps me stand in front of crowds without fear." —Brandon Yuker

"I am studying theater, speech, and French in college to be a high school teacher, and storytelling is really a part of all three. I learned to be expressive and speak clearly in Talespinners, which really helps when speaking another language, especially for teaching that language." —Heidi Bennett

"Well, I'm a writer, like it or not. I earned a minor in creative writing (in addition to being an English major) by accident. Middle school was the first time I thought I could be a writer, and being in Talespinners gave me the self-confidence I needed to give it a try. I'm studying to be a teacher because I enjoy learning, and want to share that with others. I think there's a strong correlation between teaching English and storytelling. Everyday, you're in front of that audience, who is waiting to be entertained. They say there are studies that prove that teachers who read to their students improve their students' reading skills. I think a little storytelling in the classroom would be an excellent way to do that. If you love words, be they written, spoken, or read, I think that'll come through in your teaching." —Theresa Johnson

"I am in college pursuing a degree in education. I would like to teach fourth or fifth grade. I am substitute teaching. Students that know that their teachers are away will try to get away with anything. Being able to tell stories provides an opportunity to hold their attention as well as an incentive for good behavior. I also utilized my storytelling techniques in developing characters in drama classes." —Lori Stone

"I currently have an eight-month-old son. All I do is make silly faces and noises right now, but every once in a while, I'll tell him a story, and it keeps him entertained. Of course when he gets a little older I know that I'm gong to have to find some good stories because I know he is going to want one told all the time." —Mary Muzzarelli

"As a student in speech-language pathology (I'll have my master's in May!), I use the skills I learned in Talespinners when telling stories and reading books to my child clients during therapy. Talespinners was a very fun experience for me and made my middle school years a little less traumatic. It also gave me a solid group of friends, many of which I still have, more than 10 years later." —Jennifer D'Uva

"I'm going to be a special ed teacher, and I've been able to get over my fear of doing anything in front of people." —Lauren Sroka

Youthful Voices Share Their Stories

When our students discovered we were writing a book to help others build youth storytelling groups and troupes, they were ever so willing to be a part of it. Here are some of their original stories.

Assignment: A Childhood Memory

Tell a story about a childhood memory. Think of a moment that could have happened or did happen when you were younger. From that memory, create a story that uses language that a child would use and that mentions people or places that help us realize that a child is telling the story.

BEPPO: A CHILDHOOD MEMORY

by Michelle Austin

Hanford High School

It was my first day of first grade. I was so happy. I got to ride the bus too. I said good-bye to mommy, my daddy, my little brother, and my little sister. And I said good-bye to Beppo.

I went to school and Sally, Timmy, Johnny, and Marie were in my class. We played in the sandbox, on the "Spider," the monkey bars, the swings, and the slide. We had so much fun. When we left we all said, "Good-bye Ms. Shinshak, our teacher."

When I got home I was ready to tell my mommy and daddy all about my day. But my mommy and daddy were very sad. My little brother was missing. I looked at Beppo and asked, "Beppo, what happened?"

He said, "I got hungry."

I was very sad.

The next day I got up and went off to school. I said goodbye to my mommy, my daddy, and my little sister, and to Beppo. I had another great day. I played with Sally, Timmy, Johnny, and Marie on the playground. Ms. Shinshak gave us our first homework assignment. I went home ready to tell my mommy and daddy all about my day but my little sister was missing. I looked at Beppo and said, "Beppo what happened?"

"I got hungry."

I went to bed very sad because my little brother and sister were missing. I got up and went off to school. I said goodbye to my mommy, my daddy, and to Beppo.

My day was OK. Sally was sick and she was my best friend. She had a cold. The day went by very slowly. When I got home my mommy was missing. I looked at Beppo and said, "Beppo, what happened!"

"I got hungry."

Now I was very sad. The only family I had left was my daddy. Beppo had eaten everyone else. I went to bed crying. I missed my mommy. I missed my family.

The next day I got up went off to school. I said goodbye to my daddy, but I didn't say goodbye to Beppo.

I went home and guess what? After I had that long talk with Beppo for eating my family and not to eat my daddy, he did anyway. I looked at him and he said, "I got hungry."

That night I didn't get to eat dinner because I didn't know how to cook and my mommy had told me not to play with the stove. I cried myself to sleep.

The next day I went off to school and I didn't say goodbye to Beppo. I got my homework assignment back from Ms. Shinsak. I got 100%. That made me happy, but I was still mostly sad. What made me even more happy was what I saw when I got home. I got home and there was my mommy, my daddy, my little brother, and my little sister. I looked at Beppo and said, "Beppo, what happened?"

He looked at me and grinned, "I burped."

Assignment: Creation Stories

Think of something that cannot be easily explained. For example, why do we have white in our fingernails? Why does the earth shake? Why does each bird sing a different song? Create a story that explains the unexplained. Make the story almost believable. If we didn't have modern-day science, would a person believe this is the reason why something is the way it is?

THE SPARROW AND THE SEA (Based on a Russian folktale)

By Gwen Green

Hanford High School

Before the world was created, there was nothing but spirits that dwelled in an unknown place. There were two young spirits living here. They were so very much in love with each other; they knew their love would last for eternity.

Now it came to pass that the ruler over the unknown place decided that his kingdom would flourish if he created a new place. In order to do this, he had to use the spirits to bring life to this new place.

He had appointed everything on the earth to different spirits and had already sent them down to earth. The only two left in his charge were the two who were in love. The younger of the two begged that he'd let them stay together, but the ruler was an unfeeling man who believed in necessity above emotion and love. He appointed the eldest of the two to be the spirit of the sea. He sent the heartbroken younger to be the spirit of the sparrow.

The two separated and never expected to see each other again. Thus begins the story of the sparrow and the sea.

A long time ago, when the world was young, a tiny sparrow was born. It began its life among the greenery of the leaves of an oak. From the heights of her little nest, the sparrow had a perfect view of the sea. Every night she would fall asleep to the lulling sound of the waves crashing upon the ocean. Her dreams would be filled with odd answers to the questions of how the sea could be so big and loud.

The sparrow waited impatiently for the day when she could fly from her nest and talk to the sea. When that day finally came, she wasted no time and flew out immediately over the water. She flew until she could see nothing but water on either side of her.

She called out to the sea in the loudest voice she could summon, "Sea, oh sea, you are fascinating." The sea gave no response. The sparrow called out again and again, but the booming sound of the crashing waves almost drowned her out. So finally, in desperation, the little bird flew down dangerously close to the water and whispered in the sea's ear. "Sea, oh sea. You are so very fascinating."

This time the sea listened and answered back in a loud voice that echoed with the rhythm of the waves. "I, too, find you fascinating. I have watched you since the day you hatched from the egg and I have often wondered how you could be so small and quiet yet powerful."

From that day forward the little sparrow and the vast sea spent their days with pleasant conversation. The more they talked, the fonder the sparrow grew. She found herself feeling as if she had met the sea beforehand and had known him for much longer. This went on in the same fashion for about a year. Then, one bright spring morning, the sparrow went to the ocean. But, the sparrow could see that something was not right with the sea. The waves were not crashing on the shore nearly as loud as they had in the past. The sea seamed to have lost its happiness.

The little sparrow flew whispered in the sea's ear. "Sea, whatever is the matter with you?" The sparrow waited a long time before getting a murmuring response from the sea. "Oh my dear sparrow. I've known you for over a year, and I have watched you for longer. My dear, I love you."

Now, when the little sparrow heard this, something inside of her was sparked and memories she never knew began to overwhelm her. She flew up to a very high cliff overlooking the sea. Looking deep inside herself, she realized who her beloved sea was, who she had been before she was hatched into the world. Most importantly, she realized that she, too, loved the sea.

She found that the one thing she longed for more than anything else was to be embraced by the sea, to be held in his cool waters. She would do anything, even die, just to be held by the sea, even if it would be for a moment.

Without thinking the little sparrow let herself fall from the cliff. Faster and faster she traveled downward toward the sea until she found herself numbed by the chill waters surrounding her. She could feel it enter her lungs, taking away her life. With that last little beats of her heart that were filled with such love for the spirit that killed her, the tiny bird died in the strong embrace of the sea.

And there was only one that had witnessed this horrible tragedy. To this day, you can still hear the gulls cry in mourning of that little sparrow and the sea.

WHY THE RAINBOW IS SO COLORFUL

By Brittany Finch

Chatterton Middle School

Once there was a Great Spirit who lived in a beautiful house in the middle of the forest. One day it was raining and every time it rained the Great Spirit would become very tired and go to bed. While he was asleep, he had a dream and in his dream he was crying.

The sun asked, "Do you need something?"

The Great Spirit replied, "I need some help to make the sky less dreary when it rains. It makes me so sad and sleepy."

Just then he awoke and said to himself, "What a great idea. I can use the colors I gave to the animals in the forest to make something beautiful for the sky on a rainy day!"

So the Great Spirit took some red from the color of the ladybugs, yellow from the color of the sun, orange from the color of beautiful butterflies, green from the color of tree frogs, blue from the color of Blue Jays, and finally purple from the color of pretty violets.

Then the Great Spirit took these colors and arched them side-by-side across the sky in the form of a bow and called this a rainbow. This made him happy and today when people see a rainbow it makes them smile.

Assignment: Fractured Fairy Tales

Create a story using the following:

1. Three people or characters from three fairy tales. For example, "Red" from "Little Red Riding Hood," "The Giant" from "Jack and the Beanstalk," and "Dorothy" from the *Wizard of Oz*.

2. An unusual setting. For example, in the dark forest that is rumored to come alive at night or the busy city where everyone wants to be a movie star.

3. A quest or journey that they all are seeking. For example, to find the princess locked in the kingdom, to buy new shoes, and so on.

CRIMES IN NURSERY RHYME LAND

By Jose Gonzales

Hanford High School

He laid broken in pieces. He had been sitting on a wall before someone or something knocked him off. Lying in his own yoke he looked up to see young Jill peering down at him. Jill yelled for the king and all his men, but they couldn't put him together again.

While the king's men tried to put Humpty Dumpy back together, they heard a girl screaming. The sound came from the other side of the hill, the same place that the wall stood. They couldn't help Humpty, so the kings' men ventured off to the sound of the scream.

They jumped on their horses and rode toward it. Upon their arrival they found a little spider with a huge tummy sitting in an empty bowl. They did not know what to make of it. The spider didn't know what to say. The king's men asked the spider what happened.

The spider said, "I was just hungry. I crawled down to eat curds when I sat down beside a little girl and said, "Hi!" That is when she jumped up and screamed and ran down the hill toward the old lady who lives with her many kids in the shoe."

The king's men wrote the report as the spider told it to them. Then, they headed out to find the young girl to unravel the mystery.

The kingsmen got back on their horses and rode to the Old Lady that lived in the shoe. They knocked on the door and the old woman answered with small children crying in her arms. The king's men heard even more cries of children from within the shoe. Before the men could ask what they wanted, the old woman said, "I'm sorry I can't talk now. I have too many children to deal with, whatever it is you want, I would be no help." She slammed the door.

The king's men went door to door to Peter Peter Pumpkin Eater, but they found that Peter was not home. His wife, however, was and so the king's men questioned his wife to the whereabouts of her husband.

She told them that Peter had gone. "My husband went to check on Little Boy Blue and Little Bo-Peep."

The king's men asked if she had seen a little girl screaming. She said she had not, but maybe her husband would know. Everyone knows where Little Boy Blue would lie down all day and the place where Little Bo-Peep keeps all her sheep. The king's men rode off down the road. Along the way they ran into Simple Simon.

Simple Simon stopped the three kingsmen in hopes of securing a ride to the river. The men immediately knew what Simple Simon was trying to do. The king's men said they were in a hurry and could not take Simon for a ride. They did not notice the three mice trying to run across the road. But the horses did. They stopped in their tracks to let the mice cross. The king's men looked to see such a sight. "Three blind mice?" Said one of the kinsmen. "See how they run!" said the other man."

"Did you ever see such a sight in your life, as three blind mice?" said one of the horses. The mice continued to run across the road and the men rode off to find Peter with Little Boy Blue and Little Bo-Peep. They reached the field where the boy was supposed to watch the sheep. He was not there, and neither was Bo-Peep. They looked for both of them only to find them fast a-sleep near a haystack. They dared not wake Little Boy Blue for he would surely cry. Instead they woke up Little Bo-Peep, who was also supposed to be watching her sheep. She was not much help. She began to cry that she had lost her sheep.

"I was watching my sheep with Little Boy Blue when he fell asleep. I sat down next to him to take a nap and before I knew it, my sheep were gone." She began to cry and cry and cry. The men asked her where they might have gone, but she had no clue. She begged them to help her. They agreed to help her.

On the way out of the field they saw Peter with the sheep. They asked Peter if he had seen a little girl screaming across the countryside. Peter told them that the girl that they were looking for was Little Miss Muffet. She was in the crooked woods with the crooked man, who lived in the crooked house, with a crooked cat, which caught a crooked mouse. They all lived together in a little crooked house.

The king's men had to hurry to find Little Miss Muffet because it was quickly growing dark. Everyone knows that when darkness arrives, things become weird in Nursery Rhyme Land. People say that sometimes when the moon is full, that the cow jumps over it, the cats play fiddles, and dogs laugh to see such a sight, but these are not the weirdest things at close to midnight—believe it or not, the dish may just run away with the spoon.

The king's men rode off. As they approached the crooked woods, Simple Simon ran out in front. "You must come quick," he yelled. It was then that a cow almost jumped over them on the way to the moon. They heard the faintest whispers of sounds like the clanging of dishes in the background.

The king's men finally arrived to the king's castle. It was the castle of a wise king; however, he was known for his dancing. His name was Old King Cole. He was dancing a jig. He was such a merry old soul. He had called for his pipe, called for his bowl, and he called for his fiddlers three.

Every fiddler had a fiddle, and a very fine fiddle had he, oh there's none so rare as can compare with King Cole and his fiddlers three. There was a crooked man, he was standing in a crooked corner and behind him was Little Miss Muffet. At last they could find out the real answer as to what happened to the spider and her. The king's men were busy writing her side of the story when Old King Cole asked everyone to dance. He loved dancing. Everyone was having a merry old time of singing and dancing when someone ran into the castle crying, "Where is Thumbkin? Where is Thumbkin?"

The three kingsmen looked at one another and cried, "Oh, no another mystery to be solved."

Students have very active imaginations and a desire to tell their own story. The more you work with their story ideas, the more original stories will be told. Don't worry if first attempts are not polished; let them continue to build their stories. Soon your storytelling group or troupe will show more original polish than you thought possible. Empower your students by allowing them to use their own words and their stories will flourish.

End Note

We would love to know how you are doing with your youth storytelling group or troupe. Let us know ideas that worked for you, your successes and concerns, or just feel free to tell us about your group.

Contact us at the addresses below and be sure to register your troupe with Kevin for the Voices Across America Youth Storytelling Project. Kevin will send you a free startup kit, which includes contact numbers and ideas for your storytelling group. This is the first national and international concerted effort to align youth storytelling groups across the country and around the world.

"Together we can make a difference with story."

Judy Sima
Raising Voices
30053 Spring River
Southfield, MI 48076
judsim@hotmail.com

Kevin Cordi
Raising Voices
Voices Across America
Youth Storytelling Project
KCtells@youthstorytelling.com
www.youthstorytelling.com

Index

About the Authors

JUDY SIMA has been a media specialist for the Fitzgerald Public Schools in Warren, Michigan, for more than thirty years and a freelance storyteller since 1987. In the same year, she created the Chatterton Talespinners, a middle school student storytelling troupe, and The Parent-Tellers, an award-winning adult volunteer storytelling group. A frequent presenter at reading, library, and teacher conferences throughout Michigan, Judy has also been invited to present workshops at many other state and national conferences, including the National Storytelling Conference and the American Association of School Librarians. Her numerous articles on storytelling have been published nationally in *The Yarnspinner, Tales as Tools, Storytelling Magazine, Book Links, Teaching Tolerance, Library Talk,* and others. Currently Judy is the Michigan State Liaison to the National Storytelling Network and a past president of the Detroit Story League.

KEVIN CORDI holds a master's degree in Storytelling and Education from the University of Akron and is the current co-chair of the National Storytelling Network's Youth Storytelling special interest group. According to the National Storytelling Network, he is the "first full-time high school storytelling teacher in the country." He has been a high school educator for more than fourteen years and a part-time professor of storytelling at California State University in Fresno. Kevin has coached the award-winning Voices of Illusion troupe and assisted with Junior Voices since 1993. He is a Fulbright scholar, and his program has received the "National Service Award" from the National Storytelling Network. He has produced several of his own compact disks and one videotape, six audiotapes, and three compact disks of his students' performances. Voices of Illusion perform more than fifty-five shows a year and have performed at the National Storytelling Festival, National Youth Storytelling Olympics, across the country. Kevin is a frequent speaker and teller at conferences and festivals across the country and most recently in England and Japan.

Edwards Brothers Malloy
Thorofare, NJ USA
August 14, 2015